Managing e-business Projects

Springer
Berlin
Heidelberg
New York
Barcelona
Hong Kong
London
Milan
Paris
Tokyo

Thomas Stoehr

Managing e-business Projects

99 Key Success Factors

With 37 Figures and 12 Tables

Springer

Thomas Stoehr
Overbeckstr. 7
22085 Hamburg, Germany
E-mail: tstoehr@web.de

Library of Congress Cataloging-in-Publication Data applied for

Die Deutsche Bibliothek – CIP-Einheitsaufnahme

Stoehr, Thomas:
Managing e-business projects: 99 key success factors; with 12 tables/
Thomas Stoehr. – Berlin; Heidelberg; New York; Barcelona; Hong Kong;
London; Milan; Paris; Tokyo: Springer, 2002
ISBN 3-540-42165-3

ISBN 3-540-42165-3 Springer-Verlag Berlin Heidelberg New York

Springer-Verlag Berlin Heidelberg New York
a member of BertelsmannSpringer Science-Business Media GmbH

http://www.springer.de

Printed in Germany

Typesetting: Camera-ready by the author
Design: KünkelLopka, Heidelberg
Printed on acid-free paper SPIN 10841042 33/3142SR – 5 4 3 2 1 0

Preface

Motivation for e-business Project Management

Is there a need for a book called '*Managing e-business Projects*'? There are thousands of books on project management in general and hundreds on IT project management in particular. The decisive question is whether or not traditional project management works also for e-business projects. You find different answers to this question – myths about managing e-business projects continue to abound.

Some people believe that managing an e-business project does not differ from managing an IT project. In their opinion e-business can be reduced to technological factors only. They view e-business as the current wave of a technological evolution in IT. As a consequence they propagate the application of traditional IT project management techniques to e-business projects.

Other people have a completely different view. They think that e-business projects require an entirely new project management methodology that is absolutely distinct from what has been done before. The extreme finds its expression in the belief that e-business projects need not be managed at all. Some people view project management for e-business projects as an unnecessary bureaucratic burden that stifles the creativity of the project staff.

Now, what is my opinion? From my perspective, e-business projects do differ from traditional IT projects. In e-business projects there are many specifics that you do not find in IT projects. If you treat e-business projects like IT projects, you are taking unnecessary risks. You can not apply all traditional IT project management methods and techniques in e-business projects. However, this does not mean that you have to start from scratch inventing a completely new project management methodology for e-business projects. Professional e-business project management suggests a combined triplet of practices:

1. There is a widely accepted body of knowledge about general management practices that can be applied to any project. e-business projects – as the name already suggests – are *projects*. Therefore, it can be assumed that those general project management practices fit e-business projects as well.
2. e-business projects have a lot in common with IT projects. Some of the project management practices that work in IT projects work also in e-business projects, but some do not work. This book identifies those that work and describe how they can be applied when managing an e-business project.

3. There are project management practices that are unique to or have a special significance in e-business projects. While there are individual differences among e-business projects, there are also similarities that run through all projects and project management practices that can be applied to all or at least most of the e-business projects.

This book is not meant to replace the excellent literature on project management in general and on IT project management in particular. What this book brings to you is a collection of methods, experiences, and key success factors that are unique to or require special emphasis in e-business projects.

This book is written for project managers of e-business projects. It intends to dispel some of the mysteries surrounding e-business project management and to make it more tangible. In contrast to some other books on the subject, it is not an academic book: it is written by a practitioner for practitioners. It provides practical best practices on e-business project management.

The book is written from a contractor's point of view performing an e-business project for a client. This situation is typical for many e-business projects since many companies are not well prepared to perform an e-business project 'in-house'; instead they hire a contractor to perform a project. Therefore, many of the recommendations are attributed to the relationship between a client and a contractor company. However, a lot of the described principles are applicable also to e-business projects that are conducted in-house. The given recommendations on e-business project management are not limited to a specific country or industry, and are independent of the size of project and the company involved in performing a project.

Acknowledgment

Many people contributed enthusiastically to this book. I would like to thank my colleagues in the IBM e-business Innovation Center in Hamburg, Germany, for in-depth reviews and valuable suggestions on the book. In particular, Martin Koehler and Stephan Reschke provided constructive criticism on most of the book.

Over the last 15 years I have had the opportunity to work on several IT research, development, services and consulting projects in various areas. This helped me to gain and broaden my project management experience. Without that I could not have written this book. I thank the IBM Corporation for providing me with this opportunity. However, certain material in the book might be considered as controversial or might provoke a stormy response. Therefore, I would like to point out that the opinions and views expressed are solely my own and do not necessarily represent the opinions and views of the people mentioned above nor the IBM Corporation.

Hamburg, September 2001 Thomas Stoehr

Table of Contents

1 Introduction

e-business – hardly any other topic has received so much attention in the last couple of years. In the mid 1990s the Internet and the associated World Wide Web began a revolution. The number of users with access to the Web had grown to such a level that it was recognized as an attractive market for doing business. In 1997 the Internet start-up era began. Each day new players entered the market, and the 'dot-coms' appeared on the scene. The dot-com companies often built their business entirely around an e-business model. During the next two years the technology stock markets listing the 'new-economy' companies rocketed. Shares of companies claiming to be active in the e-business field doubled, tripled, or climbed several thousand per cent or more, generating huge wealth overnight for a few lucky entrepreneurs. In 1999 e-business similarly took off, culminating in a peek in the early part of 2000. It was a time of wild euphoria with unbridled optimism and the belief that e-business would re-write the laws of competition and economics.

Predictably the hype passed and was replaced by disillusionment. The users of e-business solutions opened their eyes and recognized that ordering goods via the Web was by no means cheaper than buying the traditional way – and moreover tangibility has gone. Many dot-coms had to learn that building up an e-business solution costs a lot of money while expectations on achievable revenue and profit had to be reduced dramatically. For a while the dot-coms found satisfaction in struggling for market share by counting the 'clicks', 'eyeballs' or 'web hits' of users visiting their sites. But investors in the dot-com companies discovered quickly that more users in most cases means more loss. The dot-com shares fallout was a logical consequence.

So, where are we today, in 2001? The waves of hype and disillusionment faded. Today, e-business is just business – real business. And an enormous one, especially for suppliers of e-business solution services. The Gartner Group forecasts that the worldwide e-business services market will approach U.S. $ 527 billion by 2005 [14, 15]. This unprecedented opportunity will result in hundreds of thousands of projects – *e-business projects*. Those must be managed successfully, otherwise the next wave will again be one of disillusionment.

1.1 e-business Projects

What is an *e-business project*? Looking around the literature, newspapers, journals, IT industry, and the Web itself, one can get the impression that today nearly every project is an e-business project – or at least is called one. Over the last few years the 'e' for 'electronic' has became fashionable. In the early days of the Internet and the Web, only projects with the objective of building up an information web site were called e-business projects. The e-business hype entailed an inflation of the term 'e'. The 'e' was recognized as synonym for hip, sexy, up-to-date, and cutting-edge technology. It became fashionable to put an 'e' in front of nearly everything. The dot-coms formed terms like 'e-commerce', 'e-shop', 'e-marketplace', 'e-billing', and 'e-mobile' to name just a few.

Established old-economy companies feared that they would put themselves out of business if they are not entering the 'cyber world'. Like in the rush of lemmings they jumped on the train, hastily creating organizational or business units labeled 'e-business department', 'e-business center of excellence', 'e-business innovation center', or 'e-business practice'. Even new terms for complete industries and new job titles popped up: director of 'e-health', 'e-government', 'e-automotive', 'e-insurance', and 'e-finance', – you name it. What are all those people doing? Not surprisingly, they do *e-business projects*.

Taking a closer look at many of these projects and their objectives one may find it hard to identify what the 'e' stands for. My impression is that putting the magic 'e' in front of a project raises visibility, importance, and reputation. As a result of the 'e' the project gets more acceptance, you can sell it better to your senior management, and as a consequence you can get more funding for it. I call those projects *pseudo* e-business projects.

If we put aside the *pseudo* e-business projects, what are *real* e-business projects? In approaching the definition of an e-business project from an analytical point of view, let us start with defining the term 'project'. For this term the general definition of the Project Management Institute (PMI) can be applied. PMI defines: "*A project is a temporary endeavor undertaken to create a unique product, service, or result*" [32]. Now what is a expedient definition for an *e-business project*? There are lots of definitions available, nearly as many as e-business projects itself. I do not want to add another one. Instead, I would like to list nine characteristics of e-business projects whereas the sequence does not indicate a priority of the characteristics:

1. **The Web is the core.** In principle, each e-business project is different. The similarity among all e-business projects is that their objective is to build up an e-business solution that centers around the Internet. The Web is the core and a twofold must: the solution is made available via a web server, and the web pages of the solution are accessible to users via the Internet.

2. **Cutting-edge technology.** It requires specific, cutting-edge technology to build an e-business solution. Cutting-edge technology means technology that is only recently available or must even be invented and developed during the course of a project.
3. **Dynamic content.** Dynamic content is that what is generated automatically in response to an action performed by an end-user. In contrary to static content, dynamic content can not be simply stored somewhere and brought up on the screen. Instead, it must be generated dynamically based on specific actions that an end-user has taken.
4. **Transformation of data.** To build an e-business solution a transformation of client data to the world of the Web is required. Client data can be information about the company, products, prices, product availability, etc. Usually these data are already available in databases of so-called *back-end systems*, but the format of these data is normally not suitable to be used in the web environment without prior transformation.
5. **Change client's business processes.** A typical e-business solution has effects on the way the client is doing its business. Often client business processes are not tailored to e-business; changes in the business processes are required. At the beginning of an e-business project some clients do not believe that this is necessary, but at the end when the solution is operational they recognize this need.
6. **Multiple audiences.** There are multiple audiences for the outcome of an e-business project – at least if the result is an e-business solution in the B2C field. The target audience has a wide range of interests and sometimes it can neither be foreseen nor controlled who visits a created web site. The users can be customers, researchers, the media, or even competitors of the client.
7. **Usability is key.** Due to the wide and sometimes unforeseeable audiences of the e-business solution and the tough competition on the Web, special attention must be paid to usability issues when designing the user interface. Gartner predicts that by 2003, approximately 70% of all e-businesses will lose competitive advantages and incur revenue losses of at least 10% because of usability problems [26]. Besides technological factors, psychological, sociological, and anthropological aspects have to be considered.
8. **Need to involve people from several disciplines.** Many people from different disciplines must be involved in an e-business project. Besides people with traditional IT skills, creative, consulting, and marketing skills are needed to implement an e-business solution.
9. **Short project cycle.** The duration of a typical e-business project is six months or less. Time-to-market is key for clients of e-business solutions. Competition on the Web is cut-throat. Some clients view e-business solutions and web applications as a competitive necessity rather than a competitive advantage. Many clients fear that competitors are leapfrogging them in the marketplace. As one web year is viewed to be three months only, you will seldom find a client that gives you more than two web years to deliver an e-business solution.

So, what is a *real* e-business project? You can use the list above and check which of the characteristics apply to a project. It is not really necessary in each e-business project for all nine characteristics to apply. If you can tick seven or eight out of the list, this suggests that it is a real one. If you find less than seven characteristics, you can have some doubts – it might be a *pseudo* e-business project.

In the following, when the term 'e-business project' is used I always mean a *real* e-business project. *Pseudo* e-business projects can be viewed as traditional IT projects and those are not the subject of this book.

1.2 Differences Between e-business and Traditional IT Projects

Are e-business projects different from traditional IT projects? Yes, I think so. Let us examine some characteristics of a project to compare IT and e-business projects. You will see the contrast.

Characteristics	**Traditional IT project**	**e-business project**
Scope	The project scope is clear at the beginning of the project. The client has a specific IT problem that should be solved. The scope can be specified in detail, a contractor is hired to implement what was specified.	Often the project scope is somewhat unclear at the beginning of the project. The client only knows that something must be done to keep pace with the competition.
Objective	The objective of the project is narrow and can be defined exactly, for example, to solve a specific technical problem. The client has a defined objective of what should be achieved with the project.	The objective of the project is broad and not only technical. Frequently, marketing and business aspects are part of the objectives. Often the objective is dynamic and there is a propensity for changes during the life of the project.
Audience	The end-users for whom the IT solution is implemented are well known – the target audience can be defined.	There are a wide range of audiences. You do not know who is going to visit a web site. Aspects like national language support and cultural differences have to be considered.

Table 1. Differences between e-business and traditional IT projects

Technology	Mostly well-proven technology is used. You can benefit from experiences in previous projects where the technology has been used. Often technology plays a supporting role only.	New, cutting-edge technology must be used that is only recently available or still evolving, or must even be invented and developed. Often technology plays a major role and there is a greater dependence on technology than in traditional IT projects.
Duration	The duration depends on the project scope and the project nature but is often greater than six months.	The duration is six months or less, driven by time-to-market requirements and high client expectations. This often results in a tendency to short-cut development processes.
Implementation method	Often the implementation follows the classical waterfall model, where one step after the other is approached or proven OO development techniques are used.	Due to the short project cycle many tasks have to be performed in parallel. Often the solution is implemented in an incremental manner because client expects early results to justify investment decisions.
Client involvement	In a typical, traditional IT project only the IT staff, the project manager, and the end-users of the client are involved. If they are happy with the outcome of the project everything is fine.	In an e-business project many more client staff are involved: not only the IT people, but also finance, marketing, sales, organization, and other departments of the clients company are involved and would like to approve or comment on the project outcome. In addition, senior managers of the client love to get involved to drive the e-business project in the direction they prefer.
Skills	Personnel with classic IT skills like IT architects, system designers, testers, and programmers are needed to implement the solution.	Besides classic IT skills you need creative, consulting, and marketing skills to perform an e-business project.

Table 1 (cont.)

Visibility	If a project fails – for whatever reason – it will get known. But the visibility is normally limited to the IT department and departments close to it due to the limited number of involved end-users.	If an e-business project fails, the visibility might be overwhelming, due to the high number of end-users and due to the fact that e-business is not a technological issue only. Many other departments of the client might be affected. The visibility is much bigger than in a traditional IT project. A single e-business project can make or break a complete client's company.
GUI design	The graphical user interface, if any, is designed by a few individuals. Usually a single key-user is the only individual who is involved in the GUI design.	Often nearly 'everyone' wants to be involved in designed, influencing, recommending, or approving the design of the GUI. Normally the more people are involved the bigger the challenge to agree on a GUI design that satisfies the expectations of all – or most – of the involved people.
Effect	The outcome of the solution has effects only on the IT environment of the client and does not affect the overall way the client is doing its business. The solution is designed in such a way that the established business processes of the client are reflected.	The outcome of the e-business solution often changes the way the client is doing its business. Business processes must be re-engineered, modified, tailored, or created. Sometimes even the organization and the culture of the company must be restructured.

Table 1 (cont.)

Table 1 demonstrates the main reason for the book. As you can see, there are many differences between e-business and traditional IT projects. You take an unnecessary risk if you treat e-business projects like traditional IT projects. e-business projects are not a new type of IT project, they are *more* than IT projects. You can not reduce e-business projects to new technology only. Many non-technical facets have to be considered. As a consequence, traditional IT project management techniques are not sufficient to cover this type of project. A common mistake is to apply only traditional project management techniques in e-business projects: e-business projects are special, and so require some special techniques.

e-business projects usually consists of three elements: (1) hardware, (2) software, and (3) services. The hardware is the machines – like laptops, PDAs, PCs, workstations, servers, and mainframes – and the infrastructure – like networks, modems, switches, and hubs – that are necessary to execute the software and to transfer data.

The software element is represented by the programs that provide the functionality. The software can consist of *off-the-shelf standard products* – like databases, shops, and marketplaces – that need 'only' to be customized to fit the specific needs of a client, or programs that must be developed individually for a client to fit its requirements. Often the software for an e-business project is a combination of off-the-shelf products, and their customization and integration with individually developed software components.

Providing the integrated hardware and software for an e-business project is referred throughout the book as 'building the e-business solution'. Providing the software part of the e-business solution is referred as 'implementing the e-business application'. The myriad of activities necessary to implement the e-business application is a major part of the third element of an e-business project, the *services*.

However, the services are not limited to implementation activities. Supporting and assisting the clients in all work items necessary to deploy the provided e-business solution in their environments successfully – including organizational, marketing, and strategic aspects – are further activities covered by the services element. As defining, procuring, and installing hardware for an e-business project does not differ significantly from performing the same tasks in a traditional IT project, the hardware element of an e-business project is neglected in the following. This book primarily focuses on the management of the software and services elements of e-business projects.

1.3 Challenges in e-business Projects

Many IT projects are not successful: a survey of the Standish Group shows that on average only 16.2% of IT projects are rated as successful, i.e., have been completed on time and on budget [38]. This means that 83.8% of the studied projects failed. Further results indicate a staggering 31.1% of IT projects will be cancelled before they ever get completed. For e-business projects the situation also looks bad: the Gartner Group predicts that through 2002, 75% of all e-business projects will fail to meet their objectives due to fundamental flaws in project planning [13, 24]. In order to avoid your project becoming one of the three out of four that fails, let us take a look at the specific challenges in e-business projects. What are the main challenges you are faced with in e-business projects? There are four fundamental ones:

1. **Client expectations.** Client expectations are high and sometimes unrealistic in terms of project duration and project costs. Time-to-market is key for clients of e-business

solutions due to the tough competition. Clients frantically rush to 'be there first'. Therefore, clients are consistently pressing contractors to compress the project duration. Some clients are surprised about the costs of an e-business project. They believe that developing an e-business solution is designing a few fancy web pages only. Too often they do not have a proper understanding about the effort required to make an e-business project happen; unrealistic client expectations are raised or intensified by suppliers of e-business project services: exaggerated promises to supply e-business services at a lower prize or within a shorter time frame than competitors are sometimes used as arguments by sales people to acquire business. Clients who rely on these promises are disappointed when these can not be fulfilled afterwards. Setting client expectations at a realistic level is therefore imperative. The client must be managed in such a way that its expectations are satisfied to the highest possible extend but professional project management techniques are not sacrificed.

2. **Scope changes.** Often the scope of an e-business project is somewhat unclear at the beginning. If you finally succeed in nailing down the scope during the first few weeks of the project, this does not mean that the scope remains stable until the end of the project. Instead, the scope is dynamic and changes during the life of the project. Sometimes a reason for propensity for scope changes is the involvement of client senior management. In contrast to the situation in many traditional IT projects, client senior managers often feel that they understand the developed e-business solution in detail. They see a couple of colored pages and love bringing in their own view on layout and content – without knowing that they have put their feet in. The client project team often takes their manager's views as new directions, asking the contractor to change the scope and to adopt the solution. Another possible reason for scope changes is that the client company simply grows with a phenomenal speed – as many of the start-up dot-coms demonstrate – which has a great influence on the project scope. In order to deal with frequent scope changes, a proper change management process needs to be established.
3. **Lack of skilled resources.** For e-business projects human resources with specialized e-business skills are required. People with appropriate skills are rare and asked for by many other projects. Market demand for relevant e-business skills and knowledge currently outstrips supply. In such a labor market, the expectations of skilled people regarding salary and perks are high. Tedious efforts have to be invested to attract the proper people, to recruit them for a project, and to keep them in a project.
4. **Unproven and changing technology.** Cutting-edge technology used in e-business projects is often unproven and full of bugs. Why is there a need to use latest technology? The Web has enabled a shift in power from the supplier to the customer. Customers have a much bigger choice among suppliers and are demanding an increased level of quality of service. A competitive quality of service enforces an easy-to-use, reliable, and attractive e-business solution implemented with newest technology. During the project lifetime new hardware, software, or network technology might

come up. You or the client might find it appealing over what was originally planned to be used. In order to exploit best-of-breed technology and be able to provide competitive quality of service, some or all components may have to be exchanged.

What are the decisive determinants to cope with these challenges? I see three: (1) a project team with proper skills, (2) a qualified project manager, and (3) an adequate project implementation approach.

1.4 Skills Required for e-business Projects

What skills and people are required to perform an e-business project? From my perspective you need people from four critical skills disciplines (see Tables 2 – 5):

1. **Information Technology.** Not surprisingly, you need people with IT skills covering the technology part of the project. Cutting-edge technology needs to be invented, designed, developed, integrated, packaged, installed, customized, and deployed.
2. **Creative.** The layout of web pages has to be designed, a concept for the navigation must be developed, the content must be sourced, and graphics must be arranged. Especially the graphical user interface of an e-business application is a decisive factor for its *usability*. As usability is key for the success of an e-business solution, special emphasis must be put on the GUI design. For the design of a GUI, a high level of creativity is needed; the respective activities have to be performed by people from creative disciplines.
3. **Consulting.** An e-business strategy is required, business processes have to be evaluated and re-designed, organizational changes have to be proposed. For those activities consulting skills are required.
4. **Marketing.** Market research, online advertising, branding, media planning, promoting solution launch, etc. have to be performed by marketing specialists.

In addition to the four skills disciplines, another one is required: that is yours – the *project manager*. The skills requirements of a project manager are discussed in Sect. 1.6.

Skills/role	Description/responsibilities
IT architect	An IT architect is skilled in current web architectures and standards, familiar with software packages of leading suppliers, and has knowledge of common hardware platforms. An IT architect is responsible for developing the overall IT architecture and the IT high-level design of the e-business solution. The architecture and the design cover the application, the data, and the infrastructure/network layer of the solution. In bigger e-business projects with a wide range of technologies often a couple of specialized IT architect roles is required. In these projects roles such as CMS architect, network architect, security architect, and hardware architect are common categories of IT architects.
Programmer	A programmer for e-business projects is skilled in current languages, scripts, macros, and techniques, such as Java, JSP, ASP, PHB, C, C++, cgi, and Perl. A programmer is responsible for low-level designing, coding, and integrating the IT part of the e-business solution.
Web developer	A web developer is skilled in the current web script languages HTML and XML, as well as in programming javascript and Flash. A web developer is responsible for coding the front-end of the e-business application.
Content management systems specialist	A content management systems specialist is familiar with the content management systems of leading suppliers. The responsibility of the content management systems specialist is to define together with the conceptor the workflow, roles, and groups, and to integrate a content management system into the e-business solution.
Network specialist	A network specialist is skilled in current network protocols, like tcp/ip and http, and is familiar with aspects of performance and network capacity. The responsibility of the network specialist is to plan, evaluate, select, and design the network infrastructure for the e-business solution taking bandwidth and performance aspects into account.
Database designer/programmer	A database designer/programmer is experienced in widespread database technologies, like Oracle, DB2, and Sybase. The responsibility of the database designer/programmer is to design and implement the model for the data that is used, updated, and produced by the e-business solution.

Table 2. IT discipline roles and responsibilities

Security specialist	A security specialist is experienced in security requirements like, integrity, non-repudiation, authentication, and privacy, and familiar with security concepts of digital signatures, certificates, firewalls, and cryptographic technologies. The responsibility of the security specialist is to enhance design and coding of the e-business solution with security components so that security requirements of a client are met.
Search-engine specialist	A search-engine specialist is familiar with the current search-engines used on the Web. The responsibility of the search-engine specialist is to ensure that a developed B2C e-business solution is appropriately positioned in widely used search-engines.
Quality assurance specialist	A quality assurance specialist is familiar with quality assurance standards, techniques, and procedures. The responsibility of the quality assurance specialist is to ensure that the developed e-business solution is of a sufficient level of quality to meet the expectations of the client. The quality assurance specialist facilitates reviews and provides guidance to the team in all areas relevant to quality.
Tester	A tester is skilled in testing techniques and procedure. The responsibility of the tester is to develop appropriate test plans, procedures, test environments, test cases, test data, and to execute defined system and performance tests.

Table 2 (cont.)

Skills/role	**Description/responsibilities**
Art director	An art director is the head of the creative people. The responsibility of the art director is to determine the creative vision and high-level view of the solution, to ensure the logical integration of information, design, and content into the framework of the aesthetic design, and to oversee the development of the creative solution throughout the course of design, coding, and testing.
Conceptor	A conceptor is skilled in developing the interaction design of a web site considering aspects of navigation, style, usability, orientation, and content integration. The responsibility of a conceptor is to create a low-level view of the web site, describing each web page in detail. This determines the functionality of the e-business solution and influences the IT architecture. A conceptor is one of the key roles in an e-business project.

Table 3. Creative discipline roles and responsibilities

Screen designer	A screen designer is skilled in designing web pages. The design includes format, layout, style, and screen elements. A screen designer is experienced in graphic design software like 'PhotoShop' and 'Illustrator'. The responsibility of a screen designer is to prepare proposals for the screen design to be discussed with the client.
Content designer	A content designer is skilled in planning the content and in planning the structure and the portrayal of the content. The content may include but is not limited to text, animated GIFs, illustrations, 2 D and 3 D graphics, photographs, music, video, and film.
Editor	An editor is a technical writer specialized in writing the text parts of the content. The responsibility of the editor is to produce the text for the web pages and to write internal and external project documentation.
Graphic/video artist	A graphic/video artist is a specialist in handling the graphical content. The responsibility of the graphic/video artist is to prepare the graphics for the content of the web site and to produce video clips that are integrated into the web pages.
Audio/sound artist	A audio/sound artist is a specialist in handling the audio content. The responsibility of the audio/sound artist is to prepare the audio part of the content for integration into the web pages.

Table 3 (cont.)

Skills/role	**Description/responsibilities**
e-business strategy analyst	An e-business strategy analyst is familiar with all questions about vision and strategy in the area of e-business. The responsibility of the e-business strategy analyst is to assist the client in clarifying where it wants to go with e-business. Based on the vision, the e-business strategy analyst supports a client in developing its e-business strategy.
Business analyst	A business analyst is skilled in the business aspects of a specific industry or branch. A business analyst must have an in-depth understanding of the business of the client. The responsibility of the business analyst is to identify, document, and analyze the client's requirements from a business perspective to ensure proper transition of business requirements to e-business solution requirements.

Table 4. Consulting discipline roles and responsibilities

Process consultant	A process consultant is skilled in analyzing, defining, and modifying business processes. The responsibility of the process consultant is to support the customer in reorganizing its business processes in such a way that they fit into the developed e-business solution.
Organization change consultant	The organization change consultant is a specialist in organizational issues. The responsibility of the organization change consultant is to assist the client during the transition and adopting its organizational structures so that the developed e-business provides most value to the client's business.

Table 4 (cont.)

Skills/role	**Description/responsibilities**
Online market researcher	An online market researcher is familiar with current market research techniques such as online surveys, interviewing focal groups, and web site checking. The responsibility of the online market researcher is to analyze the characteristics of the potential end-users to influence the e-business solution in such a way that it is most attractive to the expected audience.
Media planner	A media planner is skilled in developing media strategies, media plans for a flight, and techniques to verify the success of a web site. The responsibility of the media planner is to support the client in generating more traffic on the web site and to find ways to get reimbursement for the investments in the site from the end-users.
Digital branding specialist	A digital branding specialist is skilled in assessing, creating, and managing digital brands. The responsibility of the digital branding specialist is to assist the client in developing a brand strategy and in managing its digital brand.
Online advertising specialist	An online advertising specialist is skilled in defining measures to communicate a new offer on a web site and to make it more attractive. The responsibility of the online advertising specialist is to organize the online advertising services or to support the client in doing so.
Promotion specialist	A promotion specialist is skilled in developing strategies for short-term Internet campaigns in order to raise awareness for a web site, attract new end-users, and keep existing ones. The responsibility of the promotion specialist is to plan and organize respective campaigns or to assist the client in doing so.

Table 5. Marketing discipline roles and responsibilities

In addition to the roles listed in the Tables 2 – 5 you will find others in an e-business project; e.g., administrative assistants, hardware specialists, project office staff, and technical support staff. However those roles can be found in any other non-e-business project, and so I did not include them in the tables. The listed roles should not imply that all of them are needed in each e-business project. The skills requirements depends on the specific project. Nevertheless, in a typical e-business project you will find at least someone from each discipline.

1.5 The Project Manager in e-business Projects

The previous paragraph outlines the skills and roles you typically find in e-business projects. One essential role is missing in this list, which is yours as the *project manager*. What is the role of the project manager in an e-business project?

Before discussing the role we briefly have to clarify the terminology since there is another term sometimes used in e-business projects that causes misunderstandings: the term is *producer*. There are two different opinions regarding what constitutes a producer:

1. Some companies call the project manager of an e-business project as a 'producer'. They view the producer as the person who is responsible for the day-to-day activities, responsible for delivering the e-business solution and managing staff, cost, schedule, quality, etc. Those companies simply do not use the term project manager, they simply call it *producer*. Consequently, the term 'project manager' does not show up in their terminology.
2. In other companies the term producer exists with a different meaning. Those companies call the person who is responsible for the production process – coding of web pages, programming e-business solutions, etc. – a producer. Similar to the art director who is the head of the creative people, the producer is seen as the head of the IT people, providing guidance to them as well as overseeing, documenting, and improving the production process. In e-business projects of those companies the roles of project manager and producer exist, whereas the producer is a member of the project team managed by the project manager.

If you are confronted in the e-business environment with the term producer make sure that you understand what is meant: a person responsible for the overall project or a person responsible for the production process only. In order to avoid misunderstandings the term producer is not used in this book. In analogy to traditional IT projects, the person who is responsible for the day-to-day activities is called *project manager*. In bigger projects, if there is a need for someone heading the IT people, this person is called the *subteam leader*.

Now, what is the responsibility of the project manager in an e-business project? It does not differ too much form the project manager's role in an traditional IT project – the basic role of a project manager has not changed [27, 34, 39]. A project manager is responsible for delivering the e-business solution to the client. In short, the project manager is responsible for 'everything' – but with very little authority. Too short for you? Then let us take a look on five typical roles of an e-business project manager:

1. **Communication interface.** The project manager is responsible for communication (1) within the project team, (2) between the project team and others in the contractor's company like senior management and functional organizations, (3) between the project team and the client, and (4) between the project team and subcontractors, if any.
2. **Project team leader.** The project manager is responsible for managing the project team. This includes recruiting people, organizing work environment, defining project organization, conducting team building exercises, clarifying roles and responsibilities, and resolving interpersonal conflicts.
3. **Planner and controller.** The project manager plans the project in terms of scope, schedule, budget, quality, and risk. He or she is continuously comparing the actuals against the developed plan and taking actions to manage deviations.
4. **Decision maker.** The project manager is the final authority in the project team to make decisions that are not or can not be made by other team members. Typically these are decisions that influence the overall project schedule, budget, or quality.
5. **Administrative wizard.** The project manager has to deal with all the administrative tasks that must be handled in order to maintain clean records on the project. One of the bigger challenges for the project manager is to remove administrative road blocks for the team. For the team, administrative tasks must be low key and largely invisible.

Of course there are numerous other assignments for the project manager, but I have listed the five that are the most important ones from my point of view.

1.6 The Qualifications of an e-business Project Manager

What makes a good e-business project manager? The three fundamental qualifications of an e-business project manager are (see Fig. 1):

1. **Hard-skills project management knowledge.** Understanding project management techniques, processes, and tools, as well as knowing when and how to apply them is a basic qualification of an e-business project manager. The theory on project management techniques, processes, and tools can be learned from textbooks. One source

of information is, for example, the *Project Management Body of Knowledge* [32]. A good project manager must have this knowledge at his or her fingertips. However, knowledge of the theory is not sufficient; applying the appropriate techniques, processes, and tools in a given project is much more important. This can not be learned from textbooks. The best way to do this is through practical experience, the more the better.

2. **Soft-skills project management knowledge.** Understanding the soft skills of project management and the ability to apply these skills properly throughout the project lifetime is crucial for a project manager. What are required soft skills for successful e-business project management?
   - **Communication.** A project manager must be able to communicate effectively. Giving client presentations, passing on information to the team, listening to problems, negotiating contractual issues are only some examples of numerous situations where good communication skills are essential.
   - **Engagement.** Working in an e-business project is not easy living, neither for the project manager nor for the other members of the team. Often personal time must be sacrificed due to project constraints stretching the work versus family life balance. The project manager should be a hard worker, a plodder who gets a job done acting as a role model for the team.
   - **Social competence.** A big portion of project management is attributable to people management. A project manager must have a sound feeling for interpersonal relationships and conflicts. He or she should be a consummate diplomat.
   - **Creativity.** e-business projects require a high level of creativity, not only from the people from the creative discipline but also from the project manager. A project manager's creativity is required to find new ways and to adapt to new situations quickly since change is a cornerstone of e-business projects.
   - **Power of endurance.** An e-business project manager is exposed to a high-level of stress. Overall responsibility for the project with often limited direct authority puts a large burden on the shoulders of the project manager. A high power of endurance is needed to sustain this pressure for the whole life of a project.
   - **Trustworthiness.** A project manager must be able to convey that he or she can be trusted to do always what is adequate at the right time to keep all project stakeholders satisfied.
   - **Common sense.** Last but not least, common sense should not be underestimated. e-business project management is not a mystery or magic, it is real life with hard facts. Having common sense is not a disadvantage.

   The above list of soft-skills is not all-inclusive – I have listed only those that are, in my experience, the most important ones.
3. **Basic e-business knowledge.** The emphasis is on *basic*, rather than in-depth knowledge of latest e-business technology. As project manager of an e-business project you must be willing to give up technical expertise and become a generalist. Because

the technical skills spans from IT, to marketing, creative, and consulting, it is simply not feasible to be the technical expert in all those areas. However, it is important that the project manager has a reasonable knowledge of all those areas so that he or she is able to ask the right questions and to understand what the team is doing. As the project manager is not the technical expert, it is important to recruit people who have in-depth technical knowledge and can assist him or her in decision making.

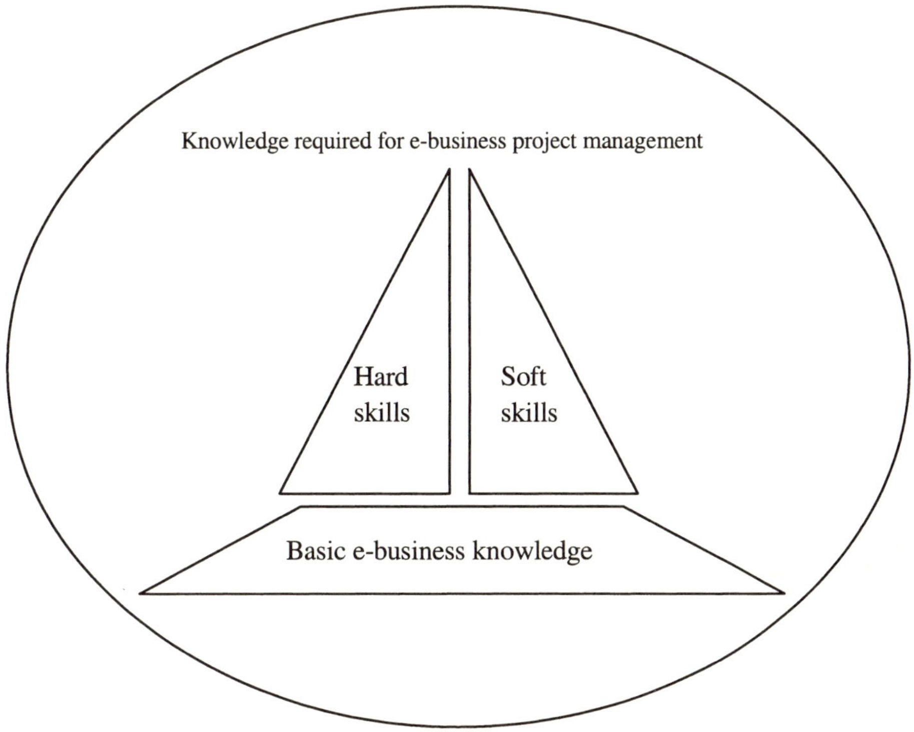

Fig. 1. Qualifications of an e-business project manager

A sound combination of the three fundamental qualifications is a good basis for an e-business project manager. In addition, knowledge about the industry that a client is in is an advantage.

An e-business project must translate into business value for the client in order for it to be considered successful. A basic understanding of the client's industry, what is critical to the success of the client, and who are the major competitors of the client can be extremely beneficial. There are of course a lot of different industries and an individual can not be skilled in all of them. In the absence of basic skills in the specific industry of a client, the project manager should at least be willing and able to extract some information about the client's business during the project lifetime. Combining this specific information with knowledge of standard business processes will provide a sufficient understanding of the client's business to make a project successful. However, being an effective e-business project manager is an ongoing challenge.

1.7 The First Key Success Factor

This book discusses 99 so-called *key success factors*. A key success factor can be a recommendation, a piece of advice, a rule of thumb, or an insight. The overall objective of the described key success factors is to provide you with guidance and support in managing e-business projects. The common element of the listed key success factors is that they are derived from real-world business experiences – they are not theoretical or academic. Furthermore, in general they are neither limited to a specific country or industry in which a project is performed, nor do they assume a certain size of a project or the company that is conducting a project.

While each of the discussed key success factors might contain an element that provides some benefit to you, there is an outstanding factor that is superior to all others. To emphasize its importance I decided to list it as the first one and under a separate heading:

@ 1 e-business projects require proper project management

Some people believe that e-business projects need *not* to be managed. From their perspective introducing project management would raise some inevitable obstacles: slowing down progress, introducing unnecessary bureaucracy, and hampering the creativity of the team members involved are only a few of their arguments. However, just the opposite is true: a reasonable amount of structure and organization can fuel e-business progress without any bureaucratic burden and in fact can help you to move faster – in the right direction. And you do not have to rely on the inspiration of creative geniuses only, since their work can be planned and controlled as well.

Other people accept that e-business projects require management. But due to the magic term 'e' involved they view the management of these types of project as a mystery. They suspect that traditional project management is no longer viable in an e-business environment and look for some new, mysterious techniques. Rather than performing the proven 'hard work' of project management, they search for an easy way out when asked to manage an e-business project.

I am convinced that professional project management is required for e-business projects, maybe even more so than for any other type of project. e-business projects – as the name already suggests – are *projects* and as such most – not all – of the well-known project management techniques proven in numerous other project types can also be applied to e-business projects. There is no need to suspend the rules of good project management just because it is 'e-business'. Nonetheless, since e-business projects raise some specific challenges the sole use of traditional project management techniques is not sufficient – those have to be complemented by some that are specific to e-business.

To summarize: e-business projects require project management. You have to accept that there are no shortcuts or a magic silver bullet. Proper e-business project management is a sound mixture of traditional project management techniques and specific e-business ones. And this is exactly what this whole book is about.

1.8 e-business Solution Implementation Approach

What is the best and fastest implementation approach to use when developing an e-business solution? There is not always a perfect answer. In most of the traditional IT projects solution development and delivery follows a monolithic implementation process: one path of consecutive phases, often named 'assessing', 'planning', 'designing', 'coding', 'building', 'testing', 'installing', and 'supporting', is followed [36]. Each phase is conducted once. One phase is performed after the other in a sequential order while each phase builds upon those that precede it. This is the classical 'waterfall model'.

Does this monolithic implementation approach – the waterfall model – work for e-business solutions as well? I do not think so! What are arguments against such an approach? Perhaps the most simple is the fact that it would not cope with the challenges of e-business projects. You might remember Sect. 1.3 where I listed four of them. Clients expect a solution delivery in a short time. Performing the project activities one after the other is time-consuming – the solution can not be delivered quickly. The logical consequence is: you have to work in parallel as much as feasible.

Due to the specific skills needed in e-business projects, a large number of different people are required. Human resources skilled for e-business projects are scarce and expensive. Doing one phase after the other can lead to the situation where people have to wait for items to be completed before the following activities can be started. The result is that the team members are not fully deployed with project work. You can not afford to have these talents sitting around. Planning the work in such a way that many activities can be performed in parallel is the correct solution to this problem.

Using cutting-edge, unproven technology is always risky. You can reduce the risk by performing early tests to verify whether the technology works as expected. If you follow the monolithic implementation approach, the testing is planned to take place rather late in the process. This means that issues arising from technology are discovered very late. This problem can be overcome by implementing a first release of a solution with limited functionality – sometimes called a 'prototype' – early in the project. The technology used can be verified with the prototype. The first release is afterwards enhanced incrementally until the full functionality is implemented. Moreover, as the scope is sometimes somewhat unclear at the beginning of an e-business project and often changes during the project, an implementation approach is needed that allows the introduction of scope changes in a flexible manner.

In summary, the key requirements of an implementation approach that is well suited for e-business projects are: (1) performing work in parallel, (2) planning for an early prototype and tests, and (3) allowing flexibility for changes. What does such an implementation approach look like? Of course there is not *one* approach as a single answer to every project. I would like to describe briefly a suitable approach.

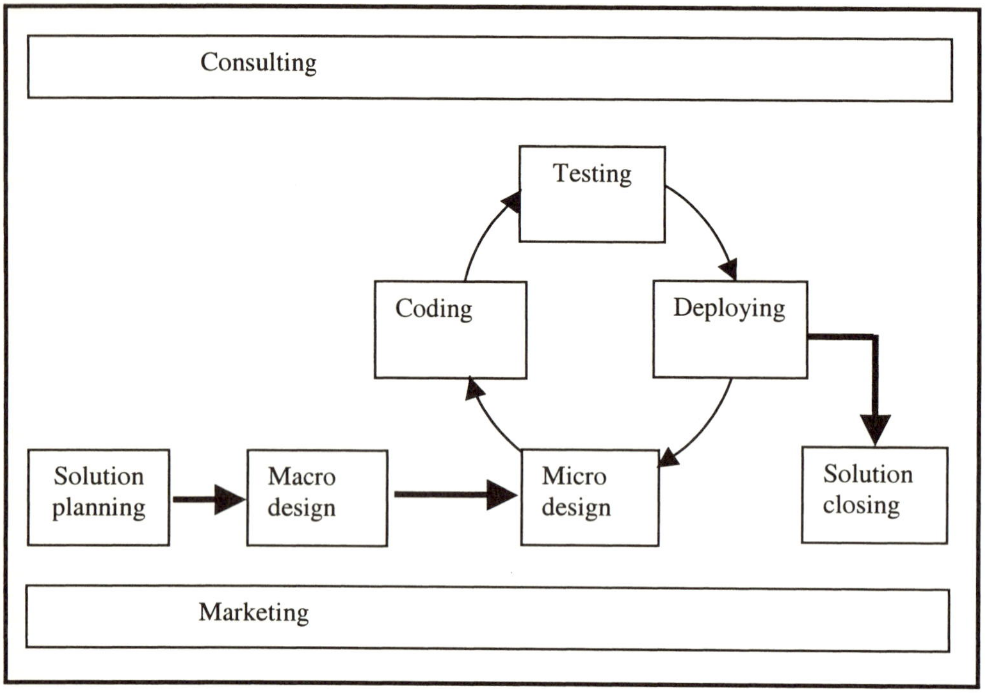

Fig. 2. e-business solution implementation approach

As shown in Fig. 2, the main idea of the approach is that the phases of solution planning, macro design, and solution closing are conducted once, while the phases of micro design, coding, testing, and deploying are conducted several times – 'iteratively' – during a project. Conducting the latter four phases more than once allows incremental development of the solution in form of *releases*. From release-to-release the functionality is enriched until the target solution is achieved. Each release is designed, coded, tested, and deployed. Experiences from one release are taken to benefit and improve the subsequent one. Instead of a waterfall model with consecutive phases such an iterative approach is recommended for e-business projects.

This approach fulfills the three requirements listed above. Work can be performed in parallel; i.e., the team can work in parallel on two releases to avoid idle times. Doing activities in parallel reduces the overall project time frame. Unproven technology can be tested in one of the first releases so that there is time left for taking measures if the technology does not work as expected. Scope changes arising during the project lifetime can be responded to easily by adjusting the design and implementing the change within one of the subsequent releases. Let us take a closer look at each phase:

- **Solution planning.** The purpose of the solution planning phase is to capture the functional and non-functional requirements of the solution, to define the initial scope, to determine the complexity of the solution, and to prepare a detailed plan for the following phases. This plan normally contains in particular an adaptive release strategy for the construction of the final e-business solution. Typically in the solution planning phase, e-business consultants support the client to position the to-be-developed solution in the context of the client company strategy. This might include the development and definition of an *e-business strategy* and an analysis of the current client business processes. In addition, recommendations of required organizational or business process changes can be developed and discussed with the client, because in contrast to traditional IT projects, e-business projects almost always require a transformation of established business processes and organizational structures of a client to reflect the new requirements of the 'cyber world'.
- **Macro design.** The purpose of the macro design phase is to develop a high-level architecture framework upon which the single releases of the solution can be built up. The macro design lays the groundwork and addresses the architectural issues that are common to all releases. The high-level architecture includes a component model defining the overall structure of the solution, and an organizational model defining how the components of the solution are distributed over infrastructure nodes. In order to develop a macro design that leads to a solution satisfying the needs of the intended end-users, the macro design phase is flanked by marketing activities to identify and to analyze the target audiences and their expectations. This might include market research activities to investigate competitors of a client or the selection of focus groups for online marketing research tasks.
- **Micro design.** The purpose of the micro design phase is to prepare the coding and the testing of a specific release. The micro design phase narrows the scope of a release by selecting and specifying the functionality that should be covered. For the specified functions, a low-level design is performed that models and refines components of the solution. On the user-interface side the low-level design covers aspects such as the format and layout of web pages, navigation among pages, and content handling. Here especially usability aspects – including the 'look-and-feel' of the solution – have to be considered [29]. In contrast to many traditional IT projects, the proper design of the graphical user-interface is one of the decisive factors for project success. At the application level the low-level design covers, if appropriate, the integration of content management and back-end systems while considering aspects of security and infrastructure. The micro design phase often includes the development of a *digital brand* for the e-business solution. The digital brand development comprises activities such as performing a brand assessment, developing a brand architecture and a brand strategy, and inventing a communication strategy to introduce the digital brand.

- **Coding.** The purpose of the coding phase is to build a specific release of the solution. The coding includes the creation of web pages with editing, formatting, and optimizing content as well as the coding of application modules. In the coding phase a close cooperation between the 'creative' team members coding the GUI and the 'techies' coding the application modules must be ensured. After the coding activities of the web pages and the modules of the application are completed, the elements are put together into an integrated solution.
- **Testing.** The purpose of the testing phase is to verify the quality of the integrated solution. Aspects of quality are, for example, that the solution provides all functions that have been specified for a specific release, and that reliability, usability, and performance requirements are fulfilled. If deviations are discovered between the specification and the built solution, re-working is performed in order to improve the quality. As usability is a key factor for an e-business solution, the testing activities often include an evaluation of usability aspects as part of the flanking marketing activities.
- **Deploying.** The purpose of the deployment phase is to bring a specific release into production at the client's facilities. The deployment starts with installing the solution in the test or production environment of the client and performing a production readiness test. Each release is evaluated by client personnel or end-users, and the results fed back into the assessment of the next release. The launch of an e-business solution is often supported by online advertising campaigns to raise awareness for the launched solution.
- **Solution closing.** The purpose of the solution-closing phase is to capture the results of the project. This phase takes place after completion of the last release cycle. Closing the solution includes obtaining acceptance of the final solution by the client, getting a client satisfaction report, performing lessons learned, and administrative closure.

It is important to understand that the approach outlined above is only one out of numerous alternatives. It is not necessary to follow this approach exactly when you are implementing an e-business solution; it might be tailored to specific needs or a completely different approach might be useful. However, it is good practice to take an approach that addresses the three requirements, i.e., allowing work to be performed in parallel, early testing, and flexibility for changes through iterations.

Regardless of which implementation approach you use, you have to perform project management activities to make the solution delivery happen. This book focuses on project management aspects – the aspects of technical solution delivery are not covered in detail. Project management aspects are not completely independent from the selected implementation approach. However, most of the project management processes, techniques, and methods can be applied to all approaches. The project management activities can be grouped into three primary categories [41]:

1. Project management activities performed only *once*. Typically those activities are executed at the start or close of a project. Activities of this category are, for example, defining the initial scope, estimating the project costs, defining an initial project time plan, defining project procedures for change, risk, and communication management, setting up the work environment, performing lessons learned, and administrative closure.
2. Project management activities performed *periodically* throughout the project at defined intervals. Activities of this category are, for example, tracking project progress, producing project status reports, updating the project time plan, monitoring the risk management plan, and building and motivating the project team.
3. Project management activities performed *as needed*, based on events that occur during the project. Activities of this category are, for example, handling of change requests, responding to risks that occur, and sorting out issues with the client.

Another alternative way of structuring the project management effort is using *domains*. All project management aspects that deal with a specific topic, for example, recruiting the team, defining an organizational structure, or managing the team are put together into one domain called '*managing the team*'. This is exactly the structuring approach used in this book.

1.9 How the Book Is Organized

The structure of the book is relatively straightforward: The introduction of the book sets the stage. It is followed by 12 chapters, each presenting one domain relevant for managing e-business projects. Each chapter discusses a single management domain. The 12 chapters are organized in the same basic manner. A chapter starts with an overview on the management domain, giving a brief motivation for the need for the domain and explaining which processes are required to cover the topic. Each identified process is described in terms of input, activities, techniques, and output.

The *input* section lists the elements that are required as input for performing the activities. Attention is given to where the input comes from, for which activity it is needed, and how it is used. The *activity* section looks at the single activities that must be performed within a process. For each activity it is defined who has to perform it and what the output of the activity is. The *techniques* section discusses possible tools, methods, and techniques that are good practice and can be applied to perform an activity. If meaningful, templates or examples of tools, methods, and techniques are presented. The *output* section traces the outcome of a process. The final section discusses *key success factors* that are best practice when performing the described process.

The flow of the 12 chapters is according to an obvious sequence when approaching an e-business project. Chapter 2 discusses the planning and the definition of the *project scope*. An approach for capturing requirements jointly with the client is outlined. It is described how the requirements can be transformed into a written scope description determining the overall scope of the project. Attention is given to developing a *work breakdown structure* to organize the project work.

Chapter 3 deals with the *project schedule*. It suggests a way for developing and controlling the project schedule. This includes the sequencing and estimating the effort required for each work package, the creation of a *project time plan*, and tracking the project progress.

Chapter 4 focuses on the *project team*. A process for recruiting the human resources required to carry out the project work is outlined. A description of how to define and document the project organization by identifying and assigning project roles, responsibilities, and relationships between the team members is given. In addition, some team building exercises are proposed.

Chapter 5 deals with the *costs* of an e-business project. It outlines a procedure for cost estimation, an approach for budget planning, and a proposal for cost tracking and control.

Chapter 6 treats the *client* as one element of a project that must be managed. It explains the vital role of a client as one factor for project success, how a contractor can help a client to achieve its objectives, and how a client can be involved in the project. In addition, problem management in the form of dealing with *project issues* is discussed.

Chapter 7 looks at *project risks*. Typical risks of e-business projects are listed and a process for the identification and quantification of risks is recommended. This chapter identifies alternatives for responding to project risks and discusses a process for tracking risks.

Chapter 8 focuses on managing e-business *technology*. It outlines the challenges raised by the use of cutting-edge e-business technology and gives recommendations for implementing and deploying technology.

Chapter 9 provides a view on *quality* management. A process for quality planning, quality assurance, and quality control is outlined and explained with examples.

Chapter 10 explains the *change* management process in e-business projects. A process for handling *change requests* is outlined and a sample template for a change request form is depicted.

Chapter 11 discusses the management of *subcontractors*. It suggests a procedure for subcontractor selection, and deals with issues of contracting. In addition, means of monitoring and controlling the progress of a subcontractor's work are discussed.

Chapter 12 outlines the *communications* process in e-business projects. It identifies the stakeholders of a project who take part in project communication and gives recommendations on information distribution and performance reporting.

Chapter 13 looks at the *documentation* for e-business projects. It gives an overview on the different kinds of documentation that are useful for e-business projects, and discusses ways of producing and handling technical and legal documents.

Appendix A is a list of the acronyms used throughout the book. Appendix B provides a glossary of project management and e-business-specific terms. The References section contains useful sources on project management and e-business topics.

The book closes with two indices: the first index lists the 99 key success factors, and the second is a subject index of the topics discussed in the book.

To finalize the outline of the organization of the book, just a short comment on the subtitle: You might ask why exactly *99* key success factors are listed. Are there really 99, why not more, why not less? In fact, to be honest, the answer is quite simple: it is just *marketing*. When I got the idea of writing a book on e-business project management I started with a list of 79 factors which I viewed as critical for project success. While writing the first few chapters the list increased steadily and I ended up with 116. But would you like a book with a subtitle called *116 key success factors*? For me the number did not look appealing. I thought of a better one that might make the title more attractive, and the number 99 came to mind. In order to avoid holding back substantial information by simply not listing the 17 remaining ones, I contemplated a little bit, sometimes combining two factors into a single one, and, as you see, I finally managed to present 99 success factors.

1.10 What Is in This Book for the Reader

The book is primarily intended for current and prospective e-business project managers who wish to share ideas, experiences, and best practices. It is written from a project manager's point of view working in a *contractor* company performing an e-business project for a *client*. However, I believe that many of the aspects discussed in the book will also prove useful for project managers on the client side. e-business project managers on the client side can obtain insights into the way contractors are performing their work which might help them to better understand the attitudes of the contractor project manager.

A prerequisite for performing an e-business project for a client is that a legal relationship between a client and a contractor – usually in terms of a contract – is established. Before a contract is signed several activities usually take place: The client company sources and evaluates potential contractors before one is finally selected. A contractor company applies to perform a project, often in competition with other potential contractors. The activities that take place on the contractor side to obtain a project contract are not a core project management topic and as such are not discussed explicitly in this book. Usually those items are referred to as 'sales' or 'acquisition' activities. Sometimes a contractor project manager is involved in those 'pre-project' activities. Therefore, some of those activities are sketched in brief where they are closely linked to project management issues.

What level of knowledge on project management and e-business should the 'ideal' reader of the book have? First, I believe that the 'ideal' reader does not exist. Each individual has its own previous experiences and its own expectations. However, the reader should have a well-grounded knowledge on project management basics. This book is not intended to serve as an introduction to project management fundamentals – it is not a primer although it has to cover some 'basics' to set the stage and the context. I do not expect that the book will be of much value to individuals who are beginners in project management. There is excellent literature on project management fundamentals, and some recommendations can be found in the References section of the book.

A basic knowledge of e-business would be an advantage for the reader. Without knowing the specific terminology used in the field of e-business, it might be hard to follow some parts of the book. Two categories of people might benefit most from the book: (1) project managers with wide experiences in traditional IT projects who are now asked to take over an e-business project, and (2) individuals and practitioners who are experts in the field of e-business but who possess limited project management experience, and who would like to improve their operational project management expertise.

The key success factors are the core of the book. They provide specific guidelines for managing e-business projects – managing them in a *profitable* way for a contractor. However, many of the listed key success factors may be true for other projects as well. This is not a surprising, since e-business projects – as the name already suggests – are *projects*. Therefore, there is no reason why some of the guidelines given should not work in other projects, for example, traditional IT ones.

Not all 99 listed success factors may be applicable in your project. Each project is specific and provides its own challenges. Simple replication of experiences is not sufficient in any case – tailoring the listed factors to unique needs is sometimes more likely to be successful. Or, for certain reasons, in your project only a subset of the management domains are of interest so that some of the problems addressed do not show up. Be happy about this! e-business projects are complex and challenging by themselves. If you have a chance to reduce the project management challenges, take the chance and limit your attention to the subset of the listed success factors that are applicable to your project.

There are several ways of reading the book. You can proceed through the book sequentially reading one page after the other. If you would not like to take the time to read the book cover to cover, you can consult the Table of Contents to see which management domains are of most interest to you so that you can concentrate on selected chapters only. Another alternative is to start with the index listing the 99 key success factors, and jump directly into the topics that are most applicable to your project.

2 Managing the Scope

The scope of a project defines the work that has to be performed. When the idea for a project is born, typically defining the project scope is one of the initial activities. Planning and defining the scope of an IT project is usually performed by the company that recognizes the business need for initiating a project. When a project is not conducted inhouse, a different company – usually called the *contractor* – for performing the work is sourced, selected, and contracted. Often a *request for proposal* (RfP) is issued to potential contractors in order to obtain offers for performing the project work. In a traditional IT project the contribution of a potential contractor is limited to evaluate whether the defined project work can be performed and to quote a price for it. From a contractor's point of view managing the project scope is ensuring that the contracted project work is delivered. Normally a *work breakdown structure* (WBS) is developed to structure and organize the contracted work. A scope change control process ensures that changes of the project scope required during the course of the project are handled properly.

In e-business projects a potential contractor is often involved earlier in a project to support a client in planning and defining the project scope. Therefore, the responsibility of a contractor in scope management is usually much broader in an e-business project than in a traditional IT project.

In e-business projects the managing scope domain can be divided in three major processes: (1) *planning the project scope* by identifying the project requirements and by evaluating project scope options, (2) *defining the project scope* by documenting the project scope and project goals, and (3) *developing a WBS* for the defined project scope to structure and organize the project work. In the following these three managing project scope processes are discussed in detail from a contractor's point of view.

2.1 Planning the Project Scope

In many traditional IT projects planning the scope of a project is an area where a potential contractor is *not* involved. The scope of a project is planned by a client based on defined requirements addressing a specific IT problem. In IT projects clients mostly have a clear understanding of the requirements of a project and on the objectives they wish to achieve. This allows a client to plan the project scope independently from a contractor. Planning the project scope is normally completed before a potential contractor for performing the work of a project appears on the scene.

In an e-business environment the situation is often completely different: many clients have no clear view on what they want to do. They only know that they want – or must – be active in e-business. What are typical reasons for this? Predictions of enormous business opportunities published in the media forecasting exponential growth in e-commerce inspire many client's addictive desire to get a piece of the pie. Overwhelming fears of putting themselves out of business when competitors launch e-business solutions on the Web or announce that they will soon do so drive clients to jump on the e-business train. CEOs are afraid of disappointing the expectations of their shareholders if they tell them that the company is not active in the e-business field. There are numerous other reasons why clients would like to take part in e-business.

Unfortunately, the entire e-business market is not settled and is relatively immature in nature. Today, no-one knows precisely what business model is viable and successful, which e-business solution attracts most end-users, and in which area the big money can be made. In this environment many clients are rattled and experiment with different approaches. They want to initiate an e-business project, but their intention is often the only thing that they can be definitive about. As a consequence many clients are unable to plan and define the scope of a project by themselves and are therefore looking for help. It is typical in e-business projects that potential contractors for performing the project work are involved early in supporting the planning of the project scope. Planning the scope of a project in an e-business context means identifying the requirements that should be fulfilled by a project and evaluating options for a possible project scope.

For contractors this situation is both an opportunity and a risk. On the one hand they are embroiled in a project from near the beginning and can define project requirements jointly with a client. This provides a contractor with a fair chance of fully understanding the client's business problem and to recommend solutions that probably will fulfill the client's expectations. On the other hand, supporting a client in scope planning bears a risk: planning the scope of a project is often conducted before a contract for performing a project is signed by a client and a contractor. Project scope planning is mostly a *pre-project* activity. When a contractor provides this support for free there is always a risk that the client will award the project to another supplier when the project scope is planned and defined. Some clients agree to compensate the contractor's efforts. Others view this support as an investment on the part of a potential contractor to acquire a project.

In the following the project scope planning process is described in terms of the *input* required to perform the process, *activities* that represent single steps to be undertaken, *techniques* that can be applied to support the activities, *output* that can be expected from this process, and some *key success factors* that might facilitate you in executing the process. Fig. 3 provides an overview of these process constituents.

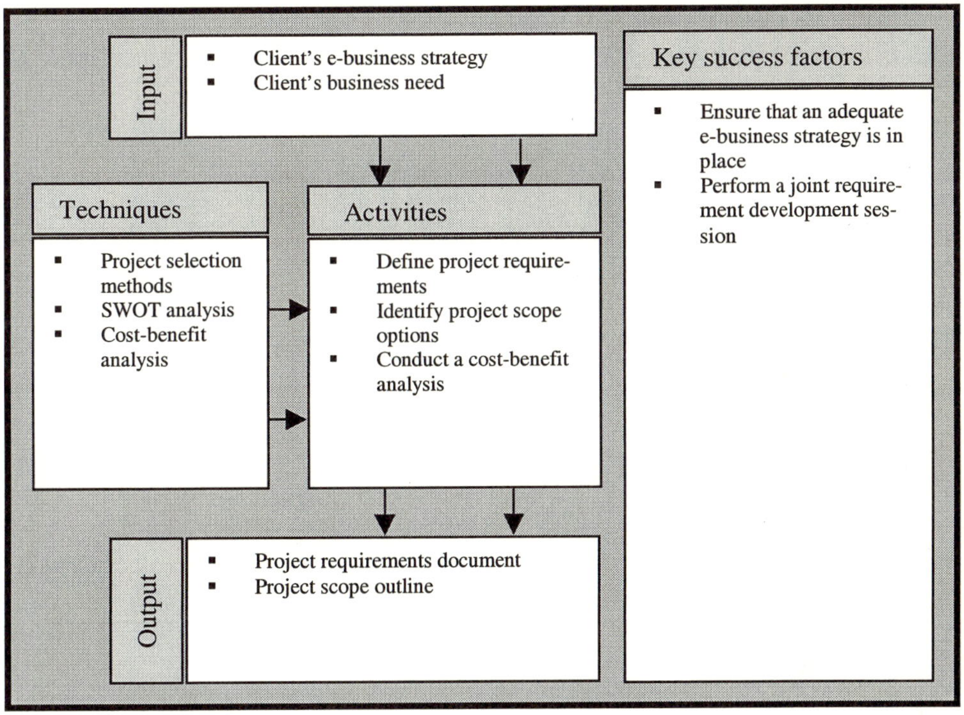

Fig. 3. Planning the project scope

2.1.1 Inputs

Client's e-business strategy

A fundament input for planning the scope of a project is the *e-business strategy* of the client. An e-business strategy defines the approach a client company plans to take to implement its *e-business vision.* The e-business vision of a client company determines where it wants to go with e-business in general. It sketches the direction in which a company wants to evolve in the e-business area. An e-business vision of a company usually answers questions like: What are the core business objectives that should be addressed with e-business? Which end-users do the company want to attract? How does the company want to position itself against competitors? Is e-business a means to make money or to save money? Which of the company products and services are included and excluded from the e-business initiative?

An e-business strategy determines the way a client wants to go to implement its e-business vision. It usually defines but is not limited to aspects like: Which e-business initiatives should be implemented and with what priority? What information should be disseminated to end-users, suppliers, and partners of the company and how do those interact with each other? How can the e-business activities be integrated with other company activities? How can current company business processes be transformed or tailored to e-business? What level of financial and personnel support is dedicated to e-business?

Client's business need

The initiation of an e-business project by a client is usually triggered by a *business need.* Typical client's business needs for initiating an e-business project are: (1) to cope with competitors who are already online with e-business solutions, or plan to do so; (2) to satisfy the demand of partners or suppliers who want to interact with a company via a B2B solution; (3) to defend or increase market share by providing better services for end-users through exploiting the latest Internet technology; (4) to implement a new business idea for making money via the Web; and (5) to save money by replacing internal company business processes or by streamlining existing ones with the support of e-business.

There are numerous other business needs that can act as stimuli for initiating an e-business project. The bottom line of all these triggers is that a client has to make a decision about how to respond. Usually the business need only determines a framework and a target audience for a to-be-developed e-business solution, for example, whether it should be a B2B, B2C, or C2C solution.

2.1.2 Activities

Define project requirements

Triggered by a specific business need and guided by the e-business strategy, identifying and capturing the requirements that a client wishes to address is the first activity in planning the scope of a project. Typically a client has a good understanding of its business need but little idea about how to address it with an e-business project. A *joint requirement development session* (see Sect. 2.1.5) between a client and a potential contractor is a good starting point to achieve a common understanding of the client's requirements regarding a future project. The objective of defining requirements for a project is to build a basis in sufficient detail for devising an e-business solution and for imagining how to develop it so that options for an adequate project scope can be identified.

Project requirements can be categorized in *functional* and *non-functional.* Functional requirements mainly address the functionality of the to-be-developed e-business solution in terms of features and functions that the solution should provide.

On the one hand, non-functional requirements address qualitative and non-technical characteristics of the to-be-developed e-business solution, like usability, branding, availability, performance, portability, and maintainability. On the other hand, non-functional requirements cover project constraints, like a restricted project budget on the client side for e-business, a specific launch date limiting the project duration, technical standards that the solution must satisfy, or a specific technology that should be exploited. Although non-functional requirements are important in traditional IT projects, in e-business projects non-functional requirements are an absolute key aspect. Fulfillment of non-functional requirements is a fundamental prerequisite for client satisfaction and the overall success of an e-business project.

The outcome of the define project requirements activity is normally a *project requirements document* (see Sect. 2.1.4) that serves as the input for identifying project scope options.

Identify project scope options

The next activity after development and definition of the project requirements is to identify options for a possible project scope, since normally there are several options available that can be taken to satisfy the defined requirements. When planning the scope for a project it is good practice to identify, in a first step, valid options, and in a second step select the best option out of these available ones. Options might be expressed in terms of possible whole projects or possible components within one project. The identified options for a possible project scope should be sketched in a sufficient level of detail so that a further evaluation allows selection of the 'best' option as the scope for the future project.

Selecting the best options can be supported by using appropriate *selection methods* or by performing a *SWOT analysis* (see Sect. 2.1.3).While the identification of project scope options can be performed as a joint effort by a client and a potential contractor, the selection of one option is usually performed by a client alone. When a decision for one project scope option is taken, the third and last step of this activity is to describe the scope in a high-level form as a *project scope outline* (see Sect. 2.1.4).The project scope outline serves as the basis for defining the project scope in detail and for justifying the establishment of the project.

Conduct a cost–benefit analysis

When one project scope option has been selected and outlined, the next activity is to justify the formal establishment of the project and to obtain the approval of the client's senior management to proceed with scope definition. This is because an e-business project normally requires a considerable investment by the client company, and such investments need to be justified in order to raise the funding for the project. Obviously, a justification needs to be prepared by the client. Nevertheless, clients often ask potential contractors for their support in collecting sufficient and appropriate arguments for project establishment.

A common method for project justification is to perform a *cost–benefit analysis* (see Sect. 2.1.3). The cost–benefit analysis should be commensurate with the size, complexity, and cost of thc intended project, and prepared at a sufficient level of detail to justify the project establishment. When conducting a cost–benefit analysis for an e-business project it is important to consider the costs that the transformation of client organizational structures and client business processes incur, because exploiting the intended benefits from using an e-business solution requires usually changes to current organizational structures and current business processes of a client. Often a client is not aware of this fact and associated costs caused by the required changes are forgotten to be considered in the cost–benefit analysis.

Nonetheless, a cost–benefit analysis focuses on the economic aspects of a project. An e-business project might fuel other benefits such as capturing market share or 'mind share', or strengthening end-user loyalty. These factors can also be used to support project justification.

The outcome of a cost–benefit analysis is a recommendation to the client's senior management as to whether or not to conduct a project with the outlined scope. In the following it is assumed that the recommendation is in favor of performing the project and that the client's senior management approves proceeding with the project scope definition.

2.1.3 Techniques

Project selection methods

Project selection methods can be used to evaluate different project scope options and to support the decision of choosing one of them. Project selection methods measure the benefit or the attractiveness of the available options from the perspective of the project owner – the client. There are a variety of project selection methods [20]. For e-business projects the *comparative approach model* and the *scoring model* seem to be the most appropriate ones for selecting a scope option.

With the comparative approach model the benefits provided by different available options are assessed and compared based on defined evaluation criteria. The outcome of the comparison is a ranking of the different scope options. The option at the top of the ranking list is the 'best' one.

With the scoring model a *balanced project scorecard* is built. The scorecard methodology was introduced by R Kaplan and D Norton [21, 22]. The basic idea of a project scorecard is to evaluate a project in terms of weighted measurement categories. Single project measurements are defined and placed into measurement categories. For each measurement category a weighting factor determined by the overall importance of the category is assigned. Scores are assessed by judgment experts for the defined measurements. The overall project score results from a simple calculation of the category scores. If the scoring process is performed for each of the project scope options, the option with the highest project score is the 'best' one.

It has to be kept in mind that the outcome of applying a project selection method is only as good as the input to this process. Assigning scores or comparing benefits has to be performed by carefully chosen representatives of the client.

SWOT analysis

SWOT stands for strength, weaknesses, opportunities, and threats. A SWOT analysis is a popular method of dealing with complex decision situations in a limited amount of time. In the context of project selection a SWOT analysis is a systematic approach to exploring how the outcome of different possible projects would influence the position of the client's company.

The idea of the method is to evaluate the current position of the client company in terms of four dimensions: (1) *s*trengths are internal positive factors and particularly represent assets that a company is the holder of or things that a company can do better than its competitors; (2) *w*eaknesses are also internal to the company, but they are negative factors and the opposite of strengths; (3) opportunities are external positive future possibilities raised by market conditions; and (4) threats are also external factors and are the opposite to opportunities. Threats are negative forces in the market.

To assess the current position of a company normally a diagram with four sectors as depicted in Fig. 4 is used. In each sector the respective factors are listed, usually limited to not more than 10 points per heading.

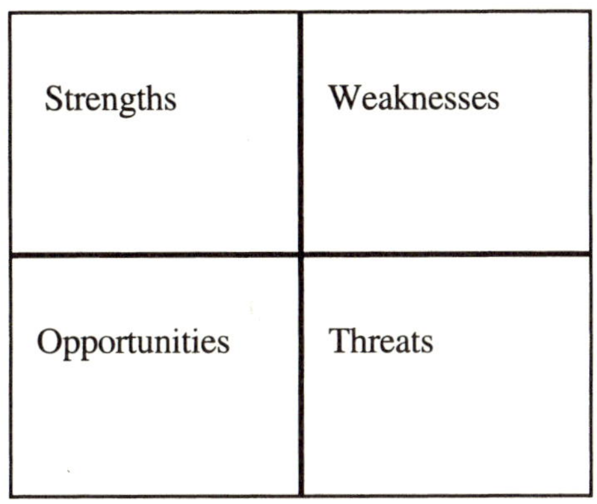

Fig. 4. SWOT analysis diagram

When the current position of the client company has been evaluated in terms of the four dimensions, it is assessed for each of the different project options how those would probably influence the factors in the future in the event that the project is performed. Obviously the desired influence and direction is to build on and enhance strengths, to reduce and minimize weaknesses, to seize upon and assess the benefits of opportunities, and to counteract threats.

The advantage of a SWOT analysis is that the technique is easy to apply and to understand, and it forces you to take a structured decision approach and to focus on critical key issues.

Cost–benefit analysis

A cost–benefit analysis is a systematic, quantitative method of evaluating the costs and benefits of a possible project with an assumed scope. It involves collecting and assessing the tangible and intangible costs and benefits in an intended project.

Costs are all investments that are required on the client side in order to perform a project. The full life cycle of a project needs to be considered. Benefits are financial or non-financial advantages that are estimated to be received from a project. Examples of possible benefits for a company are productivity gains, higher revenues, increased market share, or improved business process effectiveness. Performing a cost–benefit analysis requires assigning monetary values to expected non-financial benefits.

When formally assessing the economic aspects of a project the financial technique of *discounting future monetary values* has to be applied. Discounting future monetary values means transforming future costs and benefits to their *present value*. The *benefit–cost ratio* for a project is calculated by dividing the total discounted benefits by the total discounted costs. A benefit–cost ratio greater than one indicates a positive contribution to a company's profit, whereas a benefit–cost ratio less than one indicates a negative contribution.

Another way of expressing the benefit–cost ratio is in terms of a *return on investment* (RoI) statement. The return on investment is the total net present value (total discounted benefits minus total discounted costs) divided by the total discounted costs. A calculated return on investment number is usually multiplied by 100 to convert the decimal rate to a percentage figure.

Regardless of how the financial aspects are evaluated and how the results are quoted, the standard criterion for justifying an e-business project is that the benefits exceeds the costs over the life cycle of a project.

2.1.4 Outputs

Project requirements document

A project requirements document is the outcome of the define project requirements activity. A project requirements document describes the functional and non-functional requirements that should be addressed by an e-business project. Typically created as the output of a joint requirements development session, the document serves as a guide and a roadmap to identify project scope options.

When the scope of a specific project is defined, the project requirements document can be taken to verify that all project requirements are covered by the intended project scope.

Project scope outline

A project scope outline describes the scope of a possible e-business project at a high level. It is the output from the identify project scope options activity. The document serves as input when defining the project scope at a greater level of detail (see Sect. 2.2).

2.1.5 Key Success Factors

@ 2 Ensure that an adequate e-business strategy is in place

A vital prerequisite for proper planning of the project scope is that the client company has a clear and focused e-business strategy in place. The e-business strategy determines how a company approaches the implementation of its e-business vision. If an e-business strategy is not in place, it is not clear where a company wants to go with e-business and how to get there. Too often clients intend to start an e-business project with the vague idea that "*something new, something better than the solution of competitors*" should be implemented. But if an e-business project is not aligned with an overall e-business strategy, planning the scope of a project happens in a vacuum.

Unfortunately, having a well-defined e-business strategy in place is not a matter of course. Dr. Glazer from the University of California at Berkeley found in a recent survey of 600 managers that more than 75% of the responding companies believe that they do not have a well-developed e-business strategy [16]. Less than 50% of the companies do not even have an e-business vision. Planning the scope of an e-business project without a proper e-business strategy, or even worse without an e-business vision, is like poking in fog.

When a client company claims to have an e-business strategy, it is important to verify that it is an appropriate one that fits into the overall corporate strategy. According to an Auerbach report [2], a company can be at one of three distinct levels of *e-business readiness*: (1) at level 1, no e-business strategy is in place or there is one but it is not linked to the corporate strategy; (2) at level 2, the defined e-business strategy supports the corporate strategy as it is currently; or (3) at level 3, the e-business strategy is a driver of the corporate strategy. Only companies at level 2 or 3 can expect to capitalize on the unprecedented potential of e-business.

If you discover that a client does not have an adequate e-business strategy in place, you should encourage the client to define one before starting to plan the scope of an e-business project. Supporting a client in defining an e-business strategy can be offered by a contractor as a separate consulting effort that is performed prior to the planned e-business project.

@ 3 Perform a joint requirement development session

Often clients are overcharged when they try to define requirements for an e-business project by themselves. When a client asks you – as a potential contractor – for support, the approach that appears to work best in an e-business environment is to perform a joint requirement development session. Such a session can be organized in the form of a workshop where representatives of a client and contractor define the requirements jointly. The main idea of a joint session is that the experiences and strengths of both parties can be exploited to their best advantage.

A client contributes to such a session with the understanding of its business and its business need as well as the knowledge of project constraints that might limit the possible project scope. The contractor's contribution is mainly its understanding of specific requirements that are typical for e-business projects. Although each e-business project is unique, there are a lot of requirements that are common to almost all of them. Normally a contractor has conducted numerous e-business projects for different clients before. Based on the experiences gathered in all those projects, it is not surprisingly that a contractor has often a better understanding of the e-business project requirements than does a client. Especially non-functional requirements are a key factor for the overall success of an e-business projects. Often clients forget defining non-functional requirements or they are not aware of their importance. Based on experiences with numerous other e-business projects a contractor can complement the requirement list with aspects that a client might never have thought about.

A joint requirement development session is also an advantage for a contractor, because usually the contractor obtains a sound understanding of the client's project requirements. The requirements development is usually performed long before a project is officially established, a contractor selected, and a contract between client and selected contractor is negotiated. A sound understanding of the project requirements ensures that a potential contractor can evaluate the effort required to perform the intended project better than competitors who are not embroiled in the requirements definition. As a consequence, the involved contractor is probably able to quote a more expedient price for performing the project work compared to other potential contractors who have not obtained the same level of understanding of the client's project requirements. This is a competitive advantage for you.

2.2 Defining the Project Scope

Defining the project scope is the process of identifying and documenting in detail what *is in* and what *is not in* the scope of a project (see Fig. 5). Normally this process is performed by the client of a project. Ideally, the company who is later contracted to perform the defined project work is already involved in this activity. This provides the contractor company with an excellent opportunity to understand and influence the scope of a project. A client company can benefit from the contractor's experience gained from defining and conducting similar projects for other clients.

The objective of defining and documenting the project scope is to build a basis for sourcing and selecting a contractor to whom the project work is given. A description of the project scope and documented project goals serve as aid to communicate and discuss the project work with potential contractors.

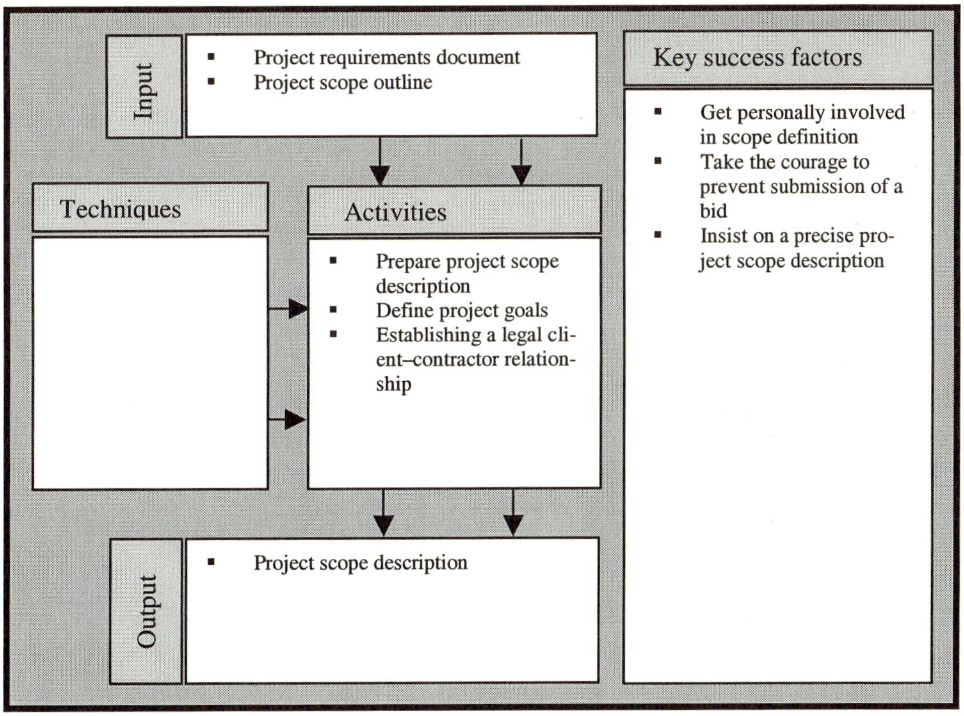

Fig. 5. Defining the project scope

2.2.1 Inputs

Project requirements document

The project requirements document produced as output from the scope planning process serves as the input to the scope definition process. The documented functional and non-functional project requirements build the framework for defining a project scope that satisfies these requirements.

Project scope outline

The project scope outline produced by the scope planning process describes the scope of the project at a high level. This document is the starting base for defining and documenting the project scope at a greater level of detail.

2.2.2 Activities

Prepare project scope description

The objective of this activity is to describe in detail what is in and what is not in the scope of the project. Normally this activity is performed by a client with support of a potential contractor for performing the defined project work. It usually starts with a review of the project requirements and the project scope outline. The outcome of this activity is a *project scope description* (see Sect. 2.2.4).

Define project goals

Defining project goals is an activity that is normally performed in close relation with preparing the project scope description. The objective of the activity is to identify and document the goals that should be achieved by performing the project. Ideally the project goals are defined by the client. Documented project goals give a potential contractor a concrete starting point from which to understand the objectives that a client wants to achieve. It is critical for a contractor to understand the project goals in order to be able to satisfy a client's expectations. Defining and documenting project goals helps to ensure that all project stakeholders agree on the same project objectives. If project goals are not clear, the project may be driven or influenced by technical or political factors and not by the client's business need.

Project goals should mainly answer two questions: (1) what should be accomplished with the project and (2) why is the project performed? Measurable project goals – either qualitative or quantitative – are used at project completion to verify whether or not the intended project objectives have been achieved. It is always valuable to encourage a client to be very precise and rigorous in this area. The outcome of the define project goals activity is a *project goals description* that is normally a part of the project scope description.

Establishing a legal client–contractor relationship

When the project scope and the project goals are defined and documented this is usually the point at which a formal, legal relationship between a client and a contractor is established. Normally, a client sources potential contractors and selects one of the candidates to perform the project work. In the best case the selected contractor is the one who has already been embroiled in the project by supporting the client in planning and defining the project scope. But this is not a matter of course. Sometimes economic, technical, or political reasons prevent a client from choosing the contractor company that is already involved. In the following it is assumed that the embroiled contractor is the one who is selected by the client to conduct the project.

When a contractor is asked to perform a project the contractor has to evaluate and decide whether or not it is willing and able to perform the project for a client under the given conditions. This decision has to be considered carefully. When a contractor accepts to perform the project work, the next step is to negotiate a contract (see Sect. 13.2.2). If the contract negotiations are successful, a legal relationship between client and contractor is established when both parties sign the respective legal documents.

2.2.3 Techniques

None.

2.2.4 Outputs

Project scope description
The project scope description provides a documented basis for structuring and organizing the work that has to be performed in a project. It supports confirming and developing a common understanding of the scope of the project among its stakeholders. A scope description of an e-business project usually covers six main areas:

1. **Project justification.** A brief description of the business need that should be addressed by the project, a justification for performing the project, and a list of intended benefits.
2. **Project solution.** An outline of the to-be-developed e-business solution, its intended audience, and its integration into the technical and organizational infrastructure of the client company.
3. **Project deliverables.** A list of deliverables that represent the outcome of the project at a high level. The complete list of deliverables normally reflects the work required to build the e-business solution.
4. **Project goals.** The business goals that should be achieved by performing the project.
5. **Project constraints.** Any constraints that limit the degrees of freedom when building the e-business solution.
6. **Project exclusions.** A list of work items, deliverables, or any other aspects that are explicitly excluded from the project.

The project scope description is the basis for structuring and defining the project work in terms of a WBS. Often the project scope description is part of the contract establishing the legal relationship between a client and a contractor.

2.2.5 Key Success Factors

@ 4 Get personally involved in scope definition
Usually it requires a considerable amount of time for an e-business project to be formally established by a client, and for a company for performing the project work to be contracted. The early days before and around project establishment are often fuzzy and full of uncertainty: the client is planning and defining the project scope, trying to find a justification for the project investment, and looking for potential contractors who are able and

willing to perform the project work. First contacts and informal talks between a client and potential contractors take place. Sales people from contractor companies frequently contact client representatives demonstrating contractor company capabilities in order to increase the likelihood of being awarded a project. Typically this is the point when you, the designated contractor project manager, appears on the scene.

In this pre-project phase it is usually your colleagues from the sales department that are the leading ones who are responsible for acquiring the project for your company. Naturally it is your job to support your sales colleagues. In fact, mostly they appreciate such support and love to present an individual who will probably be the project manager if the project is awarded to your company.

It is an advantage for you to be involved at this early phase in the project. Take this as an opportunity to lay the basis for a successful project execution. Try especially to become involved in project scope definition. Defining the project scope is the point when it is decided what is in and what is not in the scope of the project. Working closely with the client helps you to understand the client's requirements and the project goals in detail. This provides you with an excellent opportunity to recognize whether or not you and your company are able to perform the defined project work under the given project conditions and constraints. This allows you to make – or at least contribute to – an informed decision as to whether your company should bid for the project. Do not leave this decision to the sales people of your company alone. Their job is to acquire new projects, your job is to deliver the contracted work. In their enthusiasm to acquire new projects your sales colleagues often underestimate or overlook the risks that are involved in project delivery. When you are involved in scope definition, you can either influence the project scope in a direction that makes the risks acceptable, or you can simply recommend not to bid for the project

@ 5 Take the courage to prevent submission of a bid

When the scope of a project is defined and a client asks potential contractors whether they would like to submit a bid for performing the project, "*no*" is a valid and sometimes the right answer for a contractor. Too often, the option to decline a request from a client to perform a project is neglected or seems unknown to some people – most frequently you find such individuals in the sales department of a contractor company.

What is a reason for a contractor *not* doing a project? It is quite simple: declining to perform a project is the best option in a situation where a contractor company expects that a defined project can not be performed successfully. In this context 'successfully' can be reduced to two major aspects: delivering a project to a client's satisfaction and performing it with a financial profit for the contractor. If you, as designated manager of a potential project, are of the opinion that a successful project execution is not possible or highly risky, you should vote to not submit a bid in order to prevent your company from serious damage.

However, I have to admit that voting for not bidding often requires a significant amount of courage from you. You may realize that voting to decline a project is an unpopular recommendation. Your sales colleagues – with big dollar signs in their eyes – will probably not wish to hear your concerns. And your senior management might be afraid of missing a potential opportunity to generate more revenue for the company. Nevertheless, if you, as the person responsible for delivering the project, do not have the confidence that the project can be made a success, you should take the courage to say "*no*".

Driven by competition in the e-business market, contractors too often accept e-business projects although it is obvious from the beginning that they can not be successful – at least from a financial point of view. The balance sheets of many companies supplying e-business project services are the irrefutable proof: often the loss is equal to or greater than the revenue of a company. The decline of the technology stock markets forced many companies to change their view. 'Burning' money is no longer tolerated, so today everyone tries to concentrate on 'profitable' e-business projects. If you discover that the potential project will probably not result in success, it is your duty to say "*no*".

Of course, it might happen that other people in your company out-vote you and the project is contracted and conducted despite your concerns. In this case a valid option for you is to abdicate serving as project manager for this particular project and simply dare to walk away. If a replacement for you is identified a discreet hint on your appraisal of the project and some background information of the project history might be appreciated by your project management colleague.

@ 6 Insist on a precise project scope description

When you are not able to become involved in defining the project scope, you should at least insist that a precise and detailed project scope description is available as the basis for project contraction and execution. This holds especially true if a project is performed under a firm-fixed-price contract, because if the project scope description is vague or at an insufficient level of detail, you do not have a solid basis for knowing what has to be delivered to a client. Problems relating to getting project deliverables accepted by a client are inevitable.

Even if a precise project scope description is available, it might leave room for 'interpretation'. If you have not been involved in preparing the scope description, you should at least arrange for a joint in-depth review of the description with key people who have been involved. This is an opportunity to get explanations for unclear or open points and to ask for aspects written 'between-the-lines'. Using detailed checklists with problems typical for e-business projects can make the review more 'systematic' and 'objective' and might discover aspects that have not been considered when the scope description was prepared.

Moreover, e-business projects are prone to change. e-business technology and the e-business environment is changing and evolving at a breath-taking speed. There is always a considerable risk that these evolutions influence the client's expectations of the project outcome. This might require adjusting the project scope during the course of a project. A scope change almost always causes additional effort for the contractor. If the project scope is not described precisely, you might run into problems getting a commitment from the client that the scope really changed. This is a prerequisite to having the additional effort compensated for by the client. Otherwise your project might fall victim to so-called *scope creep*. This means that the client's expectations and as a consequence the project scope changes during the course of a project, but those changes are not recognized as changes and as such not handled via a change management process.

A prerequisite for recognizing scope changes and for avoiding scope creep problems is a precise project scope description. If the project scope is well documented, you can handle scope changes in accordance with a controlled change management process. This is a sound basis for getting additional costs reimbursed by the client.

2.3 Developing the Work Breakdown Structure

When the project scope is defined and described, the next logical step is to develop a WBS (see Fig. 6). A WBS represents a deliverable-oriented grouping of the work that has to be performed for a project. While the project scope description is mainly prepared by a client, the WBS is developed by a contractor.

Developing a proper WBS is an essential project management process. A WBS is the backbone of every project and critical to project success. It serves multiple purposes, four important ones are:

1. A WBS is a fundamental basis for project communication. It eases the comprehension of the project scope for a contractor and supports achieving a common understanding between a client and a contractor of the project scope.
2. It is a baseline for a contractor for developing the project time plan (see Sect. 3.1.4) and for estimating the project costs (see Sect. 5.1).
3. It allows recognition and tracking of scope changes, and verification during the course of a project whether all planned work items are performed and delivered.
4. It supports defining the organizational structure of the project and assigning roles and responsibilities to project team members (see Sect. 4.2).

Developing a WBS is a classic project management process performed mainly by the project manager. Usually he or she is supported by key project team members.

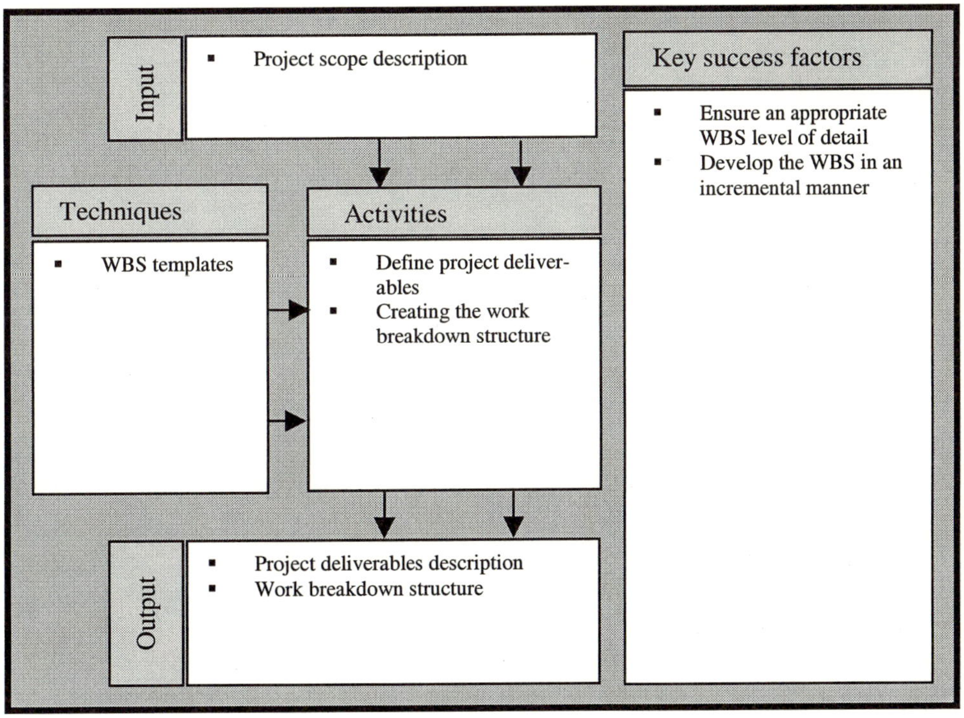

Fig. 6 Developing the work breakdown structure

2.3.1 Inputs

Project scope description

The project scope description serves as input for defining the project deliverables and for developing the WBS. Usually the project scope description already contains a list with project deliverables that have to be handed over to a client. This deliverables list has to be detailed. Other elements of the project scope description, project goals and an outline of the e-business solution, are the baseline for developing the WBS.

2.3.2 Activities

Define project deliverables

The objective of this activity is to describe the project deliverables from a contractor's point of view in sufficient detail to clarify what has to be produced by a project. Project deliverables can be classified in two types. *External* project deliverables have to be handed-over and accepted by a client. External deliverables are normally listed in the project scope description. Those are mostly technical deliverables that constitute the e-business solution. Examples of technical deliverables are pieces of hardware, system and application software, services like consulting for organizational change, marketing and branding, or documentation like installation instructions, user manuals, and training material. *Internal* project deliverables that are used by a contractor to support the production of external deliverables. Examples of internal deliverables are design descriptions, feasibility studies, and project management deliverables like the project time plan, project status reports, or project procedure descriptions.

Defining project deliverables is the activity of describing both external and internal deliverables in detail. Although the external deliverables are already listed in the project scope description, their definition is normally not sufficiently detailed for project planning and execution. The deliverables list initially prepared by a client must be expanded and further detailed by a contractor in order to achieve a common understanding with a client on what has to be delivered.

Describing the internal project deliverables is a valuable effort that is required to identify what has to be produced in a project beyond the external project deliverables. Identifying and describing the internal deliverables is a basic prerequisite for creating the WBS. The output of the define project deliverables activity is a *project deliverables description* (see Sect. 2.3.4).

Creating the work breakdown structure

Based on the defined project deliverables, a WBS for the project can be created. The WBS is used to structure the work required to produce the project deliverables.

Creating a WBS is an analytical activity that sometimes has to be performed iteratively. It starts by identifying and subdividing the work required to produce a deliverable into smaller, more manageable well-defined work items until a sufficient level of detail is achieved that allows identification of which single work steps are necessary to produce an element of a deliverable. This activity is repeated for all defined project deliverables.

Afterwards you have to verify that all work that is required to be performed in the project is listed in the WBS. Work items not in the WBS are outside the scope of the project from a contractor's point of view. It is therefore important to ensure that all work items required to cover the scope as described in the project scope description are part of the WBS; otherwise a discrepancy between the contractor's and the client's perspective regarding the project scope might exist.

Breaking the work into smaller work items has to be performed not necessarily according to the sequence in which work items are carried out. Bringing the work items into a sequence and identifying dependencies among them is an activity that is performed when developing the project schedule (see Sect. 3.1). A WBS can be presented in the form of a chart or a list. When presenting a WBS in the form of a structured list, the deliverables or deliverable elements expected as outcomes from performing a work item can be referenced (see Sect. 2.3.4).

When creating a WBS for a specific e-business project, the use of a WBS Template (see Sect. 2.3.3) can support the activity and reduce the risk of omissions and mistakes.

You can use project management software or other planning tools to support the semi-automatic generation and presentation of a WBS.

The output of this activity is a WBS that serves as the basis for further project planning and control. While the initial creation of a WBS has to be performed in an rather early stage of a project, it may require revision when the project matures. There are mainly two reasons for a revision of a WBS: (1) when the scope of a project changes, which is usually triggered by a *scope change request* issued by the client (see Sect. 10.2); and (2) when you discover a major flaw in the created WBS. A typical mistake is that you overlooked required work items and hence omit them in the WBS.

In e-business projects it is often not feasible to develop a WBS at a sufficient level of detail for all work items at a rather early stage of the project. Instead several versions of a WBS have to be created so that the WBS development is performed in an incremental manner.

2.3.3 Techniques

WBS templates

When a WBS for a specific project has to be developed, often one from a previous, similar project can be used as a template. Although each e-business project is unique, usually they have many elements in common, and often one or more other projects exist that resemble the current one. A contractor normally applies the same implementation approach and methodology when performing projects. As a consequence the work items of similar projects are either identical or resemble each other to a high degree. When developing a WBS for a specific project it is therefore not necessary to start from 'scratch'.

The 'reuse' of a WBS from another project provides the advantage that the applicability and validity of the WBS has already been proved in the previous project. Changes to the WBS that were required due to overlooked or mis-planned work items normally have been reflected by appropriate revisions of the WBS. Such a revised WBS is a good starting basis for developing one that avoids the omissions and the planning mistakes of previous projects.

2.3.4 Outputs

Project deliverables description

The output of the project deliverables definition activity is a *project deliverables description.* The content of project deliverables and the format in which they are described is highly dependent on the type of the deliverables and the overall project context. The project deliverables description should clearly describe for external deliverables what is being committed by a contractor to be delivered to a client. The description of internal project deliverables should clearly identify what is required on the contractor side to produce the external deliverables.

Work breakdown structure

A WBS is normally created to a sufficient level of detail that it can be used for developing the project schedule and for estimating the project costs. The work items at the lowest level are often referred to as *work packages*. Each work item in a WBS is usually assigned a unique identifier. A hierarchical numbering scheme helps in the comprehension of the structure of the work items.

Fig. 7 depicts an extract of a sample WBS to illustrate its general structure and organization. The small example is taken from developing the front-end application in an Intranet project and covers a part of storyboard development.

WBS item	Deliverable / deliverable element
…	
7 Developing storyboard	Storyboard
7.1 Reviewing site context	
7.1.1 Reviewing usability goals	
7.1.2 Performing comparative site survey	
7.1.3 Identifying target audience	
7.1.4 Creating end-user profiles	End-user profiles
7.1.5 Reviewing editorial style guide	
7.2 Defining UI concept	UI concept
7.2 1 Gathering creative concepts	
7.2.2 Preparing content plan	Content plan
7.2.2.1 Analyzing media content	
7.2.2.2 Generating feature map	
7.2.2.3 Generating content matrix	
7.3 Preparing navigation concept	Navigation concept
7.3.1 Developing navigational flow	
…	

Fig. 7. Sample WBS extract

The left-hand side of Fig. 7 shows the work items listed. Work packages are those work items at the lowest level; e.g., work items '7.1.1 Reviewing usability goals' and '7.2.2.1 Analyze media content'. On the right-hand side you can see the deliverable or element of a deliverable that is the expected outcome from performing the respective work item.

In an e-business project often several versions of a WBS are prepared, each version contains more work items at work package level than the proceeding one.

2.3.5 Key Success Factors

@ 7 Ensure an appropriate WBS level of detail

When the work of a project is broken down to create a WBS, it is important to decompose the work items until an appropriate level of detail is reached. The interesting question is determining what level of detail is appropriate for your project. In general, the work should be broken down until you can identify what single work steps are necessary to produce an element of a deliverable.

The nature of a deliverable element and the size and complexity of a specific project determines the level of detail that respective work items have to be broken down to. Obviously, the work breakdown should be more detailed when the work item is more complex or 'unknown'. The PMI recommends that work items should not require more than two calendar weeks to be completed [32]. e-business projects are usually rather short. Therefore, a decomposition to work packages that require no longer than one calendar week is generally more appropriate.

Reducing the upper limit to one calendar week for an e-business project does not suggest that more detailed is better. Breaking down work into items of 1 – 2 days only – or even a few hours – turn out to be less favorable. This is because if you choose such a level of detail you will end up with several hundreds of work packages even for small e-business projects. For larger projects the number of work packages quickly add up to several thousand. Such a high number of work packages can not be overseen, managed, and controlled.

Taking one calendar week or five working days as a rule of thumb for e-business projects does not mean that you should press all work packages into a 5-day corset. The five days timeline is only a number that should be aimed at on average.

It might not be feasible to decompose some work items that have to be performed at later stages of a project. It might therefore be necessary to create several versions of the WBS by developing it in an incremental manner.

The objective to ensure is that you reach a level of detail in each version of the WBS that allows you to communicate the work packages to the relevant project stakeholders, and to develop and control the project schedule.

@ 8 Develop the WBS in an incremental manner

In a traditional IT project the WBS is usually developed once at an early stage of the project based on a detailed project scope description and a complete project deliverables description. During the course of a project normally only small refinements are required, so main parts of the WBS are stable throughout the project. Unfortunately this approach does not work in e-business projects.

In an e-business project the scope is often somewhat unclear at the beginning of the project. Even when big efforts were expended on preparing a project deliverables description, often many project deliverables can not be described at a sufficient level of detail to prepare a WBS at a required level of detail. The reason for this is normally missing information; required information only becomes available or known through the course of the project.

The solution to address this problem – that is mostly specific to e-business projects – is developing the WBS in an *incremental* manner. 'Incremental' means that early in the project an initial WBS is developed that covers all work items that have to be performed throughout the project. Work items that can not be specified due to lack of information at this point are not detailed down to work package level. Only for a first release of the e-business solution all required work items are specified at work package level. When the first release is coded, tested, and deployed, a new version of the WBS is developed that details the next release on work package level. A new version of the WBS is generated for each of the following release so that it is developed in an incremental manner. Only the last version of the WBS covers all work items at work package level. Experiences from coding, testing, and deploying one release can flow into the development of the next version of the WBS.

3 Managing the Schedule

Managing the schedule is a core project management discipline – and often it is the most challenging for a project manager. In an e-business project you are normally on a race against time. Making the project schedule is an imperative criterion for project success. Commonly, a project is rated as successful when it is completed *in time* and *on budget* with an outcome at a defined *level of quality*. From these three criteria, quality is the most important one on the long run. However, the first one – completion in time – is more visible. Normally, a project has a fixed deadline. Whether or not this deadline is met can easily be traced by all project stakeholders. You, as the project manager, are ultimately responsible for the project schedule. As a consequence, the decisive test of your capabilities and your reputation as project manager is whether you made the schedule. Managing the project schedule is therefore a domain that deserves your special attention.

Managing the project schedule includes mainly two processes: (1) developing a realistic project schedule in terms of an initial project time plan that lists which work packages have to be performed when and by whom, and (2) controlling the developed project schedule to ensure that the project progresses according to the defined project time plan.

3.1 Developing the Project Schedule

Developing the project schedule is mainly the process of planning the sequence in which work packages are executed, of evaluating the duration of work packages, and of assigning human resources to single work packages (see Fig. 8). The process is usually performed early in the planning phase of a project. The output of developing the project schedule is an initial *project time plan* (see Sect. 3.1.4).

The initial project time plan usually covers all work packages identified in the WBS. The point when the first work package is planned to start and the point when the last work package is planned to be completed determine the total project duration. Some people call this total project duration determined by the project time plan the 'project schedule'. In this book the term *project schedule* is used as a synonym for the project time plan. 'Making' the project schedule means conducting a project in accordance with a defined project time plan.

Developing the project schedule is a process that is mainly performed by you, the project manager of the contractor company. Theoretically, in a perfect world you base your scheduling efforts only on the amount of work to be performed and the amount of resources available. When all work packages are scheduled, the planned completion of the last one determines the project end. However, in real life determining the project completion date – that is close to the date when the solution is delivered – is often influenced by various constraints. Some clients insist on a particular delivery date due to political or economical reasons. Therefore, developing the project schedule sometimes requires negotiations with a client to agree on a schedule that fulfills not only the expectations of a client but provides also a contractor with a fair chance to perform the planned work within the defined time frame.

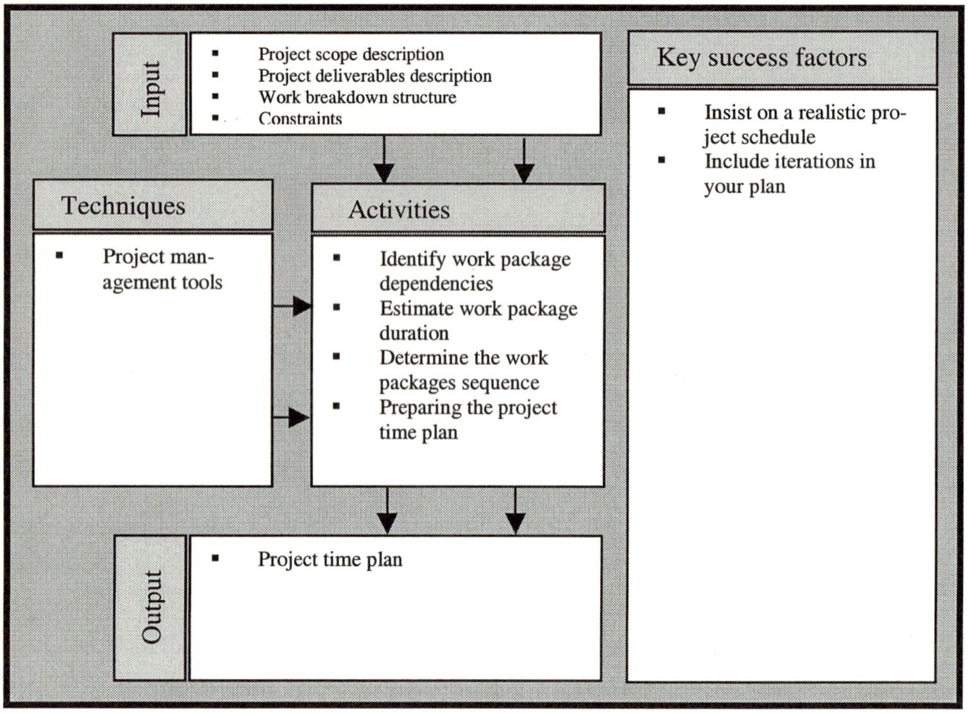

Fig. 8. Developing the project schedule

3.1.1 Inputs

Project scope description

The project scope description serves as a framework for setting up the project schedule. It specifies from a client's point of view what has to be delivered by a contractor, as well as the project goals. This is essential information for defining the project time plan.

Project deliverables description

The project deliverables description documents in detail what has to be delivered to a client. This information serves as one input for estimating the duration required to perform work packages.

Work breakdown structure

The WBS lists all work packages required to be performed for the project in a structured manner. It is a good starting point for identifying dependencies among work packages and for bringing them into a sequence.

Constraints

Constraints are factors that limit your freedom of choice in defining the project time plan that determines the project schedule. Three typical e-business project constraints are: (1) a client's expectations on a particular delivery date of the final solution or availability of preliminary project deliverables, (2) limited resources in terms of project budget or team members available to perform the project work, and (3) a limited feasibility of a client being able to fulfill defined responsibilities.

3.1.2 Activities

Identify work package dependencies

The objective of this activity is to identify the constraints that limit your choice of the sequence in which work packages can be performed and the point when work packages can be started. The constraints can be classified in *internal* and *external* dependencies.

Internal dependencies are logical relationships among work packages. These are mostly inherent in the nature of the work packages. For example, the work package 'to code HTML pages' is dependent on the work package 'to develop a storyboard'. The availability of the storyboard is simply a prerequisite for HTML coding. As a consequence, the work package to develop the storyboard must be performed and completed before the work package to code the pages can be started.

External dependencies are those that involve a relationship between a work package and an event that is outside the project. Typical examples of such events are responsibilities that have to be fulfilled by a client. Take for example a situation in which a work package is 'the integration of a content management solution', and the client has to deliver the content. Obviously the work package can not be performed before the content is delivered by the client. Another example for an external dependency is the availability of hardware or software. For example, the work package 'to install the e-business application' is dependent from the availability of the respective hardware.

An accurate and comprehensive identification of all dependencies is an imperative prerequisite for evaluating the sequence in which the work packages should be performed.

Estimate work package duration

The objective of this activity is to estimate the duration of each single work package. The duration is the time required to perform a work package. Normally the duration is estimated in terms of 'days'. Not surprisingly, the work package duration is determined by two factors: (1) the effort required to perform a work package and (2) the amount of human resources assigned to perform the work.

Estimating the effort required to perform work packages is discussed in terms of the *cost management domain* (see Sect. 5.1.2). Deciding on the amount of resources to be assigned to a work package needs to be evaluated carefully. Take for example the situation in which you have estimated that an effort of five person-days is required to perform a single work package. If you assign one person to do the work, the estimated duration is five days – that's simple, isn't it? If you assign two persons to do the job, you might assume that the estimated duration is 2.5 days – this might be correct, but it might not be. It depends largely on the nature of the work package especially whether or not it can be split up in such a way that two persons can work on it in parallel with full productivity.

Distributing the work of a work package to numerous human resources can theoretically be performed indefinitely. In the example mentioned above, 5 persons would do the job in 1 day, 10 persons in half a day, and so on. But this only works perfectly in theory. In practice you have to consider many factors when deciding how much human resources to assign to a single work product. Some factors are: the nature of the work, the skills required to perform the work, the availability of human resources with the required skills, and the 'urgency' of the work package. In general, increasing the number of human resources assigned to perform a work package does not reduce the duration at the same rate. At a certain point – sometimes called the *point of diminishing returns* – the overhead of work distribution, administration, and communication required negates the increased work that can actually be performed.

Deciding on the amount of resources to be assigned to work packages needs to be performed in close interaction with activities discussed in Chap. 4.

The duration of a work package must be distinguished from its *elapsed time*. The elapsed time is the difference between the planned end and start date of a work package. When weekend days and public holidays are not treated as working days, the duration of a work package may differ from the required elapsed time. Take for example a work package with an estimated duration of three days. If you plan to start with work package execution on Monday morning its planned start is Wednesday evening. In this case the duration is identical to the elapsed time – both are three. However, if you plan to start the work package execution on Friday, the planned end date is Tuesday, based on the assumption that the weekend days are not considered as working days. In this case the elapsed time for the work package is five days.

The outcome of this activity is an estimate of the duration of each work package. This estimate is taken as the input for preparing the project time plan.

Determine the work packages sequence

Obviously the work packages required to be performed in a project can not be executed simultaneously in parallel. Internal dependencies and the limited availability of human resources require that the work packages are executed sequentially – at least to a certain extent. Determining an adequate sequence of work package execution by considering internal and external dependencies, the duration of work packages, and the availability of human resources is the objective of this activity. Although dependencies and resource availability will probably limit the number of possible sequences, normally there will be several acceptable sequences in which the work packages can be executed. Determining the 'best' one is usually based to a large extent on the experience of the project manager.

Although determining the work package sequence and estimating the work package duration are presented here as discrete activities, in practice they are tightly linked. Normally they overlap each other and are performed iteratively.

Preparing the project time plan

Preparing the project time plan is the activity of planning and documenting the planned start and end date of each work package. Preparing the project time plan can be supported by using appropriate project management tools (see Sect. 3.1.3). The main input for this activity are overall project constraints, the determined work package sequences, and the availability of human resources assigned to perform the work packages. In addition, a calendar indicating weekend days and other non-working days is fundamental to preparing the project time plan.

Preparing an initial project time plan is usually performed at an early planning stage of the project. The initial plan normally remains valid throughout the total project lifetime. However, adjustments or refinements of the initial project time plan might be required during the course of the project. Typical reasons suggesting a project time plan adjustment are scope change requests (see Sect. 10.2) or the introduction of corrective actions required to keep the project on track. Not surprisingly, the outcome of this activity is a project time plan (see Sect. 3.1.4).

3.1.3 Techniques

Project management tools

Commercially available project management tools like 'Microsoft Project' [9] can be a big help when preparing the project time plan. The advantage of project management tools is that many planning activities can be performed automatically. Calculating the elapsed time of a work package when the work package duration is given as input, automatically considering dependencies in work package sequencing, or balancing resources, are only a few examples of activities that a project management tool can do for you. In addition, such tools normally provide several alternatives for the graphical presentation of the resulting project time plan. Using the graphical presentation techniques of a tool releases you from having to invent something yourself. Moreover, project management tools can also be of benefit in tracking and controlling the project progress (see Sect. 3.2).

3.1.4 Outputs

Project time plan

A project time plan is the main output from developing the project schedule. A project time plan usually comprises of the work packages that have to be performed in the project, a planned start and end date for each work package including dependencies among work packages, and an indication of which team members are assigned to perform particular work packages. In some projects, the work packages are arranged in terms of *project phases*. A project phase is normally a defined time frame in which it is planned that specific work packages are to be performed.

The level of detail of a project time plan depends on the nature, complexity, size, and duration of a project. Often several representations of a project time plan are prepared: a detailed project time plan that covers all single work packages and their distribution over defined project phases, and a less-detailed, high-level project time plan that summarize only the work to be performed in terms of phases and major project milestones.

A common way to present a project time plan is in form of a 'Gantt Chart'. Although it is one of the oldest techniques of presenting project activities – it was invented by Henry Gantt in 1917 – the advantages of this techniques are still valid. A Gantt chart is an easy-to-understand way of presenting work packages, their sequence including start and end dates, and dependencies among work packages.

3.1.5 Key Success Factors

@ 9 Insist on a realistic project schedule

Sometimes you might be confronted with a project schedule that is unrealistic from your point of view. 'Unrealistic' means that you do not believe that a schedule represented by a project time plan can be adhered to. There are two common situations in which you have to deal with an unrealistic project time plan: (1) you are asked to develop one and (2) you are asked to take a given one. Let us take a closer look at each situation separately.

A typical trigger for the first situation are a client's expectations regarding the availability of a planned e-business solution. Misunderstanding on the effort required to develop a solution or an unlimited ambition to beat the competition sometimes can seduce a client into requesting a contractor to commit to an unrealistic delivery date. When you prepare a project time plan based on a WBS and on an estimation of the duration of the work packages, the defined delivery date might be far beyond the date expected by a client. In such a situation the client might request you to 'adjust' the project time plan so that the planned delivery date meets its expectations. Refuse to do so! If your planning shows that a project can not be completed within a time frame set by a client, you should stand up and refuse to develop a 'fitting' project time plan only to please the client.

Unfortunately, such behavior from a project manager is not a matter of course. Driven by competition in the e-business project-supplier market some suppliers promise clients to deliver e-business solutions at a requested date even they are aware of that they will not be able to fulfill their promises. This is poor business practice and you should not follow such an approach. If you have to develop a project time plan, prepare one that is realistic!

If there are compelling reasons for a client to launch an e-business solution earlier than a realistic project schedule allows, the 'silver bullet' is often to go live with a first release that offers only reduced functionality instead of waiting for the final release with complete functionality. An incremental e-business solution implementation approach (see Sect. 1.8) is of course a prerequisite for such a strategy.

In the second situation you have to deal with a given project schedule. Consider, for example, that you have to take over the responsibility for a project from another project manager. Ask yourself: *"is the schedule realistic?"* If you recognize that the defined project time plan is invalid and that you probably will not be able to make the schedule, this is the time to make others aware of this fact. Inform first your senior management and secondly the client that you do not believe that the schedule can be made. And do this at the beginning, when you take over, not at the end.

More than once I heard from project managers who were unable to make a schedule statements like "*It was obvious to me at the beginning that the schedule could not be made, but (*the client, senior management, whoever*) forced me to take the schedule*". Project managers often use this as an excuse for missing the project deadline. Such an excuse is invalid and absolutely not in line with professional project manager behavior!

You, as the project manager, are responsible for delivering the project in time and on budget. It is your responsibility to ensure that a realistic project time plan is in place. Allow neither your client nor your senior management, nor any other project stakeholder, to force you to follow a schedule that you believe that it can not be kept to. It is part of your job to ensure that a realistic project schedule is in place; otherwise the project could turn out to be your worst nightmare.

@ 10 Include iterations in your plan

When preparing the project time plan – in particular when determining the sequence in which the defined work packages are planned to be executed – it is good practice to include *iterations* in the plan. 'Iterations' mean that the e-business solution is implementation in terms of 'cycles'. Parts or preliminary releases of the intended e-business solution are developed in one project cycle, and those parts or preliminary releases are enhanced, improved, and complemented in a subsequent project cycle. This iterative solution development provides benefits for both client and contractor.

An iterative project implementation approach allows a client to earn early business benefits from the developed e-business solution. A preliminary or a first release of a developed e-business solution can represent a 'quick win' for a client. To take the solution to test its attractiveness to end-users, to introduce a first release earlier in the market than competitors, or to raise additional funding for future developments, are only a few examples of possible quick wins for a client.

For a contractor an iterative implementation approach usually reduces technology project risks. An iterative implementation approach – in contrary to a 'big bang' implementation approach – allows development of the e-business solution in a series of consecutive steps. In each subsequent step *lessons learned* from the preceding step can be applied so that the solution is continuously improved and enhanced. This is a good way to mitigate risks resulting from technical uncertainties.

3.2 Controlling the Project Schedule

Controlling the project schedule is the process of ensuring that a project is proceeding according to a defined project time plan (see Fig. 9). This involves tracking the project progress and taking appropriate corrective actions if a variance is discovered between planned and actual progress. The tracking of project progress is closely linked to the tracking of project costs. Tracking project costs ensures that a project is completed within a defined budget. Tracking project costs is covered by the cost management domain discussed in Sect. 5.2.

Tracking the project progress should be performed by the project manager throughout the course of a project at frequent intervals, normally weekly. The basis for the progress tracking activities is the defined project time plan. Progress tracking means comparing the actual with the planned progress.

Controlling the project schedule is an important project management process, particularly in an e-business environment. A recent survey [31] indicates that nearly two-thirds of all investigated e-business projects suffer from schedule slippage that results in late completion. As time-to-market is key for many clients, falling behind schedule can be assumed as a major drawback in achieving client satisfaction. Avoiding running behind schedule is therefore an imperative project management task.

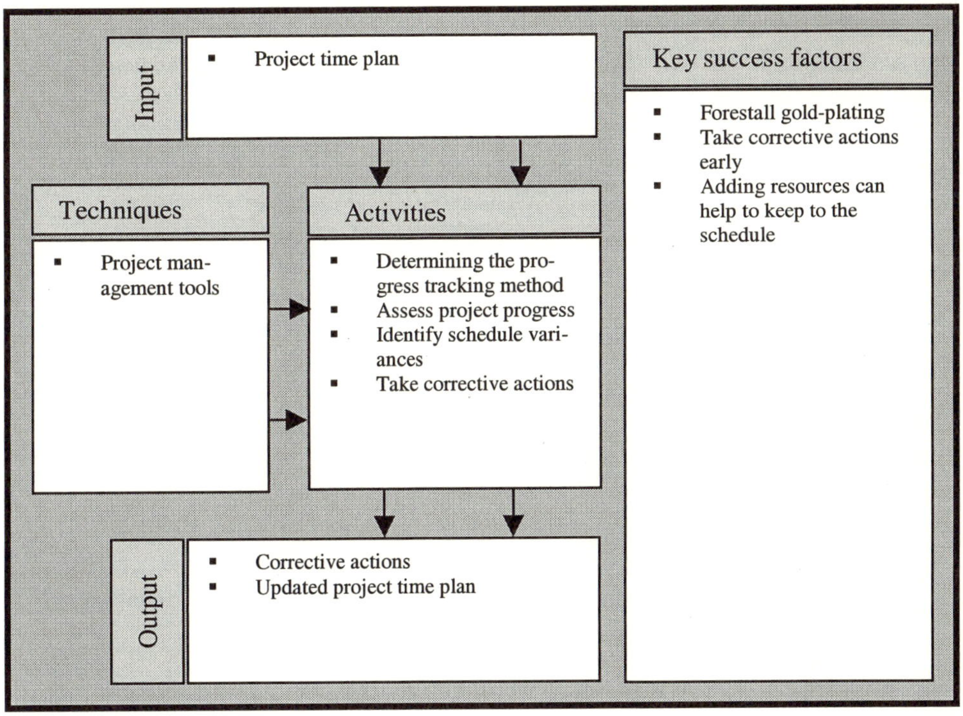

Fig. 9. Controlling the project schedule

3.2.1 Inputs

Project time plan

The fundamental basis for controlling the project schedule is the project time plan (see Sect. 3.1.4). The defined project time plan contains the relevant information on the planned project progress: the work packages that have to be performed, the planned start and end dates of each work package, and the resources assigned to perform the work packages.

3.2.2 Activities

Determining the progress tracking method

The basic idea of any progress tracking method is the comparison of planned and actual progress. However, a variety of different progress tracking methods are known and applied in projects, and they can be classified into two major groups: (1) effort measurement methods and (2) percent complete tracking methods. Effort measurement methods are usually used in close interaction with cost management methods like the *earned value technique*. The earned value technique is discussed in more detail in Sect. 5.2.3).

The percent complete tracking method is relative simple and straightforward. At defined points in time, for each work package that is scheduled to be completed or at least started, the percentage of work that has been performed is assessed. At a higher tracking level this can be reduced to assessing whether or not defined project milestones have been reached.

Often it is useful or necessary to use multiple ways of tracking the project progress. It is therefore important to determine which progress tracking methods should be applied in a particular project.

Assess project progress

A prerequisite for a comparison between planned and actual progress is that information on both are available. The planned progress can be derived from the project time plan, but the actual progress has to be assessed.

Assessing the project progress is mainly identifying which work packages have been completed. This includes assessing the quality of the outcome that has resulted from executing a work package. The effort required to perform the work has to be considered as well, but this factor is more important to controlling the project costs (see Sect. 5.2) than to controlling the project progress.

Identify schedule variances

When both planned and actual progress data are available, identifying schedule variances is relative straightforward. A schedule variance is simply a deviation between planned and actual project progress. A schedule variance can be positive, when your project is ahead of schedule, or negative, when your project is behind schedule.

The first situation occurs relative seldom in e-business projects – be happy when you discover a positive schedule variance in your project. If the situation lasts for a considerable length of time the likelihood is that you will complete the project in time. Unfortunately, the second situation occurs more frequently, and this is a situation that requires your special attention because otherwise the risk that you will not be able to complete the project in time increases. This situation requires taking corrective actions as soon as possible.

Identifying and visualizing schedule variances can be supported by using appropriate project management tools (see Sect. 3.2.3).

Take corrective actions

The objective of taking corrective actions is twofold: (1) to bring the future project progress in line with the project time plan and (2) to recover past schedule delays. What corrective actions are appropriate to bring a project back on track depends heavily on the reason for the schedule variance. A useful first step in taking corrective actions is therefore a careful analysis of the reason for the schedule variance.

In general there are numerous possible reasons for schedule variances. In e-business projects those normally origin from two typical situations: (1) external dependencies that are outside the control of the project preventing the execution of dependent work packages and (2) the execution of work packages requiring a greater effort than was initially estimated.

For the first situation there are two 'classical' corrective actions that you can take. The first is re-scheduling of work packages. This means that you postpone the execution of work packages whose start is dependent on external events until those events really happen; instead you schedule other work packages that are independent of external events to start earlier as originally planned. The second corrective action is performing work packages in parallel. The basic idea of this action – sometimes called 'fast tracking' – is to execute work packages in parallel that were originally planned to be executed in series. This normally decreases the total project duration.

For the second situation there are also two classical corrective actions that are widely applied. The first is adding human resources. The effectiveness of this corrective action is not accepted by all people and as such is widely debated. Take a look at the discussion of key success factor @ 13 to learn more about this debate. Obviously, a prerequisite for applying this corrective action is that additional human resources with adequate skills are available. As a consequence of adding these resources the project costs will probably increase. Therefore schedule and cost tradeoffs have to be analyzed carefully before taking this corrective action. The second corrective action is reducing the project scope. The idea of this corrective action is relative simple. In order to keep a fixed deadline for delivering a solution, some originally planned features of the designed solution are removed to reduce the magnitude of the project. This reduces the amount of work to be performed within a given time frame. Here the tradeoffs between keeping the schedule and reducing functionality have to be analyzed carefully.

Planning and taking corrective actions has to be reflected by the project time plan. As a consequence, the project time plan needs to be updated to document the current status of a project and the actual future planning.

3.2.3 Techniques

Project management tools

Controlling the project schedule – in particular tracking the project progress by comparing planned and actual progress – can be supported by using appropriate project management tools. Naturally the same tools should be used for schedule control as used for schedule development (see Sect. 3.1.3).

3.2.4 Outputs

Corrective actions

One output of controlling the project schedule are corrective actions taken to bring a project back on track. Obviously this output will occur only in the event that there is a need for corrective actions. If a project always progresses as planned, no corrective actions need to be applied. However, I have to admit that I have seldom witnessed such an e-business project.

Updated project time plan

If corrective actions have to be applied to a project, normally the project time plan needs to be updated to reflect the new planning. An updated project time plan is therefore a typical output from the controlling project schedule process.

3.2.5 Key Success Factors

@ 11 Forestall gold-plating

One classic reason why projects fall behind schedule is that the effort spent on performing work packages is higher than estimated. This can happen for two reasons: (1) the effort required to perform a work package is really higher than estimated, which means that the estimation is simply incorrect; and (2) the work package *can* be performed with the estimated effort, but more effort than is really *required* is spent. The latter cause is also known as *gold-plating* and can often be observed in e-business projects.

The concept of gold-plating is rather simple: when a person is assigned to produce a specific outcome, the outcome is made bigger, more brilliant, with more features, or at a higher level of quality than planned and expected by a client. The behavior of this person can be explained by psychological factors. He or she wants to demonstrate and to showcase outstanding technical or creative talent. Using the latest and greatest technology, highly sophisticated technical solutions, or multiple re-working of screen design and layout are only a few examples of temptations that can inveigle team members – in particular from creative and technical disciplines – to perform gold-plating.

You might argue that making an outcome 'better' than required is not a negative. In fact, you will probably find a big advocate for this opinion – your client. Because if a client receives a better result without a price increase it can be expected that the client is happy. Nonetheless, there is one loser: the contractor. This is because when the effort is higher than estimated the project costs increase and the project might even fall behind schedule. To avoid those consequences, monitoring whether gold-plating happens in your project is essential, and if it does occur forestalling it is the obvious countermeasure. However, keep in mind that forestalling gold-plating is a sensitive job that has to be done with care and a certain instinct. Otherwise the motivation and moral of team members might suffer when you attempt to temper their enthusiasm.

@ 12 Take corrective actions early

When you discover a variance between planned and actual project progress taking appropriate corrective actions early appears to work best. Some project manager tend to follow a 'wait-and-see' attitude when they discover that certain work packages or work areas of a project do not progress as planned. Their assumption and hope is that schedule slippage can be recovered without taking corrective actions. Often some motivating words to the involved team members or an increased pressure on specific individuals are the only thing they do. They hope that the schedule problem will disappear, but unfortunately it seldom does; the 'head-in-the-sand' strategy is not suitable for e-business projects.

Normally when a schedule slippage occurs in a certain project area there is a tendency for the slippage to become bigger over time. Many project managers take corrective actions late – often too late, at a point when the schedule slippage is so big that it can not be recovered until the planned completion date. A missed project deadline and a delayed project completion is almost always the woeful result. Normally a schedule slippage does not disappear by itself, so you have to do something. The only useful countermeasure is to take appropriate corrective actions, and the sooner they are taken the higher the probability that the overall project schedule can be made. It is therefore good practice to take corrective actions as early as possible.

@ 13 Adding resources can help to keep to the schedule

Adding resources – basically in the form of additional people – is a well-known corrective action that is often taken by a project manager when he or she recognizes that the project has fallen behind schedule. The question is whether such a measure really helps you to bring an e-business project back on track.

For IT projects many people are sceptical. You might remember the theorem of one of the forefathers of software development, Frederick Brooks, who stated that "*adding manpower to a late software project makes it later*" [5]. According to him adding programmers early in a project can speed it up, but adding them towards the end when you discover a schedule slippage might delay it even further. Experiences from numerous IT projects prove the correctness of this theorem. The question is whether the theorem is true for e-business project as well. Surprisingly, this seems not to be the case. From my experience, adding resources to an e-business project can help to keep to the schedule. The interesting question is why the theorem whose correctness was proved over many years in many IT projects seems not to be applicable to e-business projects. I do not have a definite answer, only a few assumptions.

The fundamental idea of Brook's theorem for the contra-productivity of increasing the amount of project staff is that productivity gains achieved due to the additional people are outweighed by the efforts required to get the additional staff members to work. Increasing the administrative efforts, slowing down the productivity of the assigned team members due to training of the new ones, and distributing work packages to too many staff members are only a few reasons that impact negatively upon the total productivity of an IT project.

In an e-business project those factors have to be considered as well, but normally to a lesser extent than in IT projects. The main reason for this is that in a typical e-business project you normally have many more skills disciplines involved, but from each discipline only a few people, normally one or two. Take for example a situation in which you encounter a problem in coding the web pages in a project. Normally you have one person – let us say a HTML developer – on board who is responsible for coding the web pages. If you add a second HTML developer, the total productivity in web coding does not increase by 100%, but normally by 70 – 80%. Agreeing on a suitable work distribution between two people is usually a manageable challenge, training the new HTML developer by the existing one is feasible without distracting the existing one to much, and the additional administrative effort is limited.

The situation is completely different from that in an IT project. Here you have, for example, five C++ programmers on board. If you do the same thing here – doubling the number of people – you then have to get five additional C++ programmers to work. The distraction of the five 'old' ones, and the re-distribution of the work packages probably outweighs the gains achieved by adding the new ones. Adding them can even have negative effects.

In contrary to traditional IT projects, adding resources can be a useful corrective action to keep to a project schedule or to recover from schedule slippage.

4 Managing the Team

Managing thc project team is one of the most important and most challenging activities for a project manager. If you fail to do a good job in managing the people of the team you will never make your project a success. The people of the team are the heart of the project, and they bring a project to life.

What people do you need for an e-business project? In traditional IT projects you find human resources with IT skills like solution architects, DB designers, C++ programmers, and Java programmers. These skills are also required for e-business projects. But you have to complement these IT skills with skills from the creative discipline, like screen designers, art directors, graphic artists, conceptors, information designers, cognitive architects, and content strategists. For consulting purposes you need consulting discipline skills, like business consultants, organizational change consultants, and e-business strategy analysts. Last but not least you might need marketing skills, like market researchers, branding specialists, media planners, and online advertising specialists. The people with these different skills have to be developed to *one* team.

In managing the project team you have to perform three major processes: (1) recruiting the human resources required to carry out the project work and assigning them to your project; (2) defining and documenting a project organization by identifying and assigning the project roles, responsibilities, and relationships of the team members; and (3) developing the team by exercising team building efforts and by establishing the project work environment

4.1 Recruiting Project Staff

Recruiting project staff is the process of obtaining the multidisciplinary human resources required to carry out the work assigned to the project (see Fig. 10). Many specialized skills are needed for an e-business project. The talents required are rare since they are asked for by many other projects. Market demand for relevant e-business skills and knowledge currently outstrips supply. Recruiting the appropriate people can be a long and tedious task. You find yourself battling with other project managers for the few talents that are available. How do you face this challenge? Most companies have both formal and informal guidelines for recruiting project staff. In general you have two sources where you can look for suitable resources: you can look for internal resources within your company or you can look for external resources in the market.

It depends on the overall policies and procedures of your company as to how internal recruitment is performed. In many companies you find dedicated managers with the responsibility of identifying and providing human resources for projects. In other companies you have to ask line managers for resources or you have to involve the human resources department.

For external resources you can utilize your procurement department or your informal network to source appropriate staff. Independent of the way you source the staff, it is important to have a clear understanding of your resource requirements. The resource requirements are primarily concerned with the attributes and the numbers of required project staff. After sourcing potential candidates for the project staff you have to evaluate and select the individuals who you would like to welcome to the team.

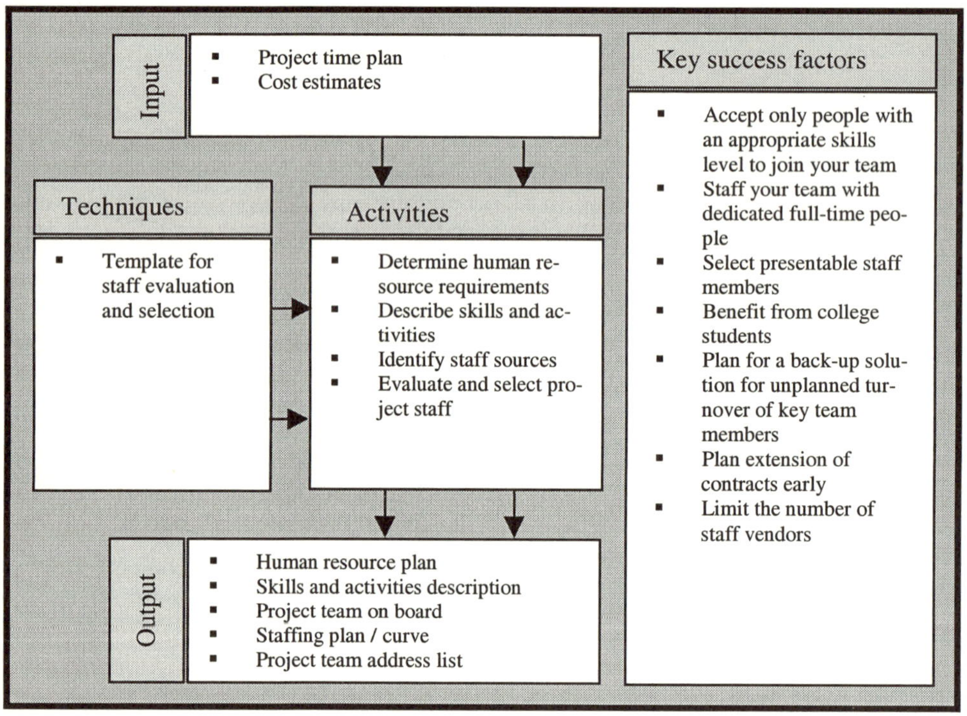

Fig. 10. Recruiting project staff

4.1.1 Inputs

Project time plan

The project time plan (see Sect. 3.1.4) provides you with information on when and how many human resources are needed.

Contractor project budget

The contractor project budget (see Sect. 5.1.4) provides you with information on the amount of money available for compensating the project staff.

4.1.2 Activities

Determine human resource requirements

The objective of this activity is to identify what human resources are required and when they are needed. The basis for this activity is the project time plan. The project time plan lists what and when activities have to be performed and how much effort is estimated for performing the activities.

In addition, the overall cost calculation must be considered since the available project budget restricts the amount of money you can spent for human resources. The output of this activity is a *human resource plan* (see Sect. 4.1.4).

Describe skills and activities

The objective of this activity is to prepare a *skills and activity description* that can be handed over together with the human resource plan to the people supporting you in obtaining the staff: i.e., recruiters, line managers, and the procurement and human resources departments.

To produce such a description, describe in detail the skills required to perform the project work. Use the outline in the human resource plan as a basis and prepare a summary of the activities that have to be performed per job category. The output of this activity is a *skills and activity description* (see Sect. 4.1.4).

Identify staff sources

The objective of this activity is to identify potential sources for project staff recruitment. Potential *internal* sources are line managers, other project managers, the human resources department, and staff members from previous projects. Potential *external* sources are staff vendors known from previous projects, employment agencies supplying temporary staff, Internet agencies, design studios, multimedia agencies, consulting companies, marketing agencies, colleges, and job sites on the Web. The more sources you identify and contact, the higher the probability of obtaining qualified staff. Hand over the human resource plan and the skills and activity description to the identified sources, and wait for feedback.

Evaluate and select project staff

When you receive results from the contacted staff sources, you have to evaluate the skills of the proposed candidates in order to select the best matching people. Perform a face-to-face interview to verify the skills of the candidates. Although resumes or CVs give a first impression of the candidate's skills level, the skills may look brighter on paper than they are in reality. In a face-to-face interview you can check the candidate for both technical expertise and personal characteristics. Especially the characteristic whether or not a candidate is a 'team-player' is an important selection criterion, because only people who are both – able and willing – to work with individuals from different disciplines in cross-functional teams are suitable resources for e-business projects. To support the comparison of candidates, it is useful to document the relevant information received in the face-to-face interview in a *staff evaluation and selection sheet* (see Sect. 4.1.3).

When you have selected the members of your team, you can build up a *staffing plan* (see Sect. 4.1.4) indicating, for each resource, when and how long it is planned to stay in the project. You can get an overview of the total staffing by producing a *staffing curve* (see Sect. 4.1.4).

The contact details of the team members you recruited can be put into a *project team address list* (see Sect. 4.1.4).

4.1.3 Techniques

Template for staff evaluation and selection

A template for evaluation and selection of staff might contain information such as that shown in Fig. 11:

- Identification of the sourcing department/organization that offers staff.
- Administrative details of sourcing organization/department.
- Contact in the department/organization responsible for the offered staff.
- Name and contact details of each candidate.
- Skills and experience per candidate.
- Availability, i.e., start date and duration.
- Job category.
- Skills types.
- Skills level.
- Experience from previous, similar projects.
- Experience with relevant methods, tools, and techniques.
- Personal characteristics.
- Team player (impression: yes/no).
- Appearance.
- Costs / daily rate.
- Living expenses, if applicable.
- Other costs, if applicable.

Fig. 11. Template for staff evaluation and selection

4.1.4 Outputs

Human resource plan

A human resource plan defines the human resources requirements of a project and the desired attributes of the people you are looking for. A human resource plan lists the job category: for example, Java programmer, XML developer, screen designer, market researcher, art director, or process consultant. For each job category the following information is specified:

- The number of staff required.
- When the staff are required and for how long: i.e., start and end dates of assignment.
- Special skills required.
- Skills level: i.e., starter, professional, or expert.
- Cost: i.e., maximum affordable rate.

Table 6 outlines a sample human resource plan for an Internet portal development project.

Job category	No.	Start	End	Skills	Skills level	Cost (per day)
Project manager	1	01/01/2001	05/31/2001	Project management	Expert	U.S. $ 1100
Art director	1	01/15/2001	04/15/2001		Expert	U.S. $ 800
Screen designer	2	01/15/2001	04/15/2001		1 Expert 1 Professional	U.S. $ 600 U.S. $ 300
Conceptor	1	01/15/2001	04/31/2001	Storyboard	Expert	U.S. $ 700
XML/HTML programmer	3	02/01/2001	05/31/2001	XML, XSL, HTML	1 Expert 2 Starters	U.S. $ 500 U.S. $ 300
Java programmer	3	01/15/2001	04/31/2001	Java, client/server, OO	2 Professionals 1 Starter	U.S. $ 600 U.S. $ 300
Tester	2	02/01/2001	05/31/2001	Quality assurance, Web testing	1 Professional 1 Expert	U.S. $ 600 U.S. $ 700
Security specialist	1	01/01/2001	04/31/2001	Security, XSL, LDAP	Professional	U.S. $ 800
Process consultant	1	01/01/2001	04/15/2001	Consulting	Professional	U.S. $ 1000

Table 6. Sample human resource plan

Skills and activities description

Table 7 outlines a sample skills and activity description for the job category of art *director.*

Required skills / education	▪ Graphic design degree. ▪ Gifted artistic and design talent. ▪ In-depth knowledge of latest graphic design software (e.g., *PhotoShop*, *Illustrator*). ▪ In-depth knowledge of all creative roles. ▪ Ability to motivate the people from the creative discipline. ▪ Good presentation and communications skills. ▪ 3–5 years experience as art director.
Activities	The major activities that have to be performed by the art director are: ▪ To determine the creative vision and high-level view of the solution. ▪ To ensure the logical integration of information, design, and content into the framework of the aesthetic design. ▪ To oversee the development of the creative solution throughout the course of design, coding, and testing. ▪ To communicate and interact with the client to get approval on the designed solution.

Table 7. Sample skills and activity description

Project team on board

The recruitment process is completed when all required human resources have been selected and are assigned to the project. The recruitment process is usually not limited to the start phase of the project. At the beginning of the project you usually recruit some people with whom you can start – the project *core team*. This project core team is then extended by recruiting further resources until a peak in the staffing plan is reached.

Staffing plan / curve

The staffing plan lists the name as well as the start and end dates of the assignment of each project team member. The staffing plan can be used as input to produce a *staffing curve* for the project. A staffing curve is a diagram illustrating how many human resources are assigned to the project at each point in time. Often the staffing curve is based on a weekly time scale. Fig. 12 outlines a sample staffing curve for an Internet portal project with a duration of 16 calendar weeks.

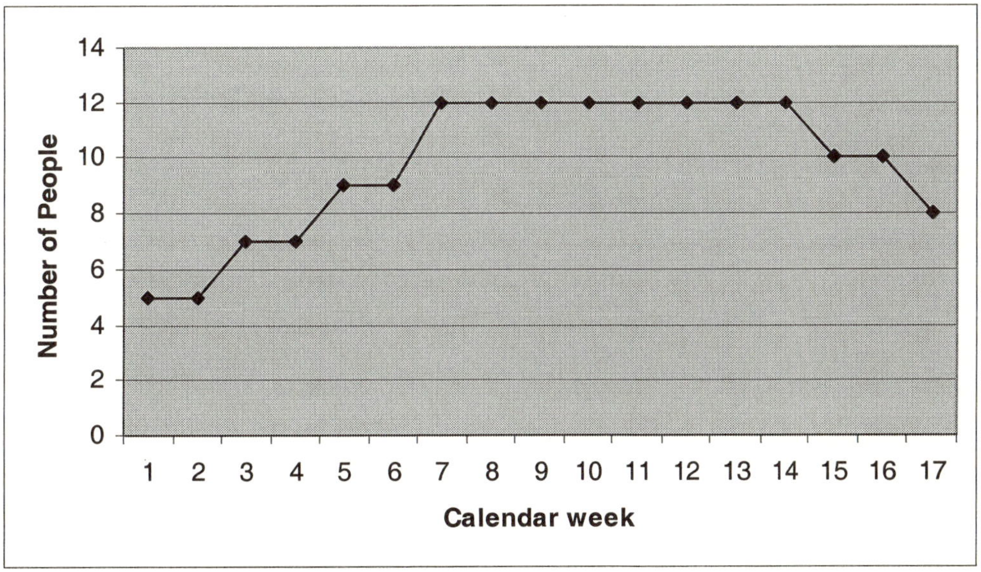

Fig. 12. Sample staffing curve

Project team address list

A project team address list contains address details of all project team members and of other project stakeholders, such as client staff members. The project team address list might be formal or informal, detailed or brief. The level of formality and detail depends on the needs of the project.

4.1.5 Key Success Factors

@ 14 Accept only people with an appropriate skills level to join your team

Leading-edge e-business skills are difficult to source: it can be hard to get the proper human resources with the required skills levels to work for your project. You find yourself battling with other project managers for the best human resources. When you encounter problems to get people with adequate skills levels you might consider accepting people with a lower level than required.

You might think: better an individual with lower qualifications than no-one. You assume that a less qualified individual can be trained during the project to achieve the required skills level. This assumption is invalid!

e-business projects usually have such a short project cycle so that there is no time for training on the job. Do not accept an individual with a lower skills level than required. Rather than settling for mediocrity, consider marking a position as 'open' in your staffing plan and continue searching. It is better to fill the opening at a later point with an individual who has the required skills level to do the job. Sometimes it is not easy to stick to this attitude when you get pressure from senior management. Too often senior manager's perspective is: "*the right people for the job are the available people*". Shun senior manager's attempts to persuade you to take on this perspective.

However, this does not mean that you should not welcome people with lower than expert skills levels in your team. You can include such people in your team – but only *in addition* to the people with the appropriate qualifications. Taking part in an e-business project is an excellent opportunity to build up skills in latest technologies. If people would like to participate in your project for training purpose, there is no reason why you should refuse that they join your team – on condition that you do not have to pay for them, and based on the assumption that they are not preventing your other team members in doing their job. The effort spent by other team members to train the lower skilled ones must be at least equalized by contributions that the additional people are performing for your project. Only in this case the productivity of the total project team is guaranteed. If those two prerequisite – no costs and stable productivity – are fulfilled, your company will benefit from this 'hands-on' training.

@ 15 Staff your team with dedicated full-time people

When human resources with appropriate skills for working in e-business projects are difficult to source, you might consider accepting *part-time* resources to fill the openings in your staffing plan. Part-time means that you have to share an individual's working time with someone else. Consider as an example a situation in which an individual is dedicated to work on two projects in parallel: 50% of the individual's working time is assigned to your project and 50% of the individual's working time is reserved for another project. Do not accept such an agreement!

Your e-business project needs the full attention of your staff. If an individual is working on two projects in parallel, you can never be sure that your project receives full attention. Even if an individual is obviously currently working for you, he or she might be distracted by thinking about work required in the other project. The 'mental' and 'physical' switch from one project to the other usually causes some overhead and inefficiency that slows down the total productivity of the individual.

In addition, there must be some sort of agreement to organize the sharing of the resource between you and the project manager of the other project. It is a simple fact of life that projects sometimes run into difficulties. A favorite measure to overcome a critical situation is to apply more resources. As e-business resources do not rain down from the sky, what is easier than trying to increase the share of a part-time worker? Be sure, if the troubled project is the other one, its project manager will inevitably get this idea – he or she will want a bigger piece of the pie.

Increasing the share of an individual's working time on the other project obviously decreases the time left for working in your project. Tough battles in vying for resources with your peer project manager are foreseeable, with the resulting time-consuming and often ugly discussions. To avoid such situations, staff your team with dedicated full-time people. Then you are in the comfortable situation of having full control over the total working time of the individuals assigned to your project.

@ 16 Select presentable staff members

When selecting the staff members for your project, do not pay attention only to technical expertise and personal characteristics of the candidates. Consider also the *appearance* of the candidate, to ensure that you have staff members that you can happily present to a client.

Even if the project work is not performed in the facilities of the client, there are numerous situations where your team members come into contact with your client. Some clients have clear expectations about the individuals working on projects for them. Some clients even put a clause in the contract entitling them to approve who works on the project. Usually this is a warning sign indicating that you are far from a trusting relationship. Nevertheless, you have to deal with this situation.

Some of the human resources who are potential candidates for e-business projects – especially those from the creative discipline – are used to demonstrate their creativity by a 'creative' appearance: green hair with blue stripes, copious body-piercing, etc. If such a person attends a meeting with a client in, for example, the insurance or banking industries, you may run into an acceptance problem. Some clients conclude from the appearance of an individual that he or she is not well-qualified for serious project work, even if you know yourself that there is no relationship between technical qualification and personal appearance. This suggests the selection of individuals whose appearance matches the expectations of your client.

However, that does not mean that you can not welcome team members with some kind of 'exotic' appearance; you only have to ensure that at least some team members in each discipline are 'presentable' from your client's viewpoint. Consider as an example a situation in which your project requires three screen designers. There is no reason not to welcome two of those hard-to-find individuals with some kind of 'exotic' appearance if you have one left who is presentable. If there is a need for client contact, for example, at a meeting to discuss issues related to screen design, it will then be obvious who to send to the client.

@ 17 Benefit from college students

In @ 15 I recommend staffing your team with full-time people only. However, in the e-business scene there are a lot of people who want to gain experience in the e-business field or to add to their e-business knowledge. Often those people are college students who want to get practical hands-on experience in real projects. Mostly these students have only low expectations regarding salary and perks. This is an ideal opportunity for you to get support for your project – with only minimal costs.

Many students have excellent technical expertise in the latest technology and are eager to do a good job. You can benefit from the students' work easing that of your full-time professionals. But be careful: students are no replacement for qualified full-time professionals; they are still *paraprofessionals*. Never count students as usual professionals of the team. The role of these paraprofessionals can be viewed as assisting the full-time people in performing their work. But those paraprofessionals will not perform the work of the dedicated professionals.

@ 18 Plan for a back-up solution for unplanned turnover of key team members

It can happen that team members leave the project unexpectedly – for personal or business reasons. If the individual leaving is a key team member, this event can disrupt your project significantly. To minimize the effects of unplanned turnover of key team members, it is good practice to plan for a back-up solution. A back-up solution consists of three components: (1) selection of a back-up person, (2) identification of a replacement, and (3) definition of hand-over procedures.

A back-up person is someone in the project who can handle the responsibilities of the leaving individual temporarily, until a permanent replacement is found. To ensure that back-up persons are available for all key team members, you should practice *cross-training* during the project. Cross-training means that you select for each key team member an individual who works closely with him or her or keeps himself or herself at least informed on the work of the person. If the key team member leaves unexpectedly, the peer takes over until a permanent replacement can be brought in.

You can proactively use the staff recruitment phase to identify potential replacements for key team members. Although you are not going to hire the identified talent immediately, it is good practice to keep the door open for later recruitment when you need the individual.

Moreover, you should spend some time defining the procedures and the manner in which a hand-over of responsibilities from the original person to the replacement might take place. This will help to make the replacement person useful as soon as possible.

Even with all these measures you can not ensure that there is no effect when a key team member leaves the project unexpectedly. However a deliberately defined back-up plan supports you to minimize the impact.

@ 19 Plan extension of contracts early

If you work with external resources you should ensure that you keep the talents on board as long as you need them. Some e-business projects are divided into consecutive phases that are contracted separately with a client. At the start of the project it might be not possible for you to recruit the project staff for the complete project: i.e., for all phases. You can only contract your staff for one phase and extend the contract when the contract with the client for the next phase is signed. As qualified e-business talents are rare, they are requested frequently in the labor market. You can find yourself in the situation where key players of your staff sign a contract early – but for a project other than yours. You should therefore place emphasis on getting the signature from your client early for the next phase. Missing this challenge could come back to haunt you. Therefore, plan ahead for a contract extension early.

@ 20 Limit the number of staff vendors

When you recruit staff externally you have to deal with vendors who provide staff to your team. Each *staff vendor* provides one or more human resources. As handling of staff vendors involves effort (e.g., administration and billing), it is good practice to keep the number of staff vendors as small as possible. If you can choose between recruiting three people from three staff vendors and recruiting three people from one staff vendor, the latter choice is the better one, on the condition that the qualifications of the proposed people are equal.

4.2 Defining the Project Organization

Defining the project organization is the process to define, build-up, and document the *project team structure* (see Fig. 13). The team structure identifies the roles, responsibilities, and relationships of the team members. The objective of the process is to achieve an appropriate team structure that will help the project manager to optimize the efforts of the team and to make the project a success.

There is a significant body of literature discussing organizational structure types such as *functional*, *projectized*, or *matrix-based* [30]. From my point of view the projectized organization type is the most favorable for e-business projects. The projectized organization suggests that the project manager has the total authority over the project. Human resources are assigned to the project and the project manager is responsible for performing the project work in time, on budget, and to the satisfaction of the client.

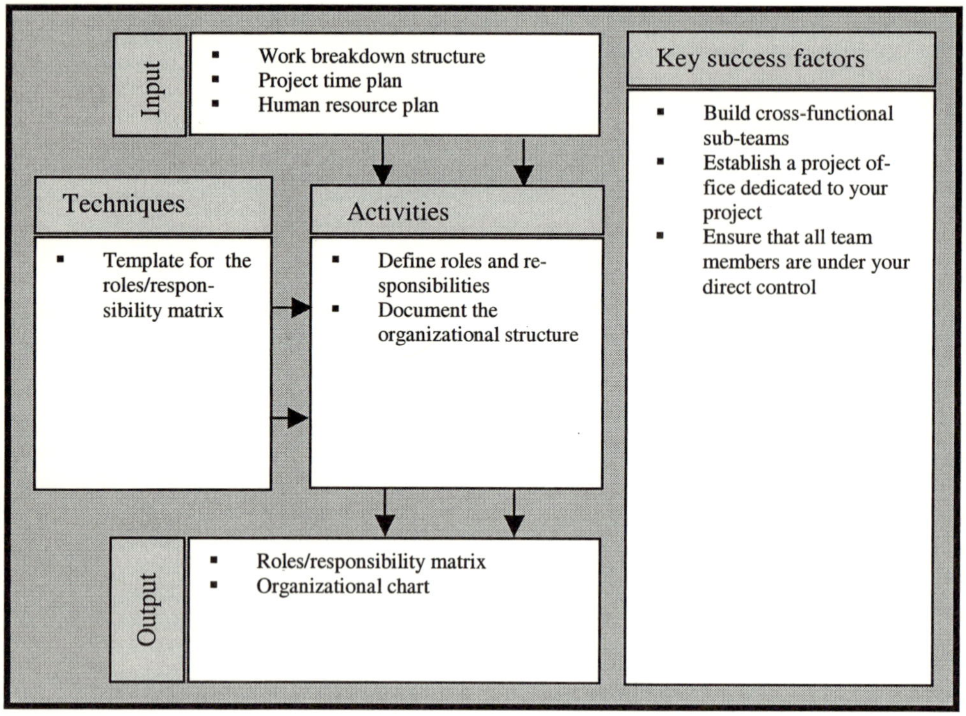

Fig. 13. Defining the project organization

4.2.1 Inputs

Work breakdown structure

The WBS (see Sect. 2.3.4) is an essential input for defining the project organization, since it outlines and structures the work that has to be performed in the project. The WBS gives you an indication on the project roles required and on the relationships between the roles.

Project time plan

The project time plan (see Sect. 3.1.4) outlines the duration, sequence, and dependencies of the work packages of the WBS. This provides you with information and restrictions as input for defining the size of sub-teams and responsibilities.

Human resource plan

The human resource plan outlines job categories and the number of human resources assigned to your project. It is essential information for defining the organizational structure and describing project roles and responsibilities.

@ 23 Ensure that all team members are under your direct control

In a project organized according to a projectized form of organization, all human resources are under direct control of the project manager – at least in theory. Too often you are asked to accept that some resources required for the project are outside your direct control. Typically such requests were issued by line managers.

Consider as an example a situation in which you have to set up and operate a network infrastructure for a project environment. A line manager offers you a group of his or her support people to perform this work. But he or she objects to these people joining your team. Instead the work is offered to be performed as a service for your project. Often his or her argument is that there are several projects requiring the same type of work and he or she will organize resource sharing so that the service requests from all projects can be fulfilled. I have never seen such a sharing of resources working properly, so you should refuse such an offer. Instead, insist on having the people required to perform the work assigned to your project under your direct control.

Another common situation is the request – typically issued by a senior line manager in your reporting chain – to assign the project office for your project to him or her. What is the main reason behind such a request? Usually, one of the tasks of a project office people is to collect the financial data of a project. By assigning the people of the project office to him or her the requester's idea is to get direct insight into the financial status of your project. First, this indicates a lack of trust in yourself, because it is part of your job to keep senior management informed on the financial health of your project. Second, the people in the project office have two bosses to serve, you and the line manager. This is often an unsatisfying situation for these people, adversely affecting team moral and motivation. You should fight hard to ensure that all team members are under your direct control. It pays off!

4.3 Developing the Project Team

Developing the project team is the process of creating a *work environment* that both enhance the ability of each staff member to contribute as individual to the team performance and enhances the ability of the team to function as a team (see Fig. 14).

Developing the project team is an important management process since a well-functioning team is much more than the sum of its parts. The basis for building the project team is a technical work environment that ensures that the staff members have all prerequisites available to execute the project work in a productive manner. With the technical work environment on a sound basis, you can build a team climate where the members share common goals and enjoy working together.

Team building for e-business projects does not differ much from team building for IT projects. You find a lot of useful team building suggestions in various publications on human resources management. The important point to remember here is that team building effort is required and must be performed – it will not come by itself and you as the project manager are the focal point for this effort. A high-performance team does not just happen, it must be made to happen through appropriate team-building activities.

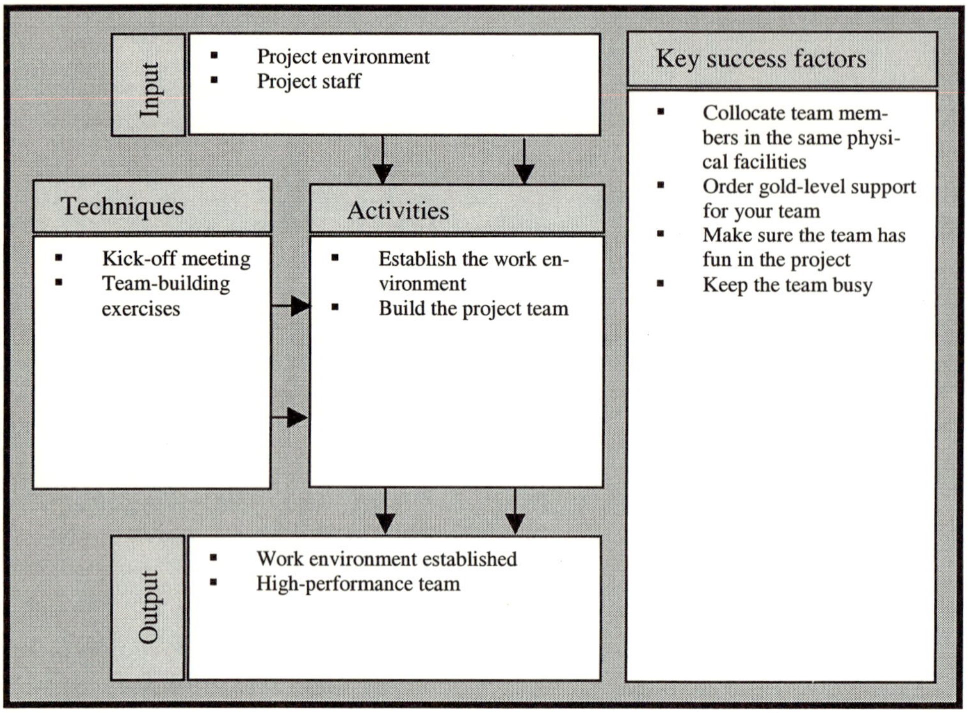

Fig. 14. Developing the project team

4.3.1 Inputs

Project environment

The project environment includes all characteristics and constraints that are relevant to the project. These include but are not limited to: duration of the project, required and available technical equipment, work location (customer side or in-house), and the importance and visibility of the project.

Project staff

The individuals who are assigned to the projects are an important input factor for the team-building efforts. The characteristics of the staff members play an important role in determining which team-building activities are most appropriate. Relevant characteristics are, for example, skills/disciplines, ages, cultural backgrounds, mentality of individuals, team size, and whether or not the individuals have already worked together in previous projects.

4.3.2 Activities

Establish the work environment

For each individual of the team, establish a work environment where all necessary prerequisites for productive work performance are available. This starts with basics like the work place environment, availability and access to required hardware, software, networks, and tools. It continues with the organization of userids/passwords and access to project information/documentation, and does not end with the ordering of pizza for long and hard working days. To make the work environment even more appealing to the team, consider enriching the office environment by providing exercise facilities, game rooms, or coffee bars.

Build the project team

Appropriate team-building activities are highly dependent on the project staff and its characteristics. However, there are three proven practices that are applicable for almost all projects: (1) conduct a *kick-off meeting* early in the project to orient the team members, (2) use *team-building exercises* like social team events to create a sense of team identity, and (3) establish a *reward system* for outstanding team performance [40]. It is important to remember that team building is not a one-time event; team building is necessary throughout the whole life of a project.

Although team building is important in traditional IT projects, in e-business projects it is an absolute necessity. This is because people from different disciplines – 'techies', creative, marketing, consulting – usually have a different 'working style' and a different mentality. This makes team building an outstanding challenge in e-business projects.

4.3.3 Techniques

Kick-off meeting

A kick-off meeting is a meeting with all project staff members. A kick-off meeting should be held at the start of the project. The main objective of the meeting is to orient the staff on the project. The meeting can be used for the following purposes:

- Getting the project team members to know each other.
- Building working and communication relationships.
- Outlining project characteristics.
- Communicating project objectives and team goals.
- Identifying project challenges.
- Communicating team structure, roles, and responsibilities.
- Achieving team buy-in and team commitments.

Team-building exercises

Team-building exercises are actions that support team consciousness and team motivation. Typical team-building exercises are team events outside the company like a sailing trip lasting a few days, going out with the team for a beer after work, or team events inside the company like recognition of special performance of individual team members or sub-teams.

4.3.4 Outputs

Work environment established

The output of the developing project team process is an established work environment. A work environment is established properly when all necessary prerequisites for productive work performance are available.

High-performance team

One output of the team development process is a *high-performance team.* Some characteristics of a high-performance team are:

- Outstanding motivation of the team members with total involvement in the project.
- Full support of decisions once they have been made by all team members.
- Trust in all team members including the project manager.
- Free discussions of issues and problems.
- Tolerance with regard to deviating ideas and thinking.
- Operational excellence and making the project schedule.

4.3.5 Key Success Factors

@ 24 Collocate team members in the same physical facilities

In my own experience the collocation of the team members is one of the most important factors for success in e-business projects. And the principle of collocation is independent of the size of the team and the complexity of a project. However, you will have no difficulties to find a lot of people who state just the opposite. Several authors praise the advantages of working in *virtual teams.* 'Virtual' means that the team members are not located at the same workplace, instead they are spread over several physical facilities, with sometimes hundreds or thousands of miles between them. Those authors claim that it does not matter *where* the work is performed, only that it *is* performed. This theorem might be true for pieces of work that can be done by a single individual where the piece of work is not dependent on any others. In e-business projects such pieces of work do not exist! Even if you believe that you may have identified such work items, you can be sure that you have overlooked some interdependencies.

Why is it so important to have the team collocated? Interdependencies and interfaces between pieces of work implies a need for communication between the team members performing the work. If those individuals are not collocated, you encounter a communication problem due to the physical distance.

The advocates of the virtual team idea do not grow weary of propagating the concept that due to the availability of new technologies like the Internet, high-bandwidth networks, mobile phones, and video-conferencing, the physical distance between team members is no longer a problem. They note that people can share information and make decisions related to a project across thousands of miles regardless of the distance between them. But the distance is still a problem – not from a technical but from a psychological and sociological point of view. Your team members will communicate less with each other if they are not all collocated in one physical facility. This fact is proven by numerous research efforts as well as by practical experience. Since communication is essential in e-business projects, your project will suffer if you work with virtual teams.

What are the reasons for virtual teams? The supporters of virtual teams claim mostly two advantages: (1) saving traveling time and (2) higher productivity. They propose having the staff members work at home – sometimes called 'home office'. The obvious advantage of the home office approach is that traveling from home to the facilities of the company is no longer necessary. Fine, since taking a look on our choked-up streets and crowded public transportation systems this would clearly be an advantage – for the public.

However, is this an advantage for your project? Based on the assumption that a staff member would spent an equal amount of time on the project when working at home and when working in the company's facilities, your project will not benefit.

So, what is left is the productivity argument. Does working at home really foster productivity? This depends heavily on the home office environment. If the team member has a big family with small children and is fully involved in social life, the productivity might even be less than working in the company's facilities. Taking these facts and the need for close communication into account, the concept of virtual teams is not suitable for e-business projects.

@ 25 Order gold-level support for your team

In e-business projects it is common for a variety of software products from *vendors* to be integrated when building up the e-business solution. The integration of vendor products mostly means more than 'plug-and-play'. For example, APIs of products must be used, special features exploited, or you simply detect a bug in the provided software components that prevents successful integration. When you buy vendor products to build up the e-business solution, you have to order and organize development support for those products from the vendors. Often there are several levels of support offered by the supplier with differing quality-of-service levels. Widespread practice is to call the levels of support 'gold', 'silver', and 'bronze', indicating a descending level of support and service. While the gold-level support frequently means that you can expect availability of service (e.g., help desk, technical experts, and download servers) 24 hours a day 7 days a week, silver-level reduces the availability to usual working hours 6 days a week, and bronze-level means a further decrease in service quality. Of course the vendor support costs money: not surprisingly, the better the service, the more you have to spend.

Usually in the project planning phase you have to decide which level of support to order. For e-business projects I strongly recommend ordering the gold-level support. There is nothing more frustrating for you and your team than being very close to achieving an important project goal on a Saturday night, with the only thing left to do is to download a bug fix from a vendor – and the door is closed only because you saved a few dollars by ordering the silver or bronze level. There are a lot of good opportunities within a project to save money, sacrificing the best possible support for your team is clearly one of the worst candidates. Therefore, always order gold-level support for your team.

@ 26 Make sure the team has fun in a project

When working in an e-business project you and your team are on the cutting edge of a new work paradigm: latest technology, high visibility, and extreme speed. Working in an e-business project is exciting by itself, however it is still work – often hard work. In e-business projects clients are always scrambling for something new, something exciting, something that has never been done before, and everything should be available overnight. Those expectations can only be met by a motivated project team.

It is your responsibility to ensure that the team motivation is high. You have to hold the team members' interest and motivation in their job assignments. Many people are not suited to the rigors of tough project deadlines. Applying hard-nosed tactics to those people can be very demoralizing. Treating the people like children will likely produce amateurish results. The best way to achieve a high team motivation resulting in professional results is to make sure that the team has fun in the project.

Fun and humor is important given the challenges and time pressures in a project. I would never claim to provide you with recommendations on how you can achieve that the team has fun – this depends highly on your personality, your working style, and the characteristics of the team – just do it! With a team that has fun you can share heartaches and triumphs whilst making your project a success.

@ 27 Keep the team busy

The level of workload for the team and for each individual team member often varies during the project. There might be times in which the workload is so high that the people are gasping for breath and other times where the workload is low – or even zero. Both situations are poison for team motivation and moral. Experience has shown that it is better for the team to be busy with too much work than to get caught in a lull.

What are the reasons for varying workload during a project? In the planning phase of a project when you identify the activities and set up a schedule, you are naturally arranging the activities and assigning the people in such a way that the workload is rather balanced. We all know that this works fine on paper. In reality you will encounter times with high workload and times with low workload. Often activities are interdependent. If an activity could not be started before a proceeding activity is completed, a delay in performing the proceeding activity will prevent the start of the subsequent one. This can result in different levels of workload for the people who are assigned to the activities. Moreover, there are other situations that are not under your control: activities are dependent on responsibilities that have to be fulfilled by the client, and the client does not always fulfill in time. In this case you will of course try to assign other activities to the team members with low workload, but due to the highly specialized skills needed for e-business projects this works only to a certain extent. You could not re-assign an activity like coding a Java servlet from a Java programmer to a screen designer. Usually the screen-designer does not have Java programming skills – be happy about exceptions. As a consequence you will not always be able to balance the workload exactly.

If some team members – or the whole project team – do not have sufficient work to do, this is a dangerous situation. If this situation lasts only for a few days, the people might even be happy about it. After a period of tough work having a few days time to surf the Web is not the worst thing that can happen. But it will become a problem when this period lasts longer than a few days and some team members or the complete team get caught in a lull. You should struggle hard to avoid this situation by keeping the team busy, otherwise the team moral will drop dramatically. In addition, although the resources are idling they have to be paid for. This might cause an overrun of your project budget. Nevertheless, the financial impact is not the decisive one, since the decreasing team motivation may even cost you more.

If it is really not feasible to re-arrange the project work by performing, for example, activities earlier than originally planned, it is better to keep the team busy by letting the people do 'something' rather than having the team idling. It would be useful if the 'something' is work that is beneficial to the project. You could, for example, let the team build tools to support the coming project activities, perform an analysis of competitors, or offer the client the performing of some pieces of work – outside the scope of the project – for free. The latter suggestion will pay twice: you are building credit on client side and you keep the team moral high. So, be creative in looking for useful work for the team to keep it busy, and avoid allowing the team or individual team members to get caught in a lull.

One last word regarding the other extreme: when there is too much work – indications are working overtime or working through the weekends – you also have to change something, especially if this situation continues for an extended period. Because otherwise people can become burned out. Symptoms of burning out are increasing absenteeism and plummeting productivity.

5 Managing the Cost

The main purpose of managing cost is to make a project successful from a financial point of view. A project can be rated as successful in terms of cost if it is completed within an approved budget that contains an acceptable level of profit for a contractor. Managing cost includes the processes required to *estimate* and to *control* cost. Cost estimation is a fundamental project management activity, and e-business projects are notoriously difficult to cost estimate. However, a reliable cost estimate is a crucial project planning element.

Who is responsible for managing cost? It is mainly you, the project manager. Estimating cost must often be performed before a project is started. The cost estimate is taken as the input for defining the price for a project. This is important since most e-business projects are performed under a *firm-fixed-price* contract. Under a firm-fixed-price contract all deliverables required to cover a defined project scope are offered by a contractor at a fixed price. With such a type of contract, the financial risk of a project is completely on the contractor side: if the deliverables can not be produced within the budget approved for the project, the financial impact is born by the contractor.

Some projects are performed under a *time-and-material* contract. With such a contract the client has to reimburse the contractor for the cost incurred in performing the project work. Here the risk is fully on the client side. If the project involves more costs, the client must reimburse the contractor. For a project performed under a firm-fixed-price contract it is obvious that estimating and controlling the cost is essential for the contractor. Nevertheless, the estimation of cost is also often required under a time-and-material contract since the client is interested prior to project start to know approximately how much the project will cost.

Before jumping into the details of cost estimation and cost control, we should clarify the relationship of *cost*, *price*, and *budget*, because those are often seen as synonymous terms – but they are not synonyms! The element common to cost, price, and budget is that they are expressed in unit of currency (e.g., dollars, euros, or yen). Costs are the monetary units required to perform the project work. The cost of a project is estimated and controlled by the contractor. Price is the total contract value – on the assumption that a firm-fixed-price contract type is used – that has to be paid by the client to the contractor as compensation for performing the project work. A budget is a spending limit for a project usually set and approved by senior management. Normally there is a budget on both the contractor and the client side (see Fig. 15).

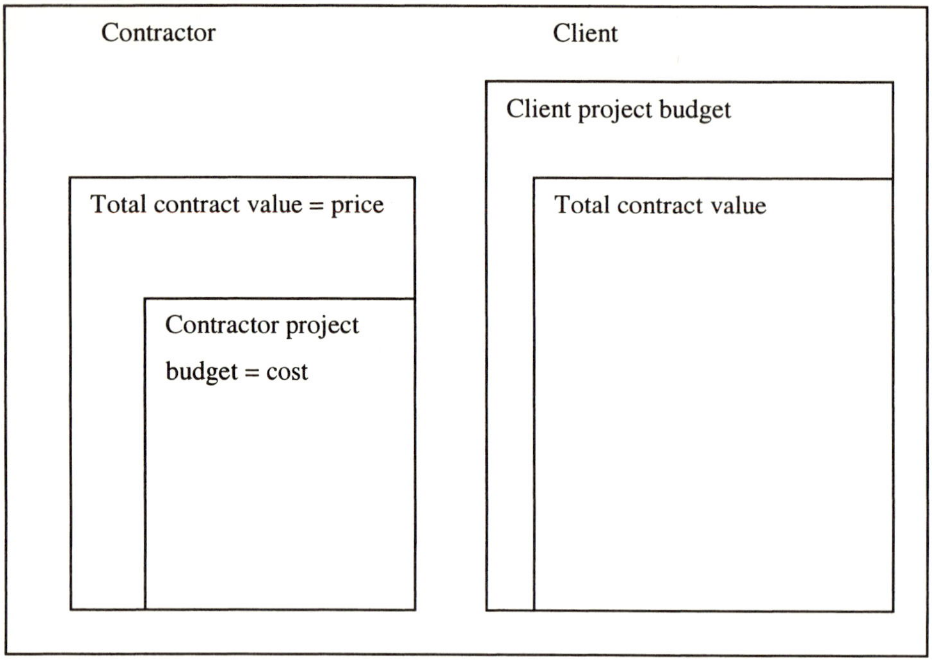

Fig. 15. Relationship between budget, cost, and price

The left-hand side of Fig. 15 has the inner box labeled 'contractor project budget = cost'. This is an estimate on the likely cost of performing the project work. This cost estimate is the contractor's budget, so it is the limit within which you should complete the project. The outer box on the left-hand side of the figure represents the project price. This is the amount of money that the contractor will charge the client for performing the project work, therefore it represents the 'total contract value'. While estimating cost is a project management responsibility, defining the price is a business decision. The cost estimate is one input to price definition. However, there may be many other aspects that have to be considered when defining a price. Those aspects are, for example, whether you are in a competitive situation and another company offers performing the project for the client, the utilization and availability of resources, and the strategy of the company. Usually the price is higher than the estimated costs, though exceptions exists. The difference between the price and the project budget is the 'calculated' or 'expected' profit. When the project is completed the difference between the price and the incurred costs is the 'real' profit for your company. If you manage to complete the project work exactly within your project budget (= estimated cost), the real profit is exactly equal to the expected one. If you manage to complete the project with lower costs than estimated, the profit is higher. If you have to encounter a cost overrun, the profit is smaller. If you complete your project with total costs that are equal to or even greater than the price, the project will have produced a financial loss.

The right-hand side of Fig. 15 depicts the client perspective. The inner box represents the total contract value that is equal to the price that the client has to pay to the customer. For the sake of brevity it is assumed that the client has engaged only a single contractor. The outer box represents the client's budget, which is the amount of money that the client project manager can spend on a project. It is the total client investment for a given project and covers also the expenses incurred by the client (e.g., client staff, training, and infrastructure).

The client project budget normally includes the *total life-cycle costs* of a project. Total life-cycle costs means that not only the costs for performing the project but also the costs for deploying and operating the developed e-business solution have to be considered. Including the costs for operating the solution is especially important in e-business projects since a considerable amount of money is required to cover e-business-specific expenses. Such expenses are, for example, network communication costs for data transfer or transaction costs when end-users can pay ordered goods via the Web.

5.1 Estimating the Project Cost

Estimating cost is the process of developing a realistic approximation of the costs of the resources required to perform a project from a contractor's point of view (see Fig. 16). The resources usually required for an e-business project can be classified into three categories:

1. **Hardware.** This is the computers and the infrastructure (network, connectors, online access fees) necessary for a project. The hardware may be divided in two subcategories: (1) hardware required by the contractor to perform the project work, i.e., mainly to develop the e-business application; and (2) hardware delivered to the client as part of the contract and used by the client to operate the e-business solution. Hardware does not need to be considered in all e-business projects. A typical situation in which no hardware costs are involved in a e-business project is when existing hardware on the contractor side can be used for developing the e-business application. The same holds true when suitable hardware already exists on client side to operate the solution, so that no new hardware needs to be delivered under the contract. Another situation is when the client does not intend to operate the e-business solution by itself. Instead the operation is 'outsourced' to another company. Of course it has to be differentiated whether hardware is *bought* or *leased* for a project. In the first case, costs for depreciation might need to be considered, while in the second case, the respective leasing costs have to be taken.
2. **Software.** These are standard software products used in a project. Also here can two subcategories be considered: (1) standard software products available on the market that have to be integrated and are delivered to the client as components of the e-business solution – typical examples of such software products are system software,

database software, web server software, web browser software, online shop software, and marketplace software; and (2) standard software in the form of software tools required by the contractor to design and build the e-business application. Typical examples of such software are PhotoShop, Java server engine, a debugger, and memory-leak checker. The standard software products have to be distinguished from the software that is developed by the contractor for an individual client. The activities involved in developing this software are part of the *services* and are covered by the costs of the people performing these services.

3. **People.** These are the project staff required to perform the project work. The work performed by the project staff is commonly summarized as 'services'. The costs of people include salaries and related costs, office space charges, and travel expenses (if any).

Estimating the cost of hardware and software is relative straightforward compared to estimating the cost of people. Usually you can identify definite prices for hardware and software, since you have 'only' to analyze which hardware and software components are needed, and then evaluate the costs of acquiring them. Estimating the cost of people is much more complicated. The biggest challenge is to estimate how many people you will need to perform the project services.

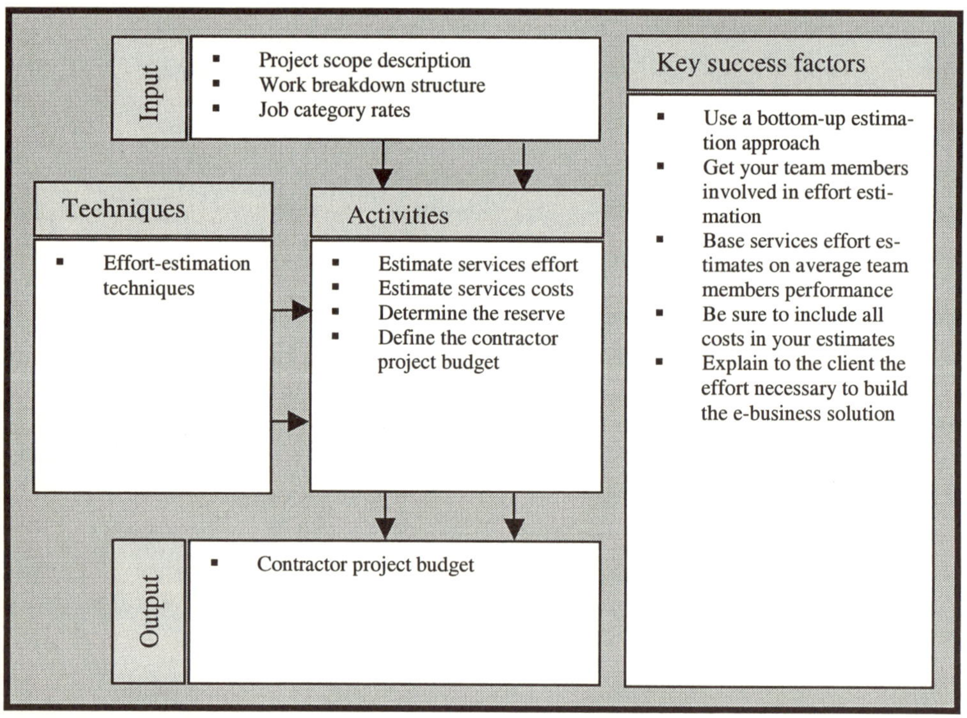

Fig. 16. Estimating the project cost

5.1.1 Input

Project scope description

The project scope defines the framework of what has to be delivered to the client in terms of functionality. From the functionality specified in the project scope description, the hardware and software that is required to build and to operate the e-business solution can be derived. The project scope description serves as input to the estimation of the hardware and software costs.

Work breakdown structure

The WBS defines the work packages that must be provided during the course of the project. The WBS is used to organize the services cost estimates in order to ensure that all identified work items are covered when preparing the cost estimates.

Job category rates

For calculating the total costs you have to know not only how many people in each job category you need to perform the work, but also how much a person from a specific job category costs. The costs for a person of a specific job category is usually given in the form of *job category rates*. A job category rate is normally expressed in monetary units per hour or per day. The rate can be given inclusive of all expenses (e.g., travel expenses and office space charges) or exclusive of these. If the expenses are not inclusive those have to be considered separately.

5.1.2 Activities

Estimate services effort

The objective of the estimate services effort activity is to assess the likely services effort that is required to carry out the project work. Unfortunately, often the services effort has to be estimated at an early stage in the project when not all information are available that are normally required to perform reliable and accurate estimates. There are several estimation techniques (see Sect. 5.1.3) that have been applied in various projects.

In principle two estimation approaches can be taken. The first is *top-down* estimating, which is also called *analogous estimating*. It means that the total project effort is estimated by using the actual effort spent in a previous, similar project. A prerequisite for this approach is that you have the data from a similar project available. Reliable estimates can be expected when the project taken as the basis is really similar – not just in appearance. The second approach is *bottom-up* estimating, which involves estimating the effort of single work items, followed by summarizing the single estimates to get the total effort. For estimating the effort of single work items one of the estimation techniques outlined in Sect. 5.1.3 can be used. My recommendation is to use the *expert judgment* technique. This suggests that you take the WBS, find an expert for each listed work item, and ask the expert to give you an estimate of the effort required. For different work items you might need to involve different experts, because due to the diversity of e-business work items, you will normally not find a single individual having the required skills to cover all the different work items that are required to perform an e-business project.

Estimate services costs

The objective of this activity is to estimate the costs in terms of monetary units that are likely to be incurred when performing the services required to complete the project. The estimation can be performed using a relative simple calculation. For the calculation you take two parameters as input: (1) the effort estimates produced by the previously described activity and (2) the job category rates. You identify for each work item the job category of the person required to perform it. The cost in monetary units is calculated by multiplying the effort value by the job category rate. The total estimated services costs are calculated by summing up all single values resulting from the multiplication. If you are not only interested in the costs of the total project but also its distribution over project phases, you can perform the calculation in steps; i.e., summing up the single values for each project phase separately. This provides you with more detailed information about the point in time when the costs are likely to be occurred during the course of the project.

Determine the reserve

Even when you estimate the services costs very accurately there is always a level of uncertainty inherent, because an estimate is only a *prediction* of the real costs. The real costs can differ from the estimated ones for two main reasons: (1) your estimate of the effort required to perform the identified work items is incorrect and (2) you overlooked certain work items that must be performed – consequently no effort for these work items is included in your estimate. When the project is completed and the real costs are much higher than the estimated ones, you have encountered a cost overrun. Such a situation will most likely cause you a lot of trouble. In order to reduce the likelihood of a cost overrun it is good practice to include a 'safety factor' in terms of a *reserve* in an estimate. The reserve is normally calculated as a specific percentage of the initial estimate. This reserve serves as a safety buffer to compensate for costs of overlooked work or incorrect estimates.

The question is what percentage to choose as a safety factor? When determining this percentage you have to consider two aspects: On the one hand it is obvious that the higher the factor, the more safety is included in the estimate, and the more comfortable you can be about a difference between estimated and real costs. On the other hand you have to pay attention to the fact that the reserve enhances the price at which you can offer to perform a project for a client. If you take a very high safety factor, there is a greater risk that a competitor will issue a lower offer, raising the risk that the contract for the project is not awarded to your company.

As a rule of thumb I found it useful to plan with a factor of about 15% as the reserve on top of the initial estimate. However this factor must be determined individually for each specific project. When determining this factor you should mainly take into account how accurately you consider the initial estimate to be. If you use the latest technology often no experience in exploiting this technology is available that would allow to verify an estimate with data from previous projects. Due to this lack of experience the safety factor chosen for e-business projects should therefore be normally higher than for traditional IT projects that use proven technology. However, in general the 'right' amount of reserve depends largely on the method used to estimate the effort and the input data available when producing the estimate.

Define the contractor project budget

To define the project budget you simply sum up the estimated costs for hardware, software, services, and the reserve. On top of the resulting total you put any additional costs that are not included in the four categories listed. Additional costs in an e-business project include the following:

1. **Warranty.** In a firm-fixed-price contract the contractor normally has to provide a guarantee for the delivered e-business solution over a limited time frame, usually 3 – 6 months. Within this time period the contractor has to warrant that the solution operates properly. This covers especially the duty to fix severe bugs that are discovered in the code of the e-business application by the client or end-users. People must be available in the warranty phase to perform any necessary fixes. The estimated costs for these people must be considered in the project budget.
2. **Travel expenses.** Most e-business projects are conducted mainly in the facilities of the contractor. However, there are some situations where the contractor's staff visit the facilities of the client. Typical examples are for project status meetings, design reviews, interviews with client end-users conducted by consultants, support in installation and deployment, and administrator training. The client's facilities might be hundreds or thousands miles away from the contractor's facilities. In this case a considerable amount of travel expenses are incurred and they must therefore be added to the project budget. The amount of travel expenses will be even higher if the complete project or parts of it are conducted in the facilities of the client. It is therefore important to clarify early in which location the project work will be performed.

The listed additional costs are examples only. There might be various other additional costs. The definition of the project budget is complete when all additional costs are collected.

5.1.3 Techniques

Effort-estimation techniques

Effort-estimation techniques can be divided into two categories: (1) estimating techniques that are based on a specific *method* using some kind of *metrics* and (2) techniques that are based on *experience*. In the following, two commonly used techniques in each category are given as examples and discussed briefly.

COCOMO method: The constructive cost model method [4] is a vehicle used to estimate software development effort. It can be applied to estimate new code development as well as to customize already existing code. A prerequisite for applying the method is that the size of existing code is known in terms of *lines of source code* (LoSC) and that a reliable estimate of the LoSC that have to be developed can be given. The idea of the method is to evaluate for a project so-called *scale drivers* and *cost drivers*. Scale drivers are, for example, development flexibility, team cohesion, and process maturity. Cost drivers are, for example, personal, product, and platform factors. The development effort is estimated by applying an equation that takes the number of LoSC and the scale and cost drivers as input. The equation is based on experiences and measurements performed on a variety of software development projects. The output of applying the equation is an effort estimate expressed in terms of person-months.

The advantage of this method is that it is relative straightforward and the effort for single project phases can be calculated separately. The disadvantage is that the method is limited to estimating the software development effort only; it can not be applied to estimate the creative, consulting, and marketing efforts of an e-business project.

Function point method: The function point method [17] measures software applications by quantifying the functionality provided to the user based primarily on logical design. The estimation is performed in terms of so-called *function points*. A function point is a quantifiable measure of the size of an application from a user's perspective. The idea of the method is to size the complexity of a software application by analyzing its data, its input and output transactions, and its end-user inquiries. Based on this analysis, function points are counted. In addition, a set of general system characteristics is defined. An influence factor is assigned to each of the defined project characteristics and out of this a value adjustment factor is calculated. The value adjustment factor is multiplied with the number of counted function points. The result is an *adjusted function point* total. For adjusted function points, effort measurement data from other projects are taken as ball-park estimates for the current project.

The advantage of the function point method is that it is independent of subjective views of people performing the estimates and independent of the programming language and technology. The disadvantage is that it requires an in-depth analysis of the software application. In addition, the effort measurement data of similar projects must be available. The estimate calculated with the function point method is limited to the software development effort and is not suitable to estimate the costs of creative, consulting, and marketing efforts.

Expert judgment method: The expert judgment method relies on the estimation experience and expertise of *subject matter experts*. Subject matter experts are individuals who are skilled in estimating the effort required for a specific piece of work in a certain subject area. The basis for an expert judgment is the identification and description – at a sufficient level of detail – of all work items that have to be performed during the course of the project. The effort of each identified work item is estimated by an appropriate expert. The total effort is calculated by summing the single estimates. A prerequisite for applying this method is that you have adequate subject matter experts available. The advantage of the method is that all work items, and not only those related to software development, are taken into consideration. The disadvantage is that the estimate is highly dependent on the subjective view of people.

Analogous method: The analogous method takes a top-down approach. The basic idea of the analogous method is to identify another project that is similar in terms of scope, complexity, and technology to the project for which you wish to estimate the effort. You simply take the actual effort required to carry out the other project and use this as an estimate of the effort needed in yours. A prerequisite for this method is that you find another project with a comparable size, scope, complexity, and technology, and that you can obtain the data on the effort spent on that project. The advantage of the analogous method is that it is generally less costly than the other methods. The disadvantage is that you might not find any other project that is similar to yours, or that the other one only looks similar, but is not similar in reality.

5.1.4 Outputs

Contractor project budget

The output of the cost estimating process is the project budget of the contractor. The contractor project budget is the amount of money that is available to the contractor project manager for completing the project work. It is a fixed amount of money that is calculated in an early phase of a project. Nevertheless, the project budget might change during the course of the project due to accepted *change requests*. Normally change requests increase the project budget.

5.1.5 Key Success Factors

@ 28 Use a bottom-up estimation approach

Many e-business projects are not successful from a contractor's point of view because they suffer from cost overruns. A cost overrun is a situation in which the costs incurred to complete a project are higher than the contractor's project budget. e-business projects often go over budget because the contractor budget is linked to inaccurate services cost estimates performed early in the project. A reliable services cost estimate is therefore crucial for improving your odds of making a project a success.

For estimating the services effort for a project, in principle either a top-down or a bottom-up estimation approach can be taken. For an e-business project the recommendation is to use the second approach. What are advantages of the bottom-up estimation approach? First, e-business technology is evolving at a dizzying pace – what was used yesterday is no longer appealing today. It might therefore be hard for you to find a previous project which you can use as a basis for a top-down approach using the analogous method. Therefore, it often happens that you take another project that is only 'rather' similar to the current one. However, a 'rather' similar project can require a significantly different services effort, so that the estimated costs are far from your real ones. In addition, 'similar' is often seen only in terms of technology and functionality. But developing the same functionality might involve different costs when performed by a different team, in a different environment, or for a different client – even when the same technology is used.

Second, both research and experience in many IT projects indicate that the accuracy and reliability of a bottom-up estimate is usually higher than that of a top-down estimate. This holds true for e-business projects as well.

Third, with the top-down approach you normally obtain an estimate for the total services effort only. The total effort is not distinguishable for separate project phases that normally result from an incremental and iterative implementation approach that is normally favorable for e-business projects. This complicates the tracking of project costs. You might only recognize at project completion when all work items are finalized that the real effort was much higher than the estimated effort. Deviations can be detected much earlier when you trace the effort at the phase or work package level. There is a two-fold benefit: (1) it gives you the chance to take countermeasures in the current project and (2) discovering major deviations between estimated and real effort for a single project phase or a specific work item provides you with valuable information in terms of *lessons learned*. If you have to estimate costs for your next project – and this includes comparable work items – you can estimate costs much more accurately. Nevertheless, I do not want to hold back that using the bottom-down estimation approach usually involves more effort than using the top-down approach. But this investment normally pays off.

@ 29 Get your team members involved in effort estimation

In Sect. 5.1.2 I suggested estimating the services effort using the expert judgment method. The fundamental idea of this method is basing the cost estimates on the judgment of individuals who are subject matter experts in the work items for which the effort has to be estimated. Your job is to put together the effort figures that you receive from the experts as input. The interesting question is: where to find these experts? The simple answer is: get your team members involved.

However, one aspect must be considered: normally you have to perform the effort estimation activity at an early point in the project – often it must be performed even before the project is started. So, you might argue that you do not have any team members at this point. Nevertheless, in most cases you have either a basic idea of the skills needed to perform the project and a rough idea of the people who have those skills, or you have already a few individuals as a 'core' team on board. This means, in the best case, that you have the key team members already assigned to the project; in the worst case you have at least an idea whom you would like to welcome into the team in the future.

Taking team members as your experts provides several advantages. First, your team members are normally specialists in their fields and their expertise usually results from performing similar work items in previous projects. The best effort judgment expert is often an individual whose knowledge is based on real-life experiences. This is exactly true for your team members – otherwise you would not have assigned them to the project.

Second, you can assume that the team members will perform the effort estimation carefully and with great accuracy. What is the reason for this assumption? The team members know that during the course of the project they have to conduct the work items for which they are asked to provide effort estimates. Not surprisingly they anticipate that you will later insist that they complete the work items within the estimated effort. This is a enormous stimulus for the team members to give realistic estimates. In addition, you can expect that the team members are wedded to conduct the work items within the estimated effort when the effort was estimated by the team members themselves. Although you can not take the team's estimate as a 'formal' commitment to conduct the work within the estimated effort, most team members take this as a 'moral' commitment. They will try harder to complete the work items with the effort estimated by themselves compared to the situation in which the estimation was performed by someone else.

Third, you have an implicit advantage: in order to prepare an accurate estimate, the team members have to analyze the work items in detail with the implicit consequence that they become familiar with the work items. If estimating the work items and performing them is done by different individuals, you have to pay twice for this activity; if the individuals are identical, you only have to pay once. You see, involving the team in effort estimation as your experts has several advantages. Why not take this approach?

@ 30 Base services effort estimates on average team members performance

When you estimate the services effort for an e-business project it is good practice to base the estimate on average team members performance. Not all people are created equal. Productivity between individuals varies – the difference can be quite significant. When you estimate the services effort in terms of 'person-months' the productivity of a 'person' is an important factor. Usually you have to estimate the services effort at a point when only a core team with few members is assigned to the project. Since many team members will be recruited later, you do not know their productivity and performance. Often the core team members are your 'best' people – highly skilled individuals with an outstanding performance. Outstanding performance means that their productivity is significantly higher than those of most other people within the same job category. Not surprisingly you will struggle to get many outperformers assigned to your team. However, you can be glad to employ a few outperformers and usually you have to accept a few underperformers. Therefore, taking all team members into account you will end up with an average performance level. When estimating the person-months you should take an average team members performance as the baseline for the productivity of a 'person'. This advice sounds obvious but real-life experience shows that it is worth mentioning.

When individuals are asked to estimate services effort they tend to give estimates based on their own productivity and performance. If you ask an outperformer the estimated figure will be lower in terms of person-months than this of an average performer. The estimated figure of an average performer will be lower than that of an underperformer. If you take your core team members as experts for the effort judgment – the core team members are often outperformers – you might receive relative low figures. Simply taking those figures as input for the project budget might result in a lot of trouble for you in avoiding cost overruns. You should therefore carefully evaluate the figures provided by your experts. Verify whether the experts took an average or their own performance as the baseline for their estimates. In case that they give you figures based on outperformer's productivity you should adjust the figures appropriately.

The remaining question is whether the average productivity of an individual working in an e-business project can be compared with the average productivity of an individual working in a traditional IT project. I am convinced that the average person's productivity in e-business projects is lower than in IT projects. Why that? The answer is simple: in e-business projects people from a variety of disciplines have to work together. Building an e-business solution requires an incredible amount of communications, coordination, and cooperation among the team members. Due to the different mentality and terminology of 'techies', creative, consulting, and marketing team members, the required communication, coordination, and cooperation significantly slow down the productivity. When estimating the services costs for an e-business project, a lower average productivity than in traditional IT projects has to be taken into account.

@ 31 Be sure to include all costs in your estimates

In @ 28 I mentioned that one typical reason for cost overruns in e-business projects is inaccurate services effort estimates. This means that the real effort in performing the project work is significantly higher than the estimated effort. Another major reason for cost overruns is that costs are simply overlooked in the cost estimates.

Most e-business projects are complex by nature. Not surprisingly, estimating the costs for an e-business project is a complex task. When putting together a cost estimate the costs for hardware, software, and people are naturally considered. But there might be a lot of 'additional' costs that are often overlooked. Those additional costs can represent a significant amount of money. If you do not include these costs in the total cost estimate, the project is prone to cost overruns.

Some of the typical additional costs in an e-business environment are: (1) *Publishing rights.* A lot of material included in an e-business solution may be restricted by publishing rights and not available free of charge. A special fee must be paid in order to obtain the authorization to publish material; (2) *Focus groups.* In the area of market research or for usability tests you might use focus groups for online surveys. Usually a special charge must be paid to get access to selected groups; (3) *Content.* If the e-business solution is, for example, to build an Internet portal you need representative and attractive content as input. Content such as equity quotes, videos, films, and music, must often be bought from content providers or information brokers; (4) *Network.* This covers all kinds of networking costs incurring during the course of the project when the e-business application is build. For example, establishing a line connection between the facilities of the contractor and client, access to the Web, and data transmission fees; (5) *Communication.* Due to the variety of disciplines required to perform an e-business project, the communication among project team members is a cost factor that should not be under-estimated. Communication, coordination and cooperation – which mostly happens in form of meetings – consume a considerable amount of time in an e-business project. Often the effort needed for these meetings is overlooked when putting cost estimates together.

Other additional costs such as *warranty, travel expenses* (see Sect. 5.1.2), and *fix costs* assigned to a project are not specific to e-business projects but should also not be overlooked. Make sure to include all additional costs – not only those listed above as example – in the total project cost estimate.

@ 32 Explain to the client the effort necessary to build the e-business solution

Many clients are surprised – or at least demonstrate surprise – when the contractor quotes the price for a project. When a proposal with a firm-fixed-price is handed over to a client, a typical first reaction is: "*Wow – I never thought that the project would cost me so much.*" Or another common one is: "*I have a proposal from a competitor of your company, and they offer me the project for a price that is 30% lower than yours.*" The typical second reaction of clients is asking contractors to show them a breakdown of the total price into hardware, software, and services parts. If a contractor accepts such a request a review of the figures by a client ends up in 90% of the situations with grumbling about the costs in the services part. While most clients accept the given costs for hardware and software without opposition, they will often rate the services costs as too high.

What is the reason for such a reaction? Many clients do not understand what is necessary to build up an e-business solution. They only want to have "*a few colored screens, some marketing, a little bit of consulting, and a simple integration of back-end systems*". For many clients it is their first e-business project, so they do not have any experience in the e-business area. Explaining to a client in detail the effort required to build its e-business solution will help give the client a better understanding of the price for the project. Moreover, by explaining the effort a client obtains a better understanding of the details of what can be expected from you. Often a proposal with a lower price is available from a competitor, but the services offered are not the same as in your proposal. If the client only compares the total price of the proposals without looking in detail into what will be provided, the project might be awarded to a competitor. You may therefore benefit from encouraging the client to compare not only the price but also the services offered.

5.2 Controlling the Project Cost

Controlling project cost is the process of tracking the financial data of a project (see Fig. 17). The overall objective of controlling cost is to ensure that the project is completed within the approved contractor project budget. Controlling cost is performed throughout the course of the project. Succeeding in completing the project significantly below budget is normally not to the disadvantage of the personal career of the project manager responsible. Controlling cost involves collecting incurred costs, determining variances between estimated and real costs, and taking appropriate actions when the real costs tend to be higher than the estimated ones.

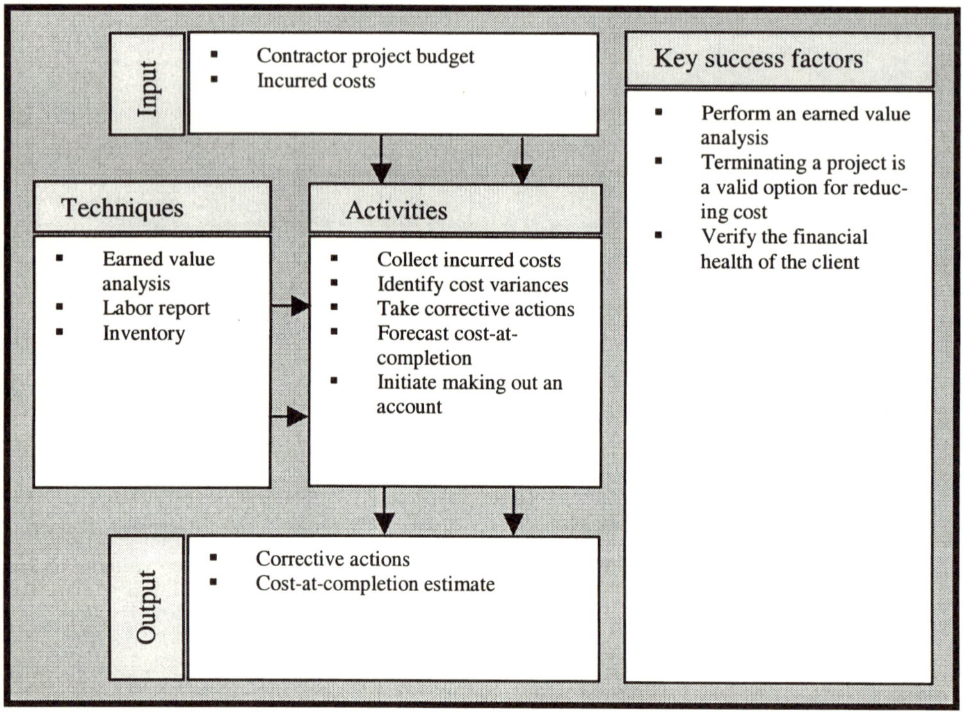

Fig. 17. Controlling the project cost

5.2.1 Input

Contractor project budget

The contractor project budget is a cost baseline and upper spending limit for the project expressed in monetary units. It results from the cost estimating process. The initial project budget is usually approved by senior management and assigned to the project manager when a project starts. It represents the upper limit for all expenses that the project manager is authorized to spend at the project level. If during the course of the project the necessary expenses are expected to exceed the project budget – for whatever reason – normally senior management has to decide on a project budget enlargement. The project budget can be influenced – increased or decreased – by approved change requests (see Chap. 10). The total budget value is often separated in terms of time – a *time-phased budget* – or in terms of categories (i.e., hardware, software, services, and additional costs).

Incurred costs

Incurred costs are all expenses spent on a project at a defined point in time. The interesting question is: When can costs be viewed as 'incurred'? To illustrate the problem, take for example a situation in which you have to include a piece of standard software supplied by a vendor in the e-business solution of your project. You order the standard software at a fixed price and the software is delivered by the vendor two weeks after the start of the project. In the package with the CDs you find a payment order with a latest payment date eight weeks later. You hand over the payment order to the accounting department of your company with the advice to make the payment in eight weeks. The accounting department follows your recommendation so the money is transferred ten weeks after project start.

Now the question is: when the cost of this piece of software occur – two weeks or ten weeks after project start? There is not a unique right answer to the question – it is a matter of definition. You can define that the costs occur when the software is physically received or when the financial flow of money happens. For cost controlling purposes the first definition seems to be more appropriate. Making the occurrence of costs independent from the financial flow of 'real' money provides an essential benefit: for some costs no 'real' money is transferred. Take for example the costs of team members recruited within the company. You do not have to issue a check to the team members for their salaries and related costs. Normally your project is charged with an internal cost rate based upon the job categories of team members. This internal rate represents the costs in terms of 'virtual' money. In the following incurred costs are defined as 'virtual' rather than 'real' money.

5.2.2 Activities

Collect incurred costs

The objective of the collect incurred costs activity is to keep track of all expenses for a project. As already outlined in Sect. 5.2.1, incurred costs are collected in terms of 'virtual' money. Collecting incurred costs is an ongoing activity. The usage of a calculation tool like a *spreadsheet* may make the activity easier. Let us take a look at how you can collect the incurred costs for various cost categories:

1. **Hardware.** Whenever you receive a piece of ordered hardware for use in your project register it in a *hardware inventory* (see Sect. 5.2.3) and put the price you will be charged beside it. Summing the single price figures gives you the total costs of purchased hardware at any point in time. If you do not buy the hardware, for example, you *lease* it, you should instead collect the leasing costs.
2. **Software.** You can do the same thing for any piece of software you received or any software licenses you are charged with. Register all software in a *software inventory* and note the price. Summing the single price figures gives you the total software costs at any point in time.
3. **Services.** Services costs are measured in terms of effort by the team members on the project. In order to keep track of the services effort, ask your team members to prepare so-called *labor reports* (see Sect.5.2.3). Any team member logs the time spent on the project in a single labor report. The effort may be recorded on an hourly or a daily basis. The duly completed labor reports are handed over to you regularly, for example, weekly or monthly. By multiplying the registered hours or days with the internal cost rate for internal staff members, or with the real rate for external staff members, you can simply calculate the incurred services costs.
4. **Additional costs.** The incurred additional costs are often the most difficult to track. Tracking the occurrence of additional costs highly depends on the specific nature of the costs. No general recommendation on a specific technique can be given here.

When collecting incurred costs, a short validation of the financial data might be of benefit. If you collect, for example, the travel expenses of team members you should validate that the expenses are associated with journeys that are approved for the project. For purchased hardware and software you can check that the costs are in line with the quotations of the vendor and, if applicable, that agreed discounts were applied. Of course, validating and checking is limited to a certain level of detail, so you might discover only obvious mistakes or inconsistencies. For many costs (e.g., the effort data specified in labor reports) you have to rely heavily on the loyalty and honesty of your team members.

Identify cost variances

The objective of this activity is to identify whether there are differences between the estimated and real costs. The activity is performed by simply comparing these two costs.

For comparing estimated and real services costs the *earned value technique* (see Sect. 5.2.3) can be applied. Identifying cost variances should be performed periodically – for example monthly – during the life of the project.

A cost variance can be positive or negative. A positive variance means that the real costs are lower than the estimated ones. Be happy about such an outcome! A negative variance means that the real costs are higher than the estimated ones. In this case a further step seems expedient: you should try to find out the cause for the variance. What are typical reasons for negative cost variances in e-business projects? Below find five common reasons:

1. **Higher services effort.** A situation in which the real services effort is higher than the estimated one can be caused by one or several factors. First, during the course of the project *new technology* become available and subsequently used instead of the originally planned one. If this factor becomes known only at a point when work items have already been performed by exploiting the original technology, the effort spent so far is wasted but nevertheless involves costs. If the new technology comes up rather early in the project, it might still influence the effort. Using this technology instead of the original one might simply require more work. Secondly, due to a *lack of experience* in using cutting-edge technology the effort required exploiting it is simply underestimated. Thirdly, often standard vendor software products have to be integrated into the e-business solution. Unfortunately such software is often full of bugs and does not fulfill quality requirements. Dealing with a vendor to get bugs fixed involves effort in terms of re-work, testing, and administration for you and your team. And finally, it is possible that *work is overlooked,* since most e-business projects are complex by nature and you might learn and understand some aspects only during the course of the project. As the effort estimation must take place rather early in the project, you might simply overlook some of the work items that have to be performed.
2. **Lower productivity.** The productivity of your team members is on average lower than estimated. What might be reasons for such a situation? In most cases when you estimate the effort required in performing the work items you do not have all team members on board. This means the productivity of a significant number of people is not known. In effort estimation it is good practice to base estimates on average team member performance (see Sect. 5.1.5). When recruiting the team members you might not be able to achieve an average skills level due to the fact that experienced e-business people are rare. Besides lower skills level, another factor leading to a lower productivity might be that you suffer from idle times, when your team members could not go forward with their work. A common showstopper in e-business projects is that the client is not well prepared to fulfill its responsibilities. When the execution of certain work items is dependent on fulfillment of client responsibilities and the

client is not able to fulfill in time, the team members assigned to perform those work items may become idle. The idling team members nevertheless incur costs.

3. **Higher labor cost rates.** When you work with external resources you might have to accept higher labor rates than estimated when recruiting the correct people for your team. Currently the demand for experienced e-business people outstrips supply. One of the oldest principles of economies applies here: when demand is high and supply is low the price goes up. The organizations or individuals offering their working capacity are of course fully aware of this situation. They might request higher rates than what you have estimated. This might not be limited to external resources only. Often higher labor costs must be accepted for internal staff as well. Another factor that influences labor costs is paid overtime. If you agreed to compensate staff members based on hourly labor rates and you base your estimate on an eight hours-a-day estimate, you have to pay overtime charges if the people work longer. This is closely related to the factor mentioned earlier, when the services effort is higher than estimated. To cover the additional effort it usually not practical to recruit additional people to perform the work. The commonly used approach is to ask your team members to work 'a little bit' longer. Of course the team members can expect to be paid fairly for this additional work.
4. **Changes without price increase.** Too often contractor project managers agree to implement scope changes with no price increase. Often the additional work caused by scope changes is significantly underestimated. Many contractor project managers want to achieve or keep a good relationship with the client by offering to implement change requests without additional charges. If the effort required to implement a change is not reimbursed by the client, the effort must be taken from the original contractor project budget.
5. **Additional costs overlooked.** One common reason for discrepancies between estimated and real costs is that additional costs are overlooked when the project estimate is put together (see Sect. 5.1.5). Often at an early stage of the project enthusiasm is high and foresight is low – in such an atmosphere significant costs are simply overlooked.

Take corrective actions

In the event of uncovering negative cost variances corrective actions should be taken to bring expected future costs in line with the estimates. It is important to remember that corrective actions are addressing the future; they will not help you to recover costs incurred in the past. Expenses spent in the past, so-called *sunk costs*, are gone. You will seldom find a way to get reimbursement for sunk costs.

The primary purpose of this activity is to find a solution for avoiding or reducing the variance between real and estimated costs in the future. Not surprisingly, it may neither be possible nor meaningful to find, for all situations where such a variance is expected, a corrective action or a countermeasure. Some deviations between estimated and real costs must simply be accepted. Those deviations are covered by the reserve included in the contractor project budget (see Sect. 5.1.2) – hopefully the size of the reserve was chosen appropriately so that all additional costs can be covered. What corrective actions might help you to reduce or avoid cost variances? Here are just a few suggestions:

1. **Charge client.** Look for a way to charge the client for costs resulting from additional effort. Some opportunities are: (1) if a client suggests to replace originally planned technology by the latest technology when implementing an e-business application, do not hesitate to ask the client to reimburse additional costs resulting from this replacement; (2) be rigid in accepting no-cost scope change requests from a client – explain to the client in detail the additional effort caused by the scope change and ask the client to accept a price increase; and (3) if the client is not able to fulfill its responsibilities and this causes your team members to be idle, let the client pay the idle time.
2. **Charge vendor.** If a vendor supplying products to you causes you supplementary costs due to the low quality of its products, ask the vendor to reimburse your additional costs. A prerequisite for taking this action is that you agreed in detail with the vendor on the quality of the delivered software and that you can prove that quality requirements are not met. Often vendors refuse to pay back money in cash. In such a situation you can offer to accept compensation in the form of human resources. You can ask the vendor, for example, that some of its experienced staff members join your team for a certain time period to support the integration of the supplied standard software into the e-business application.
3. **Reduce idle times.** Reducing the times at which team members are idle can be achieved by two activities: (1) remind the client to fulfill its responsibilities well in advance of the due date – often a client is able and willing to fulfill its responsibility but simply forgets to do so; and (2) when a situation arises such that work items can not be started or continued – for whatever reason – try to re-schedule work items or re-assign work items to idle team members.
4. **Improve productivity.** If the productivity of the team is lower as expected and this is not attributable to missing skills, perhaps an improper work environment has slowed performance. In this case try to improve the work environment. Some measures to foster the productivity by improving the work environment are: usage of better tools, realignment or simplification of processes, elimination of unnecessary tasks, and reduction of administrative work.
5. **Transfer work.** If the cost variance is due to a higher labor cost try to re-assign work to lower-cost staff or replace higher-cost staff with lower-cost staff. But be careful, since e-business projects are usually rather short. Even if you can recruit lower-cost staff during the course of the project think twice before replacing staff members. When you replace team members you have to consider that the new members must get used to the project. They have to be integrated into the team and the

work has to be handed over to the new members. All these activities involve effort. This additional effort might exceed the savings achieved by lower job rates.

If applying corrective actions is not sufficient to avoid or reduce cost variances, think about measures to cover the difference. One way might be to look for compensation. A popular opportunity for obtaining additional funding are *change requests* (see Chap. 10). Be creative in identifying functionality that is of benefit to the client but is not covered by the initial project scope. Encourage the client to enrich the e-business solution via change requests – of course change requests that result in a price increase. By enhancing the overall project budget with change requests, you might be able to compensate some of the supplementary costs. However, recovering from cost overruns by accepting and implementing change requests will work only to a certain extend.

Taking corrective actions is not limited to the setting up of actions. In fact, you have to monitor whether actions taken are really successful. Successful means that they bring the real cost in line with the estimates. If you recognize that some corrective actions are not successful, you have to change them or take different ones.

Forecast cost-at-completion

When you have completed the identification of cost variances the result is an assessment of the current project status in terms of actual costs incurred so far. Based on this assessment you can give a forecast of the cost that will be incurred by project completion. But remember when you give such a forecast during the course of the project it is still an estimate on the total project costs. The real costs can only be calculated when all work items are finalized and the project is completed. The forecasted costs will be the closer to the real costs when the forecast is given later in the project.

How can you forecast the cost-at-completion? In principle there are two different approaches. The first is to take the actual costs incurred so far and add the remaining project budget adjusted by a specific factor. The adjustment factor could be the performance deviation discovered in the past. Take for example a situation in which you identified a negative cost variance of 10%, which means that the real costs are 10% higher than the estimated ones. The adjustment factor in this case would be 1.1. The forecast would therefore be calculated by multiplying the remaining budget by 1.1 and adding this figure to the already incurred costs. You will take this approach if you assume that the cost variance observed in the past is typical for the future. The basis idea of the second approach is that the cost variances observed in the past will not continue in that form in the future. According to this approach you estimate the cost-at-completion by taking the actuals to date plus a new estimate for the remaining work. For the new estimate of the remaining work you can take, for example, the initially estimated costs.

Forecasting cost-at-completion regularly during the course of a project provides you with an indication of a 'trend' towards the real costs.

Initiate making out an account

In the previous sections 'virtual' money was taken as the basis for estimating and controlling cost. However, virtual money has to be turned into 'real' money when external parties are involved. There is a flow of money *in* and *out* of the project. It is usually the job of the project manager to initiate the money flow although the money transfer is in most cases not performed by him- or herself. Real money flowing out of the project due to purchase orders to vendors or compensation for external resources will normally be initiated when a bill is received from a vendor. Real money flowing into the project is normally the payment from a client for the project work.

Usually you will initiate your accounting department to make out an account for project work. It depends on the terms and conditions – normally fixed in the contract with the client – when a transfer of money will occur. A payment can be linked to delivery and acceptance of specific work items or achievement of milestones, or it can be agreed that it has to happen at defined points in time. It can be defined that a payment occurs only once for the complete project or the total price might be split up into parts. Independently of these aspects you have to ask the accounting department – or whoever is responsible in your company for such activities – to make out an account at the agreed date. Controlling the receipt of money in return to the bill is normally above your responsibility and does not need to be taken into account in the cost control management domain.

5.2.3 Techniques

Earned value analysis

The earned value analysis is a method of measuring the costs involved in achieving project progress [10]. The basic idea of earned value analysis is to compare the cost of work that was planned to be performed until a certain point in time with the cost that was really incurred. The earned value indicates how much work was done. The analysis points out whether the real effort is in line with the estimated effort.

Let us take a simple example to illustrate the idea of the earned value analysis. A work item to code eight web pages in XML was estimated to involve an effort of four working days when being performed by a specific web developer. The effort required for each page is rather similar. The daily rate of this specific individual is \$ 500. The total estimated cost to code the eight pages is therefore 4 x 500 = \$ 2000. Let us assume that the web developer has started to work three days ago, which makes the cost 3 x 500 = \$ 1500. That's easy, isn't it? But now, at the end of day three, you ask the web developer how much work has been performed so far. Let us assume three different responses.

1. "*I coded six pages.*" Six out of eight pages means that 75% of the work is done. The earned value is 0.75 x 2000 = \$ 1500. As your real costs are \$ 1500 there is no variance between the estimated and real costs. That's fine.
2. "*I coded five pages.*" Five out of eight pages means that approximately 62.5% of the work is done. The earned value is 0.625 x 2000 = \$ 1250. As your real costs are \$

1500 there is a difference of \$ 1250 minus \$ 1500 = minus \$ 250. This means that doing the work has cost you \$ 250 more than what you have estimated. That's bad.

3. "*I coded seven pages.*" Seven out of eight pages means that approximately 87.5% of the work is done. The earned value is 0.875 x 2000 = \$ 1750. As your real costs are \$ 1500 there is a difference of \$ 1750 minus \$ 1500 = \$ 250. This means that doing the work has cost you \$ 250 less than what you have estimated. That's fine, even better than the situation according to response 1.

To calculate the total earned value for a complete project all work items that are scheduled to be completed or started at the point at which the earned value analysis is performed must be evaluated as outlined in the example. Summing the variances provides you with an indication of the overall cost situation of the project. The single variances of activities already started but not yet completed provide you with an indication of where cost overruns occurred.

Labor report

A labor report records the effort that a single staff member is spending with project work. The labor can be reported on an hourly or a daily basis. Normally a staff member logs the point in time when project work is performed and – at a high-level – what has been done. Usually a reporting period of one calendar month is summarized in a single report. A labor report can be a simple sheet of paper or it can be based on an automated tool like a *spreadsheet*. Using a spreadsheet normally eases the reporting process and supports acceptance of labor reporting by the project staff.

Inventory

An inventory is a tool for registering project equipment. It is mainly used to keep track of hardware and standard software components used in a project. An inventory is a simple list of hardware or software components, where each item is normally labeled with a unique identifier. If the price for each item is logged as well, the inventory is a valuable tool for controlling cost. The inventory can be a simple sheet of paper or based on an automated tool.

5.2.4 Outputs

Corrective actions

Corrective actions are one output of the controlling cost process, but obviously only in case that corrective actions are needed. If the real costs are exactly in line with the estimated ones, no corrective actions are required. Corrective actions are all measures taken to bring expected future costs in line with the estimates. However, corrective actions address the future and do not retrieve sunk costs.

Cost-at-completion estimate

A cost-at-completion estimate is a forecast of the total costs that will likely occur throughout the term of the project. At project start the cost-at-completion estimate is equivalent to the project budget. When the cost-at-completion is forecasted during the course of the project, the cost estimate can be higher or lower than the project budget. Estimating the cost-at-completion several times during the project can indicate a trend towards the real cost-at-completion. The estimated cost-at-completion will be closer to the real cost when the estimation is performed later in the life of the project.

Project profit achieved

The real profit achieved by a project can not be calculated until all project work items are completed and the project is officially declared as finished. The profit achieved by a project is usually expressed in terms of monetary units. In principle the achieved project profit is the difference between the total price paid by the client and the total cost-at-completion. The real project profit achieved can be higher or lower than the project profit estimated at project start. In the worst case the project profit achieved can be zero or even negative.

5.2.5 Key Success Factors

@ 33 Perform an earned value analysis

A variance between estimated and real services costs is a common situation in e-business projects. When a project is completed the contractor may suffer from a cost overrun. However, often there is an opportunity for a project manager to avoid or reduce cost overruns by taking corrective actions in due time. A prerequisite for taking this opportunity is that you notice a difference between estimated and real services costs in sufficient time to react appropriately. Too often project managers track project costs only by monitoring consumption of the budget over time. Take for example a situation in which an e-business project with a budget of $ 1 million is scheduled to last six months. After three months 50% of the budget is spent. Believe it or not, some people are happy about such a situation without taking an interest in obtaining more information about the work accomplished! If only 25% of the planned work has been performed this is a disaster – under the assumption of a linear effort distribution. Of course, you have to evaluate how much work has been performed in order to get an indication of the financial status of your project. The best approach is to perform an earned value analysis (see Sect. 5.2.3). Although it is true that you need to invest a considerable amount of time and effort to perform such an analysis, the result is usually well worth the investment.

@ 34 Terminating a project is a valid option for reducing cost

When you serve as project manager for an e-business project, terminating the project might be something you hardly ever think about. Just to make sure what I am talking about, 'terminating' in this context means to *cancel* a project. In fact, canceling a project to reduce costs is a drastic but nevertheless valid option. In which situation might this option be the right decision? In short, canceling a project might be meaningful when the cost-at-completion estimate is significant higher than the total project price agreed in a firm-fixed-price contract. This means to complete the project you have to spent more money than that which you are going to receive from the client for the project work. Or in other words this is a situation in which you become aware that the likely profit is negative – and the project was not intended to be an 'investment case'. Let us not speculate about how and why the project falls into this ugly situation, but let us just assume that it is your job to decide what to do. Normally, the objective of a contractor is to make money and to employ people, therefore you have to do something in this situation.

When thinking about possible alternatives to solve this problem do not neglect to consider terminating the project as a valid option. As project manager it is your job to make money for your company, or if making money is not feasible then at least you should reduce the financial loss. If the likely costs to complete the project are really higher than what you will receive from the client, canceling the project fulfills the objective of reducing the financial loss. However, the pros and cons of this option must be weighed carefully. It might be an unpopular decision from the perspective of other project stakeholders and the impacts of a project cancellation are usually not limited to financial factors only.

A prominent stakeholder who would most probably be disappointed is naturally the client. If the project is cancelled by the contractor before completion, normally the client will on the one hand not pay anything but on the other hand will also not receive anything. As a consequence the project deliverables expected by the client are not available for use. The client will suffer in terms of time, money, and effort spent in dealing with you.

You can expect that your team members would be disappointed as well. Based on the assumption that they perform the project work with great enthusiasm and high personal engagement, they will be frustrated to see that the results of their work are not released and used. They might get the impression that their work is not appreciated. And moreover no-one likes to be a member of a team delivering a project that is viewed as unsuccessful.

Your senior management might not be a big proponent to prematurely terminate a project. They might worry about the reputation of the contractor company fearing that the client and competitors take this project as an opportunity to blame the contractor's capabilities to deliver successful projects. This might seriously damage the contractor's reputation in the marketplace making future business more difficult.

The advantage of reducing the financial loss by terminating a project must therefore be weighed up carefully against negative consequences that will most probably occur when a project is cancelled. However there might be situations and certain circumstances in which terminating a project is the best alternative. If you are in a position that you have to decide how to proceed in such a situation, consider the termination of a project as a valid option – sometimes it is really the best one.

@ 35 Verify the financial health of the client

Completing a project successfully, in time, on budget, and to the satisfaction of the client is fine – you as the responsible project manager will probably be praised. However, for the contractor company a project is finally successful from a financial point of view when the payment agreed with the client as compensation for the project work is received. You might believe that this is like a duck taking the water, but unfortunately the number of projects where this matter of course does not happen is increasing. The reason for not paying the bill is often not a lack of willingness but a lack of ability on the part of the client.

Many typical clients of e-business projects are start-up companies, the well-known 'dot-coms'. One year ago the financial health of a dot-com was not an issue. It was a simple matter of fact that sufficient money was available on the client side. Issuing new shares or bonds to get fresh money was not a problem for listed companies. Venture capitalist were hoggish to pump money into privately held start-ups. The well-known recent collapse of the technology markets has changed the situation completely. Floundering dot-coms with unsuccessful business models lead to the much hyped dot-com fallout. As a consequence, many dot-coms became insolvent and were not able to pay their financial obligations. If your client is one of those companies, you will never see any money for the work you delivered. Big projects with large expenses can even break a contractor's company. It is therefore in your own interests to verify the financial health of your client before you accept to start a project, and even monitor the financial situation during the course of the project in case it changes before the project ends.

What can you do if some doubts remain on the financial health of the client but you are eager to take the business? A strategy to mitigate the risk of not getting paid for the project work is to agree with a client on a *step-wise payment* mode. Step-wise means that the total compensation for the project work is not charged as a single payment when the project is finished. Instead the total sum is divided into portions that have to be paid during the course of the project at defined points in time or when specified milestones are achieved. If the financial situation of a client does not – at a certain point – allow further payments, you can stop the project work immediately. In this case you can cover your expenses, or at least a part of them, with the payments you have received so far.

6 Managing the Client

Managing the Client? You may be surprised about the title of this chapter or even about its existence. You may think "*normally the client wants to manage me, and not the other way round*". You are not the only one with this opinion. Some contractor project managers take a passive attitude and look to the client as the one who gives the directives about how to manage a project. This attitude is exactly the root cause of many unsuccessful projects.

Let us take a general look at the sensitive topic of a client contractor–relationship. The importance of the client in a business relationship has increased significantly – or at least the attention on a client's importance has increased. In the early days of IT, a supplier's major attention focused on how a product – for example, a mainframe, a PC, or a piece of software – could be produced and improved. Selling a product to a client was at the end of the production process and viewed as less important. The client, as the 'buyer' of a product, was in the background.

In those early days the IT market was dominated by a few big IT suppliers. The power resided on the supplier side – it was a *supplier's market.* Over time innumerable new IT suppliers entered the market. The upcoming competition turned the market to a *buyer's market.* The client, as the buyer of a product or services, stepped into the foreground. The power moved to client side. Today, the client is viewed as the center of any business. Contractors have to satisfy client expectations – otherwise they may put themselves out of business.

The client, as the buyer of an e-business project, requires special management attention. Many clients view themselves as the 'masters' and expect that contractors dance to their tune. From their perspective, they have the power on their side due to the fact that they are paying for a project and as a consequence they want to give the directives.

In traditional IT projects clients often view contractors simply as their 'gofer' and want to 'manage' them. Here the client plays the active role in managing a project. The contractor simply executes the client's directives. While this approach sometimes works in traditional IT projects, too often it leads to disaster in e-business projects.

What is the reason behind this? Today, you frequently find an excellent knowledge of IT and on managing IT projects on the client side. Clients have the opportunity to collect experience and knowledge in many IT projects they perform internally or with contractors over many years. Their knowledge and experience grew with every project they mastered. Their qualifications in managing IT projects are often at the same level as contractors – or even above.

For e-business projects the situation is quite different. For many clients it is the first time that they perform an e-business project, so experience in e-business project management is lacking. Too often, they want to force you to follow the traditional project management techniques which they are used to from IT projects – with the consequence that the e-business project fails.

What is the solution for the problem? It is quite simple: the contractor has to take the active role. A contractor whose business is *performing e-business projects* can usually look back on much more experience in managing these types of project than a client. Not surprisingly, the contractor should therefore rely on its experience and manage the project actively. It is up to you, the project manager, to manage the project in such a way that the client is happy with project execution and project results. Many clients appreciate benefiting from a contractor's experience in managing e-business projects. They are looking for a partner from whom they can learn for the future. They view a project as a real 'partnership' between client and contractor. Only when a contractor offers real value to a client, can it be expected that the partnership is rated as successful from a client's perspective.

This chapter provides you with some ideas on managing the relationship with your client. It focuses on three processes: (1) supporting a client to achieve its objectives; (2) involving a client in project execution; and (3) handling problems or conflicts in the form of issues.

6.1 Supporting a Client to Achieve Its Objectives

Supporting a client to achieve its project objectives is to the benefit of the contractor. The philosophy being that when the client wins, the contractor wins too. The objectives of a client can be viewed as its *expectations* on the outcome of the e-business project (see Fig. 18). It is your job to meet the client's expectations. In order to avoid disillusions on the client side you have to ensure that the client's expectations are realistic. Otherwise you and your team can work like mad, but if the client expectations are out of reach, you are unable to reach them and disappointment is inevitable [3]. Unfortunately, meeting a client's expectations is not a matter of course in e-business projects. A recent survey from American Management Systems indicates that only 14% of 131 senior managers surveyed thought that their completed e-business projects had been 'very successful'.

Supporting a client is not restricted to meeting its expectations. A second aspect is that you should make the client aware of the consequences that an e-business project might evoke. Often an e-business project changes the way a client is doing its business. Many clients are not aware of this fact and appreciate it if you bring this aspect to their attention.

The third aspect that needs to be considered in the client–contractor relationship are contributions of a client that are required for successful project execution. This is because often input in the form of information, data, know-how, or decisions are required from a client. The client has to provide this input in time and to the level of quality that is required for successful project execution. For many clients fulfillment of these responsibilities is not an easy task. It is to your own benefit when you support a client in this area.

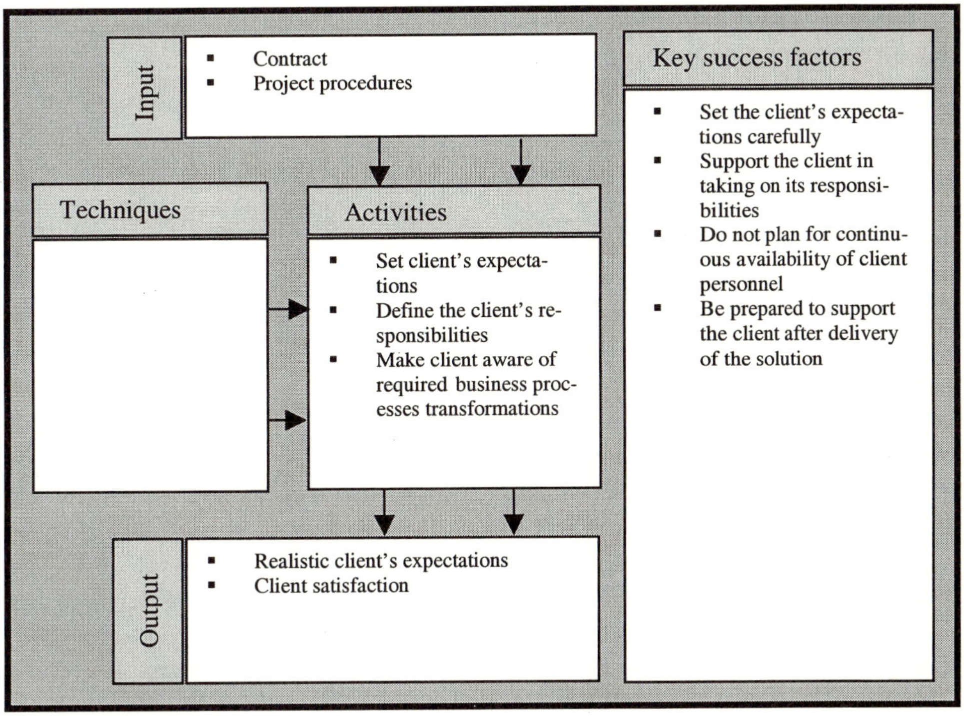

Fig. 18. Supporting a client to achieve its objectives

6.1.1 Inputs

Contract

An essential input for managing a client is the *contract.* The contract is the fundamental basis for a project. It defines the *hard facts* of the scope and of the conditions under which a project has to be performed. The hard facts define the relationship between client and contractor in a *formal* way at a high level. A contract establishes a framework for the client–contractor relationship. Often roles and responsibilities of both client and contractor are defined and basic project procedures are outlined.

Project procedures

All kinds of project procedures defined for the areas *change management, quality management, communications management,* and *documentation management* serve as input for managing a client. The project procedures specify the formal relationship between client and contractor at a detailed level.

6.1.2 Activities

Set client's expectations

The objectives of the set client's expectations activity is to ensure that both client and contractor have the same understanding of the intended outcome of an e-business project. Meeting a client's expectations is a fundamental element of achieving *client satisfaction.* Only when the client's expectations are well understood is there a fair chance of the contractor fulfilling them.

In order to avoid disillusions on the client side you have to ensure on the one hand that the client's expectations are realistic and can be met. On the other hand the capability of meeting client's expectations is not sufficient, because there is another party embroiled – the contractor. You have to ensure that the fulfillment of a client's expectation is feasible within the boundaries of your project budget. Otherwise you manage to meet the client's expectations but only by sacrificing the project profit. The client feels happy, but your senior management most probably will not have the same feelings about you. It is therefore essential to set the client's expectations in such a way that both client and contractor are satisfied when the expectations are fulfilled.

Why is there a need for *setting* a client's expectations? You might believe that the expectations of a client are clear. In fact, in most e-business projects the client's expectations are neither clear nor fixed. Of course, the project scope defined in the contract serves as a basis for the client's expectations. But in some cases clients even do not have any concrete expectations when they sign a contract and want to start a project. Often the only thing a client definitely knows is that something must be done to keep pace with the competition. There are some vague expectations that "*something new, something better than the solution of competitors*" must be made available. The attempt to fulfill such vague expectations is similar to a lottery. You might win the first prize, but the probability is low. Clarifying vague client's expectations is therefore essential.

In other cases clients have concrete expectations but they are extremely unrealistic. Two common unrealistic client expectations are on *project duration* and on *project costs.* Driven by tough competition, time-to-market is key for many clients. From their perspective a suitable e-business solution should be delivered by a contractor almost overnight. And not only the project duration should be minimal but the same should hold true for the project costs. In their belief developing an e-business solution is "*designing a few fancy web pages*" – and this "*is rather cheap, isn't it*?" You have to turn the unrealistic expectations into realistic ones. Otherwise you lose the race on fulfilling the client's expectations before you have even started.

Moreover, when you have succeeded in settling the expectations of a client, the game might not be over. During the course of a project the client's expectations can change – and often they do. What can you do in such a case? What you can *not* do is prevent a client from changing its expectation, that's for sure. The only thing you can do is to notify the changes and raise attention to this. Often a client is not aware its expectations are creeping. Whenever you recognize a change in expectations evaluate whether or not you are able to fulfill the changed ones. If fulfillment is feasible, but only by increasing the effort on the contractor side, ask the client for reimbursement of the additionally incurred costs.

Finally, I have to admit that recommending to *set client's expectations* is easy, but more difficult to enforce. However, you should try it. Experience shows that it is almost always better to discuss with a client its expectations in a rather early stage of the project – or even better before it is started – than to sit and wait until project completion. If non-fulfillment of a client's expectations results in a big 'bang' at the end of a project, it is to late to turn the situation around. In most cases you will find such an e-business project on the long list of failures.

Define the client's responsibilities

When an e-business project is performed by a contractor for a client, usually input and support from a client is required for successful project execution. The contributions of a client to a project are called a *client's responsibilities*. What are typical responsibilities of a client in an e-business project? Here are a few examples:

- Providing client-company-specific content (e.g., graphics, texts, videos, and audio) for a web site.
- Providing information on the client's business processes.
- Providing information on interfaces of back-end systems that have to be integrated into the e-business solution.
- Providing client-company-specific software and corresponding licenses that have to be integrated into the e-business solution.
- Performing an acceptance test and notifying the contractor of detected errors.
- Naming a contact person in the client's company as the client project manager who is willing and authorized to take decisions on behalf of the client.

A basic prerequisite for successful project execution is that the client's responsibilities are fulfilled. As many responsibilities might be not obvious, it is essential to define the responsibilities in detail. Defining a client's responsibilities is normally performed at the beginning of a project. When defining the client's responsibilities for a project it is important to describe them as precisely as possible. This helps a lot in avoiding misunderstandings. Besides defining *what* is required, it should be defined *when* it is required. Setting a fixed date for delivery of every client's responsibility eases the monitoring of proper fulfillment. Usually the defined client's responsibilities – or at least a summary – flows into the contract between client and contractor.

Make client aware of required business processes transformations

Many clients believe that they can deploy and operate an e-business solution while maintaining their current internal business processes. Their intention is to keep the internal business processes that have been applied in many cases for several years. They simply do not want to change their way of working. They want to do the same things as before but now only with the support of e-business. Experience shows that this attitude is almost always not successful in achieving a business value through e-business. An e-business solution is most effective when internal business processes are designed for e-business. This means in most cases that current business processes have to be changed or new processes have to be developed.

Many clients are not aware of that e-business requires a transformation of business processes. Support your client by making it aware of this fact. It is your job and to your own benefit to do so. Otherwise you might end up in a situation in which you delivered an excellent e-business solution but it is not successful because it does not fit into the client's business processes. The necessary transformation can be a simple modification, adoption, transformation, or streamlining of current processes, but might reach a full redesign or a completely new definition.

The activity of making the client aware of required business processes transformations should be performed at a rather early stage in a project. Transformation of business processes usually involves a staggering amount of effort and time. The reason for this is that usually the necessary redesign is not limited to a few business processes only. An e-business solution can impact upon business processes throughout the company: across the IT department, accounting, inventory, logistics, distribution, and out to the supply chain. And only redesigning processes is not the end of the game. The new processes have to be established, introduced, and adhered to.

A change in internal business processes changes the way the people on the client side are working. Often the change involves a change to the client's company culture. Such changes do not happen overnight. The earlier the client starts to transform its business processes the better.

6.1.3 Techniques

None.

6.1.4 Outputs

Realistic client's expectations

One output of the supporting client process are realistic client's expectations. The emphasis is on *realistic*. What does *realistic* client's expectations mean? On the one hand realistic means that a contractor has a fair chance of fulfilling the requirements of a client, and that the fulfillment can be achieved within the budget allocated for the project. On the other hand, realistic means that when the expectations are fulfilled, the client is satisfied with the overall outcome of the project. In other words, a client achieves all the objectives and benefits that were intended to be reached with the project.

Of course it would be fine if the client's expectations could be explicitly written down and documented. In reality this is rarely the case. Often a lot of expectations are expressed only implicitly. However, it is important that a contractor has a good understanding of a client's expectations, regardless of in which form they are documented or expressed.

Client satisfaction

The overall goal of managing a client is to achieve its satisfaction. What is *client satisfaction*? In the IT industry it is common to measure the level of client satisfaction in terms of quantitative data. Frequently surveys are conducted to gather metrics. The result of such a survey is that the client satisfaction is, let's say, 84%. The meaning of the figure is that the average satisfaction of all clients of a company is rated as 84%. Such a figure doesn't help you much, does it?

Metrics are suitable for indicating a trend. By monitoring the client satisfaction level over time, you can identify whether the client's satisfaction is increasing or decreasing. When the surveys used to gather those data are intelligently designed, you might also get an indication of the areas where improvements for raising the satisfaction level would be most effective.

Another field for benefiting from metrics is *benchmarking*. When client satisfaction data are gathered for several comparable contractors, each contractor receives an indication as to where the company is rated compared to its competitors. These surveys and metrics are of relevance for the overall strategy of a company and might serve as input for strategic business decisions to improve the overall client satisfaction level. Those decisions are normally the responsibility of senior management.

Your primary responsibility is to achieve the satisfaction of a single client – your client. By conducting the activities outlined in Sect. 6.1.2 and the advice given in Sect. 6.1.5, this should be a solvable assignment. Nevertheless, achieving client satisfaction for an e-business project is almost always still a challenge.

6.1.5 Key Success Factors

@ 36 Set the client's expectations carefully

Setting client's expectations is a difficult but nevertheless necessary job. Only when the client's expectations are realistic, have you a fair chance of meeting them and hence achieving client satisfaction. The client satisfaction will most probably be higher when the client's expectations are better met. If you deliver exactly what a client expects, you will be viewed as a credible business partner. If you succeed in exceeding expectations, the client will praise you as a hero. But if the project outcome falls short of expectations, you are the geek.

To increase the chances of being praised as a hero, a valuable strategy is to lower a client's expectations. If the client expects less, you have a fair chance to deliver more. In other words: *under promise* and *over deliver*. This advice sounds reasonable but you may find people who do not like this approach. The highest likelihood of finding such people is in the sales department of your company.

Not surprisingly, the objectives of sales people is *selling*. Selling a project to a client is usually one of the first activities in a client contractor–relationship. Selling a project is a hard but glorious job. Most sales people are hard-working individuals who deserve my full admiration. However, some of them tend to over promise when they want to acquire new clients and new projects. In order to get a project awarded some sales people exaggerate 'a little bit' on what a contractor can deliver. This raises the client's expectations – often to an unrealistic level. When the contract is signed and the sales person disappears you appear on the scene with the assignment to deliver the promised solution.

Burdened with this history, setting the client's expectations in such a way that you have a fair chance to over deliver might become a sensitive job, because realistic expectations might not be exactly in line with the promises of your sales colleague. However, struggling for a situation in which *you* are able to deliver more than what *you* promised pays off. A frank discussion with the client project manager at the beginning of a project is a good starting point for achieving such a comfortable situation.

@ 37 Support the client in taking on its responsibilities

Many e-business projects suffer from schedule slippages caused by missing or late fulfillment of a client's responsibilities. Timely fulfillment of defined client's responsibilities is an important element for the success of an e-business project. Supporting the client in taking on its responsibilities is therefore a worthwhile endeavor.

What can you do to ensure that a client takes on its responsibilities? A good starting point is an exact and detailed definition of the responsibilities. However, having the responsibilities well described is not sufficient. You have to ensure that the client fully understands the description so that a client knows exactly what is required and what must be delivered. A careful review of the defined responsibilities with the client project manager in an early stage of the project is an excellent opportunity to verify the client's understanding of its responsibilities.

During the course of a project, when the date for fulfillment of a responsibility approaches, it is good practice to make the client aware of the due date well in advance. This is because failures to fulfill responsibilities are often not attributed to a client's missing capabilities or willingness – often they are simply forgotten or overlooked by a client. Many clients appreciate being reminded of responsibilities well in advance of due dates.

Nevertheless, not everything works always perfectly. Despite a sound understanding of a responsibility by a client and a timely reminder on its due date, it may happen that a client does not take on its responsibility in time – for whatever reason. The notification and documentation of the non-fulfillment is a matter of course. But a simple documentation of the fact is not sufficient. And blaming the client does not help either. Instead you should evaluate – together with the client – what can be done to keep the impact as minimal as possible. Maybe you can reschedule work items, implement a workaround, or let your staff take over responsibilities that were originally intended to be performed by the client.

In any case, if a non-fulfillment of client's responsibility causes an impact on project schedule, effort, or quality of the e-business solution, make sure that the consequences are covered by the originator of the impact – the client. If additional effort is caused on your side, ask the client for reimbursement.

@ 38 Do not plan for continuous availability of client personnel

When defining a client's responsibilities, a common responsibility is the availability of the client's personnel for dealing with project affairs. Primarily it is the client project manager who is the focal point for all project related matters. In addition, other people of the client might be required to contribute to project affairs, for example, as suppliers of input information. Typically those people are from IT, marketing, or e-business strategy departments of a client company. Although you might get a strong commitment that a client's personnel are available whenever it is required, do not plan for continuous availability of client staff.

At the heart of this advice is the fact that usually the people on the client side who are designated to contribute to a project are also embroiled in other business. You can not assume that they are available continuously. These people are outside your direct control. You can not view them as members of *your* project team. Normally you do not have the power to force them to contribute to the project. If they are not available – for whatever reason – you usually have to wait until they become available. It is therefore good practice to consider this fact in project planning.

What does this mean? Simply include some slack time in planning when you expect contributions from the client side. For example, if you need a decision from the client project manager that is a prerequisite for a work activity, do not plan the start of the activity five minutes after you ask the client project manager for a decision. Planning a slack time of, say, three days between the point in time you request a decision and the point in time the decision is definitely required should provide a sufficient buffer to compensate for unavailability of the client project manager.

@ 39 Be prepared to support the client after delivery of the solution

You may assume that with the delivery of an e-business solution and the internal formal close of the contract your job on the project is completed. For many projects this assumption is invalid. Too often, a client is not well prepared to operate and maintain the delivered solution. Lack of e-business skills, missing resources, or undefined roles and responsibilities are only a few reasons that commonly hinder a client operating and maintaining an e-business solution. Such problems are of course solvable and not surprisingly clients work hard towards their resolution. However, resolving such problems requires time, usually several weeks but up to a few months. Driven by time-to-market constrains and the fear that competitors leapfrog them in the marketplace, many clients do not want to wait with the launch of a delivered e-business solution until these problems are solved. Eager to beat competitors, they often start production right after solution availability, rushing to 'be there first'. Normally they discovered rather quickly that they are not well prepared to operate the solution properly. They are desperately looking for a expedient problem resolution.

Be sure that sooner or later a client will get the idea to contact you asking for support. This idea is not bad. Who has the best knowledge about the e-business solution and how to operate it? It's *you* and *your team* as the ones who have built the solution. Members of your team would be obvious candidates for operating and maintaining the solution on behalf of a client until the client is prepared to take over. If you ask members of your team to work on the client side for a few weeks or months this is an excellent opportunity for transferring know-how from your staff to the client's staff. Both client and contractor benefit from such a solution. A client gets excellent support and the opportunity to build up know-how. For a contractor the provided support in terms of human resources is an opportunity for additional revenue.

However, a prerequisite for such a solution is that you are prepared when a support request from a client arrives. Being prepared for such a request means keeping on board a few team members that are properly skilled for such a job. Usually when a project is complete, the team members immediately take over new assignments in new projects and are no longer available. 'Blocking' a few people for potentially supporting the client is a simple action. Nevertheless, you should evaluate rather early whether you can expect such a request for support from your client. Otherwise, when keeping team members on board after the project end you might run into a problem when a support request does not happen. In this case the blocking of resources wastes the money of your company.

6.2 Involving a Client in the Project

The execution of an e-business project will probably run more smoothly if the client is more involved (see Fig. 19). Finally, a project is performed for a client and the client is paying for it. It is your job to meet the client's expectations in order to get the money for the work performed. This requires that the client buys into a project.

Your objective is to achieve a good working relationship with your client. If you succeed in doing so, this may finally lead to some sort of *partnership*. In a partnership both parties – client and contractor – benefit from a project and the benefits are fairly shared between the parties. In order to achieve the project benefits, each party supports the other wherever this is feasible.

Too often, the relationship of contractor and client is far away from a fair partnership. Each party views the other more as an 'enemy' than a partner. Each party tries to fight for advantages at the cost of the other. Not only does the working atmosphere suffer from such a relationship, but also the project deliverables. Each party spends more time in thinking about how advantages can be achieved at the expense of the other than doing real project work.

You should do your best to avoid such a situation. Instead, struggle for a fair partnership. Reaching a fair partnership can be very much helped by involving the client in the project execution. When the client has the opportunity to see directly how the project develops, this will probably raise the feeling of "*we are all sitting in the same boat*". This builds an excellent basis for reaching acceptance of project deliverables by a client.

A valuable element of client involvement is open and honest communications. From a technical point of view, communications with a client can be supported by a *project site* (see Sect. 6.2.3). However, communications can not be limited to technical aspects. It is important to always keep a client well informed on the project. Especially, project problems should be communicated as early as possible.

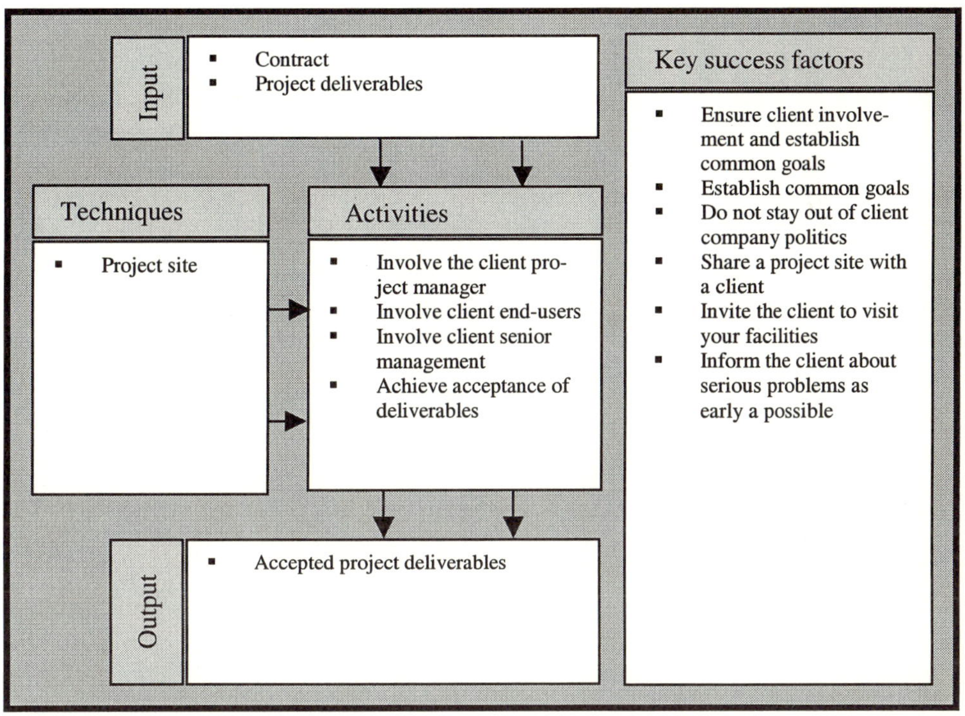

Fig. 19. Involving a client in the project

6.2.1 Inputs

Contract

The contract is the legal basis of the client–contractor relationship. It establishes a formal framework within which a working relationship can be created. Often roles and responsibilities of both client and contractor are defined in a contract. When involving the client in project execution, the defined roles and responsibilities have to be respected.

Project deliverables

Project deliverables, especially those that have to be accepted by a client, are another important input for dealing with a client. Project deliverables produced during the course of the project are the basis for project acceptance by a client.

6.2.2 Activities

Involve the client project manager

The client project manager is the most important person to involve – he or she is your direct counterpart. The client project manager is normally the person on client side who has the most influence on the project – positive as well as negative. Ensure that he or she influences the project positively.

Try to develop a good personal working relationship with this individual. If possible, establish common goals to make him or her an ally in achieving them. Often the future personal career of the client project manager depends on the outcome of the project. In this case play to the self-interest of the individual to make the project successful.

What can you do to involve the client project manager? Ask him or her to visit your facilities frequently to see the solution developing. The client project manager must be convinced that you and your team are the right people to deliver a successful project. Perform an open and honest communication with the client project manager. Sharing a project site (see Sect. 6.2.3) is a valuable support mean. Inform him or her of important matters as early as possible – especially if you have negative information. Share all relevant project management information with the client project manager. This starts by a joint development of the project time plan, the discussion of a project communications plan, and does not end with the development of a change management plan. Reviewing the project risks (see Chap. 7) and the project time plan with the client project manager on a regular basis is an excellent opportunity for involving him or her. Share all your project issues (see Sect. 6.3) with the client project manager and ask him or her for support. Offer your support to cope with his or her problems on the client side.

Involve client end-users

What are the *end-users* of an e-business solution? If the solution is for a B2B scenario, the end-users are the people on client side working directly with it. In a B2C scenario, there are usually several categories of end-users. The 'real' ones from the 'Internet community' access the solution as potential customers of the client, and the people on the client side who are responsible for operating the solution for the Internet audience and to react on action or data inserted by the 'real' end-users.

It is important to involve the end-users on the client side in the project, because these are the individuals who have to work with the outcome of the project. If they are not satisfied with what was produced, you might still receive formal acceptance from the client and the financial compensation for your work. But is such a project a successful one?

Too often, the perspective of the end-users of an e-business solution is not sufficiently considered. The client project manager and his or her staff are sometimes so engaged with defining and designing a solution that they overlook the needs of their end-users. It is your job to take an active role here by encouraging the involvement of the client end-users. If the end-users – or at least proper representatives of them – are embroiled in the specification and design of the e-business solution, the likelihood that their requirements are fulfilled by the solution increases significantly.

Involve client senior management

Try to involve client senior management in the project. Although they will probably not contribute directly to the day-to-day business of the project, they can be an important factor for project success. If they are not in favor of the project, it will be rather difficult to make it a success. Try to raise their interest in the outcome of the project and identify how the project contributes to the fulfillment of their goals.

However, be careful when interacting with client senior managers. Ensure that their involvement in the project is in the interests of the client project manager. Some client project managers do not like a direct contact between the contractor project manager and client senior management. Verify the attitude of the client project manager before establishing contacts with client senior managers.

An alternative to direct contact between yourself and client senior management is that *your* senior managers establish a contact with their counterparts. Often people like to interact with other people who are at the same management level. If you believe that this is the right way, encourage your senior management to involve the client senior management.

Achieve acceptance of deliverables

Another area where the involvement of a client is useful – and is in fact a must – is when it comes to acceptance of deliverables. When an e-business solution is performed for a client under a firm-fixed-price contract, normally there is some kind of *acceptance* required. Acceptance means that a client officially receives a deliverable and approves it. The approval is a sign-off and as such the final indication that a deliverable is complete from the perspective of a client. The acceptance can be limited to the final e-business solution or might cover intermediate deliverables such as design documentation, concepts, reports documenting consulting results, or proposals for online marketing campaigns.

It is your job to achieve the acceptance of deliverables – and it is an important job, because normally the acceptance of intermediate or final deliverables is a prerequisite for a contractor being paid for the project. And that is an important element, isn't it?

What can you do to support client acceptance? A proven practice that also works well in e-business projects is *early client involvement.* Involve the client in the production of deliverables and demonstrate the development of deliverables. Show pre-versions of deliverables to a client in advance to the official acceptance decision and ask for feedback. This gives you the opportunity to rework a deliverable before the final, official hand-over to the client. When the client discovers that its feedback was incorporated, the client is much more in favor of taking a positive acceptance decision.

When a client plans an acceptance test of the final e-business solution, offer your support. The support can span from helping to prepare a test plan only, to the provision of test data and test cases, up to supporting with human resources actually performing the test. The latter situation is a comfortable one – for you. Often clients are short on people qualified to perform the acceptance test or the client staff is not used to the e-business solution. You can offer that some members of your team support the client staff and perform the test jointly. Such a 'joint' acceptance test is an excellent basis for achieving acceptance of the final e-business solution.

6.2.3 Techniques

Project site

What is a *project site*? A project site is a project management tool to enhance the communications with a client and to support its involvement. As the name already indicates, the tool is based on a web site. A project site is hosting the information you would like to share with a client. The information flow is normally unidirectional: from a contractor to a client.

A project site can be viewed as an *extranet.* The project site is created and maintained by a contractor and can be accessed by the client project manager and his or her team members. The access is normally restricted to selected project stakeholders and is usually controlled via a password mechanism.

What are the advantages of a project site? The main advantage is that it supports *asynchronous* communications with a client. Asynchronous means that information can be exchanged at different times but through a common medium. What information should be put into a project site? The concrete information depends heavily on the scope and nature of a project. However the following information can be found in many project sites:

1. **Project schedule.** A high-level overview on the overall project schedule including start and planned end dates, project phases, and major milestones. The project schedule should not exceed one web page. The objective of this single page is to allow an overview on a project at a glance.

2. **Project team address list.** Contact information, like the phone numbers and e-mail addresses of the contractor project team members. The list may include client staff members.
3. **Major events.** Events, like meetings, reviews, and milestones that are planned for the next few weeks. This page must be updated regularly so that the highlighted events are always up-to-date.
4. **Documented project communications.** All kinds of project communications between contractor and client that is documented in written form. Examples for such documents are meeting minutes, review reports, QAP, communications plan, change management plan, project status reports, and acceptance declarations.
5. **Day-to-day project stuff.** A collection of information that you want to share with a client at a detailed level. The objective of this page is to inform on project news that might be of interest to a client. The page has to be updated daily or sometimes hourly depending on the flow of information that you want to share with a client.

Inserting information and maintaining the project site is usually performed by the contractor project manager. The client's access to the site is normally limited to a 'read-only' mode. However, in a good and long lasting relationship with a client, the unidirectional information flow might be enhanced to a bidirectional one. In this case the project site can be used to receive information from a client. A client project manager can put information that he or she wants to share with a contractor to the site.

6.2.4 Outputs

Accepted project deliverables

Accepted project deliverables are an important outcome of a project. 'Accepted' means that the client is satisfied with what you delivered and the deliverable is officially received by a client. Usually acceptance is documented with a formal *acceptance declaration* signed by the client. Normally such a declaration is a prerequisite for issuing a bill for a deliverable to a client.

6.2.5 Key Success Factors

@ 40 Ensure client involvement and establish common goals

A key factor for making a project a success is the involvement of the client. The objective of client involvement is to achieve a fair partnership between contractor and client in the execution of a project. The project stakeholders on the client and contractor sides must have the feeling that "*all are sitting in the same boat*". Such a working atmosphere reduces conflicts between a contractor and a client. And the few conflicts that might come up can be resolved much easier in a cooperative manner.

The more a client is embroiled in a project the better. Client involvement supports heading the project in the right direction. A direction that lead to results that provide the expected value for a client supports client satisfaction. Achieving formal acceptance of project deliverables is much easier when a client has been embroiled in the production of deliverables.

Which stakeholders of the client should you involve in the project? Not surprisingly, the best would be if you succeed in involving all of them. However, there are three categories of stakeholders whose involvement is of particular advantage: (1) The *client project manager* and his or her team. Usually the client project manager is the individual on the client side who has the most influence on the project. (2) The *end-users* for whom the e-business solution is designed. These are the individuals who have to work with the solution after delivery. It is important that their requirements are fulfilled by the delivered e-business solution so that they are satisfied. (3) The *client senior management* which is the sponsor of the project. They are providing the funding for the project. It is important that they are in favor of the project and notice it as being a success.

Common goals of a contractor and a client are a powerful weapon when fighting for project success. Of course, you might argue that an overall common goal is clear: both client and contractor want to make a project a success. However, this is obvious, but a key success factor is establishing common goals at a more detailed level.

For establishing common goals with a client first you have to find out what the expectations, intentions, motivations, and driving factors of the client are. Many might be obvious, but others might be hidden or not expressed explicitly. An open communication with the client project manager at a rather early stage of the project often helps to identify and understand the client's goals.

The second step is to identify your goals and the overall goals of your company. Contact your senior managers to ask how they see the project and the client. Find out whether they are more interested to make 'quick money' with a client once or in a long-lasting relationship by conducting a series of projects for a client.

Armed with the knowledge of your goals and those of your client you have to find a way to align the goals. In the best case, the client's and contractor's goals are identical. Be happy about this, since then establishing common goals is completed. In the worst case, the client's and contractor's goals are contradictory. This is a real challenge. Try to find a matching subset and concentrate on those. The usual case are not these extremes; normally you will find a mixture. Some goals are identical, some are contradictory.

Try to establish as many common goals as possible. The more common goals you share with your client, the easier it will be to solve project problems that need obligingness of client and contractor.

@ 41 Do not stay out of client company politics

Are you surprised about this recommendation? Politics are a fact of life, and they happen in a contractor's as well as in a client's company [33]. When it comes down to a client's politics, in almost all project management books you can read a simple advice, like: "*Recognize it, but definitely stay out of it*". Full stop! Hey that's it, that's great, isn't it?

Staying out of politics works perfect – in theory. But have you ever seen that this works in real life? I have never found that it is possible for a contractor project manager to stay out of client's politics in an e-business environment. Project management is a 'political business'.

An e-business project is ideally prone to company politics. Usually many departments on the client side are involved and are affected by its outcome. The interests of many people might be touched and visibility is high – also at senior management level. Is there any better environment for politics? And do you really believe that you, as the contractor project manager, can avoid becoming ensnared in a client's politics? You definitely can not! Struggling to avoid the entanglement of your project in client's politics is a waste of time. Indeed, often you and your project are the center of a political battlefield.

So, what can you do? First, you have to be aware of that client politics exists. You have to monitor what is going on and to listen to the complains of the people on the client side. Second, identify the different interests of the people involved and find out who belongs to which faction. In some books you read the advice "*not choose sides*". In real life staying *neutral* is rarely possible. You, as the project manager, will be asked for your opinion. You have to give your opinion and it should be in favor of one side. Base your opinion always on what is best for the project from your point of view.

Play an active part in the client's politics. You are part of the game. You can not be passive and stay out of it. Otherwise you may be in fact out – out of the project and out of the business. You have to be a 'political' project manager!

@ 42 Share a project site with a client

A project site is a very effective tool for sharing information with a client in asynchronous mode. In contrast to many other project management tools, its usage requires minimal prerequisites on the client side. Internet access and an Internet browser are the only media needed to make use of it. Availability of these prerequisites is a matter of course in an e-business environment. Sharing a project site with a client is of great benefit to both contractor and client. However, you have to be aware that a project site requires effort, mainly from you.

A project site is only as valuable as the information contained in it. Putting information in and maintaining this information requires time and effort. On the one hand the more time you spend on preparing and maintaining a site the better the site will most probably become. On the other hand, maintaining a project site is only one project management activity out of many that you have to perform. It is up to you to find the right balance on the effort dedicated to a project site.

When preparing and maintaining a project site, three 'golden rules' should be considered: (1) A project site is the proper place only for information that you want to share with a client. Ensure that no internal information is put on the site. The right place for communicating internal information is a *project team room* (see Sect. 12.2.3). (2) Restrict the access to those stakeholders who need to know and understand the published information. There is nothing more frustrating and time-consuming than to explain mation. There is nothing more frustrating and time-consuming than to explain information details to a project stakeholder who jumped by accident on a site asking questions about published details without proper knowledge of the project context. (3) Establish a version control and a consistent numbering scheme for information that is published in different versions or releases. A unique identification of any piece of information ensures that visitors can refer to exactly the release of information that they are interested in.

If you consider these three golden rules, a project site is a very powerful tool. Nevertheless, clients who are not used to working with a project site might need some time until they recognize its benefits. Do not give up encouraging your client to use the project site. After a while your client will love it.

@ 43 Invite the client to visit your facilities

e-business has a lot to do with *emotions*. Whether or not a client likes especially the front-end of an e-business solution often depends more on emotions and feelings than on hard facts. A client should *feel* comfortable working with you. If the client gets the impression that your company is the right contractor for doing the job, the client will probably be satisfied with what you produce as the e-business solution. One measure to make the impression indelible is to invite the client to visit your facilities.

Visiting your facilities gives the client an insight into your work environment and the opportunity to meet with members of your team. The objective of such a visit is that the client gets the opportunity to feel the enthusiasm and excitement of your team in working on the project. The client should get the impression that it can rely on you and your team, also in tough project times when nothing runs smoothly.

Who from a client should you invite to visit your facilities? The most important person is the client project manager. He or she is the individual with whom you probably have the most interaction. The second most important stakeholder to visit your facilities is client senior management. Nevertheless, the more people from the client side are investing time and energy to visit your facilities the better. This demonstrates their involvement in the project.

Encourage the client project manager to visit your facilities frequently. This gives him or her the opportunity to see how the project develops.

@ 44 Inform the client about serious problems as early a possible

Despite applying proven e-business project management techniques and considering the key success factors discussed in this book, your project might run into problems – big problems. You may have to cope with a situation in which the problems are so serious that they can only be solved by changing the defined project schedule. If the delivery date of the e-business solution can not be made despite the efforts of you and your team, you have to postpone the originally defined date. You may view this as your worst nightmare. Nevertheless, you have to communicate the schedule slippage to your client. You can expect some bumpy times.

A serious problem like a project schedule slippage might have an enormous impact on the client and its plans. Inform the client about the problem as early as possible. Immediate notification of the problem might put the client in a position to find a solution for the delayed delivery in order to keep the impact minimal. The earlier you notify the client the better.

You may believe that notifying a client immediately when one recognizes a serious problem can not be solved is a matter of course? I know of more than one project where the contractor informed the client that delivery of the e-business solution would not be possible the day before delivery date. And the information was that the delivery has to be postponed by months! Not surprisingly, you can expect that a client is not only upset about such an information but also – and even more so – about the point in time that it is communicated.

Having to admit that you encounter a schedule slippage is not good information to be communicating to a client. But you should do this as early as possible. Honest and open communication is the least you can do in such an woeful situation.

6.3 Handling Project Issues

Handling project issues is the process of coping with certain kinds of event that occur during the life of a project (see Fig. 20). Events can be positive for a project, in which case they are viewed as *opportunities,* or negative, in which this case they are viewed as *issues*. Issues are events that have to be resolved in order to avoid negative consequences for a project.

During the course of a project normally many issues arise. Most of those issues can be handled by members of your team as part of their daily work. Nevertheless, some issues are critical and beyond what your people can deal with. Those critical issues must be handled at project management level. The challenge is to identify and discover the issues that are critical for project success and to resolve them before they have a negative impact on the project.

The resolution of an issue might be possible immediately after it comes to your attention, or an issue might require a detailed analysis and evaluation prior to its resolution. In order to ensue a timely resolution of issues, a structured procedure for identifying, notifying, logging, and monitoring of issues must be established and adhered to by the project stakeholders.

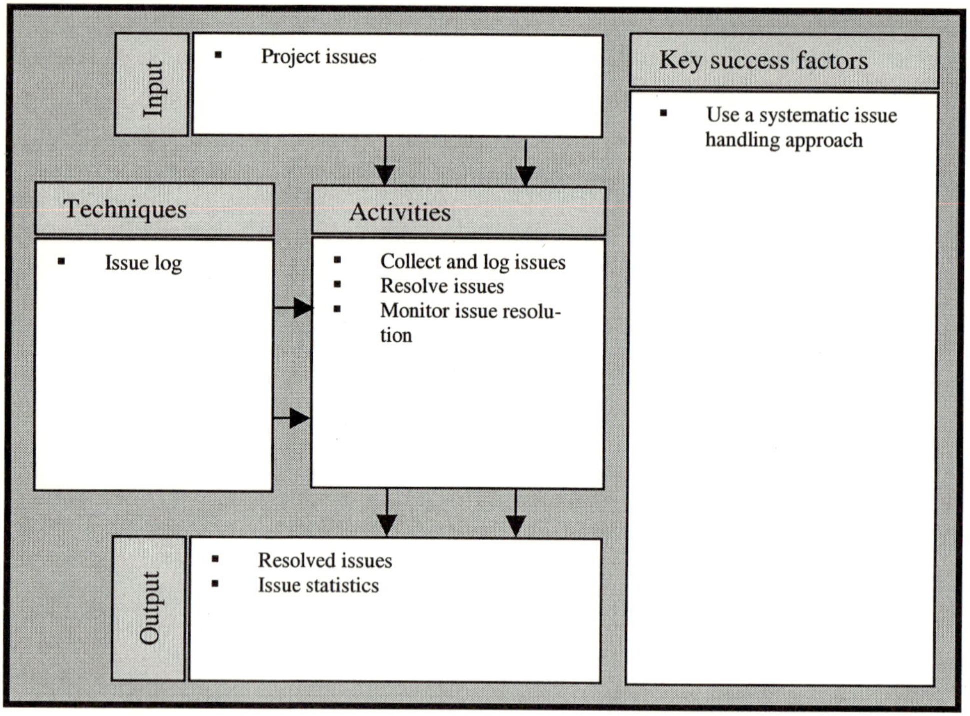

Fig. 20. Handling project issues

6.3.1 Inputs

Project issues

Not surprisingly, the input to the issue handling process are *issues*. An issue is any event that can have a negative impact on the project if it is not resolved. The characteristics of an issue is that it surfaces unplanned and in most cases can not be foreseen. Of course, you might anticipate many potential situations that would impact upon the project success if they happen. However, until such a situation really happens it is just a *risk* (see Chap. 7) and not an issue. When a risk occurs it might come in the form of an issue.

Project issues can be categorized in *internal* and *external* issues based on their origin. Internal issues are raised by members of your team or identified by yourself. Typical examples of internal issues are unplanned leave of a key team member, cost overruns, decreasing team motivation, insufficient quality of the e-business solution, or failure of subcontractors.

External issues are concerns raised by your client. Typical examples of external issues are a client not being satisfied with a deliverable or a client not fulfilling its responsibilities. The classification into internal and external is based on the origin of an issue. This does not imply that the impact of an internal issue – if it can not be resolved – is limited to internal consequences. An internal impact can impact a client and an external impact can cause internal implications. External issues usually require a more formal issue handling procedure than internal ones.

6.3.2 Activities

Collect and log issues

The activity of collecting and logging issues should be limited to the issues that require project management attention. These are typically internal issues that can not be handled by your team members as part of their day-to-day work, and external issues raised by your client. For external issues the collection activity is rather easy. Your client will inform you about its concerns and you can notify the concerns in the form of issues.

Before internal issues can be collected they have to be identified. Some issues pop up automatically and come to your attention immediately. In other cases it might take some time until you become aware of an issue. As a rule of thumb you can assume that issue resolution is less difficult the earlier an issue becomes known. Identification of internal issues is therefore a worthwhile activity. You should encourage your project team members to contribute effectively to this activity by alerting you to anything that might affect project success.

Identification and collecting issues is only the first step of the issue handling process. The next step is the logging of collected issues. Logging means recording issues in an *issue log* (see Sect. 6.3.3). Recording issues should be performed frequently to keep the issue log up-to-date. Logging issues supports traceability and the prevention of forgetting them when resolution is not immediately feasible.

Resolve issues

The logical next step after logging an issue is its *resolution*. The resolution of an issue might take place immediately after its insertion in the issue log or at a later point in time. The point in time when the resolution of an issue should be planned is determined by its urgency. The urgency of an issue is dependent on its potential impact and on its resolution deadline (see Sect. 6.3.3).

The concrete steps and measures for resolving an issue depends highly on the nature of the problem. In general it seems appropriate to start with a careful analysis of the issue, determining options for resolution, followed by an evaluation and selection of one of the options, and finally taking the actions necessary to realize the selected option.

Analyzing an issue might require the request of more information from its originator or other project stakeholders. The generation of options for resolution can be supported by involving other people. For example, you may collect resolution ideas through discussions with members of your team. When the actions taken to resolve an issue are successful, the next and last step is the documentation of its resolution and the update of the record in the issue log.

There may be situations where you are not able to resolve an issue at your management level. Do not hesitate to ask your senior management for support if you believe that this would help. Lifting a problem to a higher management level is sometimes not a bad idea. Often senior management has options and opportunities that are not available at the project manager level. However, it is essential that you brief senior managers with appropriate information when you lift a problem to their level.

You may benefit from this approach even when senior management is not able to resolve an issue. Your bosses are at least aware there is a critical project issue that can not be resolved. This eliminates the risk that they hear from other people that your project is in a critical state. Moreover, even if they are not able to resolve an issue, their concerns on your personal project management capabilities might be moderated.

Monitor issue resolution

The main purpose of the monitoring issue resolution activity is to ensure that project issues are resolved in time. The activity is performed via a regular review of the issue log with special attention to the issues in status 'OPEN'. Monitoring the issue resolution can be supported by generating statistics based on the data of the issue log. Besides the total number of issues, the relationship between the number of issues inserted as 'OPEN' and the number of issues that could be put forward to 'RESOLVED' is of interest. A negative trend (see Sect. 6.3.4) is an alarm signal and a trigger to start thinking about countermeasures.

6.3.3 Techniques

Issue log

A valuable tool for logging issues is an *issue log*. What is an issue log? An issue log is a data repository, normally realized via a database. The data repository is used to store issues in a structured and systematic manner. An issue log can be used to record internal as well as external issues. An entry or record of an issue log represents a single issue. Normally the following elements are included in each record:

- **Identification.** A unique identifier for an issue. Usually issues of a project are identified by consecutive numbers.
- **Status.** The current status of an issue. When an issue is inserted in the issue log, the status is 'OPEN', unless it could be resolved immediately. When an issue could be resolved, the status is moved forward to 'RESOLVED'. If you can not do anything to resolve an issue but to suffer from its impact, the status should be put to 'TERMINATED'.
- **Category.** An indication whether the issue is an internal or an external one.
- **Originator.** The individual who brought the issue to your attention. Where the issue was not discovered by yourself, the recording of its originator allows you to ask for more information, if necessary.

- **Description.** A short but exact description of the issue and the conditions that gave rise to it. The description should be prepared at such a level of detail that other persons can understand the issue from reading your description.
- **Impact.** A short description of the consequences that are likely to occur if the issue is not resolved.
- **Resolution deadline.** A specification of the latest point in time when a resolution of the issue must have taken place. The resolution deadline and the potential impact determine the urgency with which an issue requires attention and handling.
- **Resolution.** A short description of how the issue was resolved. Obviously this element is included when a resolution was found.

Access to the issue log in 'write mode' should be restricted to the contractor project manager. Access in 'read mode' should be granted to other project stakeholders. Moreover, it is common practice to limit the read access for outside stakeholders to external issues – read access to internal issues is reserved to internal stakeholders.

An issue log is a useful tool that requires minimal effort. The logged data can be used to generate statistics on issues and to trace the history of project problems.

6.3.4 Outputs

Resolved issues

The final output of the issue handling process are *resolved issues*. Of course, issue handling is an ongoing process that has to be performed during the full course of a project. It can be assumed that there will always be a couple of issues recorded in the issue log with status 'OPEN'. However, this is only an intermediate snapshot at a specific point in time, and sooner or later every issue should either be put forward to the status 'RESOLVED' or 'TERMINATED'. The expectation is that the number of issues in 'TERMINATED' status is diminutive compared to the number of 'RESOLVED' ones.

Issue statistics

Statistics about issue status and trends are another output from the issue handling process. You should generate issue statistics regularly from data from the issue log. Statistical data that are useful to be generated are:

- Total number of issues.
- Total number of issues per status; i.e., 'OPEN', 'RESOLVED', and 'TERMINATED'.
- Trend in increase of numbers over a certain time period.

The statistics indicating a trend deserve special attention. You can compare the number of new issues that surface with the number of issues you resolve. If the number of new issues increases more than the number of issues you can resolve, this is a negative trend that requires your attention and action.

6.3.5 Key Success Factors

@ 45 Use a systematic issue handling approach

Managing issues is an important e-business project management activity. If a critical issue or a set of issues are not resolved, this might jeopardize the overall success of the project. In extreme situations, unresolved issues may cause an e-business project to fail. In order to handle issues properly, a systematic issue handling process should be established and used. Define and agree with your client an appropriate issue handling process for external project issues.

A systematic issue handling process covers identification, notification, logging, and monitoring issue resolution. You might ask: "*Why should I spent time on establishing and adhering to a systematic approach? Can't I just simply act on issues as they surface?*" Of course you can do so. But this 'chaotic' approach might bring you into trouble. Prioritization of issues is not possible, you might 'forget' issues that you can not resolve immediately, or you might have difficulties tracing the history of issues, to name just a few disadvantages. A systematic approach for handling issues is more efficient, although it involves a little bit more effort – on the first view. When you have established a simple but efficient issue handling procedure and you and your team members get used to it, you would not like to miss it.

7 Managing Risks

Every e-business project is an adventure – there are almost always events that lead to consequences for a project. Those consequences can be positive or negative for the project. Some events can be controlled or influenced by the project team or yourself. Some events are caused by the project team or yourself. Some events are beyond the control or influence of the project team or yourself.

You are not a clairvoyant – you do not know what will happen to your project in the future. However, it is important to have an understanding of potential events or future situations that may have negative consequences for your project. Events or future situations that result in negative impacts for a project are called *risks*.

No matter how hard you and your team are working, risks may occur and your project may fall victim to them. It is always easier to deal with a risk if you have spent some time thinking about how to react before an event actually happens. Certain events can be overcome to a great extent by knowing them and taking appropriate prevention measures or corrective actions. Proper risk management is proactive rather than reactive. In order to be prepared, it is good practice to assess what can go wrong; i.e., to determine which risk is so relevant that you should spend time thinking about, and to define an action plan on how to deal with the risk.

Proper risk management is an essential element of project success. Defining an adequate risk management procedure in close cooperation with your client allows involving the client in the project by sharing information on project risks, because it is important that also the client is fully aware of the project risks.

The question is: how can risks be managed? There is no quick answer or a shortcut, but you can apply proper risk management. Risk management can be divided into the processes of (1) *analyzing project risks* and (2) *responding to project risks*.

7.1 Analyzing Project Risks

Analyzing project risks is the process of *identifying* and *quantifying* risks (see Fig. 21). The objective of this process is to provide the project stakeholders with complete and accurate information about the risks potentially facing the project.

Analyzing risks begins with identifying potential events and future situations that could have a negative impact on the project [7]. Afterwards each risk is analyzed and its characteristics are documented. Typical risks in e-business projects include lack of experience in rapidly changing technology (remember: 1 Web year = 3 months), project visibility to end-users, unrealistic client time-to-market expectations, or lack of skilled e-end-users, unrealistic client time-to-market expectations, or lack of skilled e-business resources.

To obtain a better understanding of the identified risks, each risk is quantified. Risk quantification means evaluating the probability that a risk will happen during the project, to determine the impact for the project (e.g., financial loss or client dissatisfaction) if the risk occurs, and assessing the time frame in which the risk might occur. This allows a prioritization of the identified risks. Moreover, interdependencies among the risks, i.e., the occurrence of one risk might automatically cause another risk to occur, are investigated.

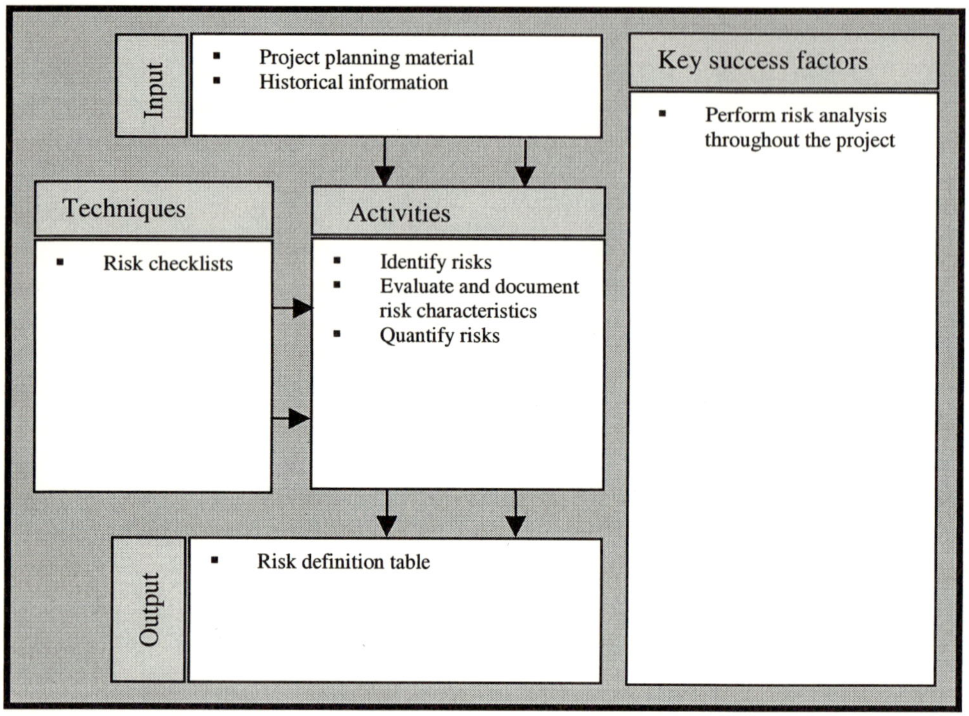

Fig. 21. Analyzing project risks

7.1.1 Input

Project planning material

All kind of project planning material that has been produced as output of other management domains is valuable input to the analysis of the risks. A careful review especially of the following project planning documents serves as a solid basis for the risk analysis: contract, WBS, project time plan, human resource plan, staffing curve, and contractor project budget.

Historical information

Historical information about previous, similar projects is also a useful input to the risk analysis process. Rich sources for historical information about projects are:

- Documented lessons learned.
- Archived project information like issue logs, project status reports, and risk management plans.
- Articles published in project management journals.
- Books about risk management in IT projects.
- Contributions in Internet news forums dealing with project management.
- Knowledge and experiences of the project staff members, the client, and yourself.

7.1.2 Activities

Identify risks

The objective of the identifying risk activity is to determine potential events and future situations that could have a negative impact on the project. Identifying risks is mainly performed by reviewing carefully the project planning documentation taking historical information into account. The output of this activity is a *list of risks* that you might face during the course of the project. To ease the further evaluation of the identified risks you can mark each risk with a unique number.

Evaluate and document risk characteristics

The objective of the evaluate and document risk characteristics activity is to reduce each identified risk to a level of detail that permits you to understand the significance of the risk and its causes. The input for this activity is the list of risks produced by the identify risks activity outlined before. By documenting the risks characteristics you can provide the project stakeholders with complete and accurate information about the risks potentially facing the project. The risk characteristics should include, for each risk, a brief description of the risk and a brief description of the conditions that lead to the risk.

The documented risk characteristics should especially be shared with the client. By reviewing and discussing the identified risks, the client becomes fully aware the risks that might face the project. This is a further mean of involving the client in the project (see Sect. 6.2).

Quantify risks

The objective of the risk quantification activity is to provide a decision-making basis for risk response planning. It is primarily concerned with determining which risks warrant a response. Risk quantification involves estimating the probability that a risk will occur and estimating the consequences of the risk, should it occur. Risk quantification includes estimating the time frame in which the risk might occur and estimating the frequency of occurrence in the case of a repeated risk. Moreover, whether there are dependencies among the identified risks is also analyzed.

The risk probability is usually expressed as a percentage within a range of 1% to 99%. Do not wonder about the fact that a probability of 0% and 100% is not included in this range. Not surprisingly, an event with a probability of 0% does not have to be considered. An event that will occur with a 100% probability can not be viewed as a risk., because if it is certain that the event will occur, this is an *issue* for the project rather than a risk. Risk consequences can be expressed in terms of financial, quality, functionality, time, or client satisfaction losses.

To quantify the financial loss, it is often recommended to use mathematical techniques like the so-called *expected monetary value* (EMV). The EMV is the product of the risk probability and the value that will be incurred if a risk occurs. I do not recommend to use such techniques for e-business projects. A financial loss expressed in terms of a simple number often creates a misleading impression of the precision and reliability of risk quantification. Estimating the risk probability and the consequences is typically a subjective effort based on your judgment or the judgment of experts you are involving.

There can be interdependency among risks. Consider as an example two risks: risk A and risk B. Two different kind of interdependencies between risk A and B can exist: (1) *inclusive* dependency – if risk A occurs, risk B will occur as well; or (2) *exclusive* dependency – if risk A occurs, risk B can not occur. Identifying the interdependencies is an important input factor for risk response planning.

The output of the risk quantification activity is a *risk definition table* (see Sect. 7.1.4).

7.1.3 Techniques

Risk checklists

Risk checklists mainly provide support in identifying risks. The objective of using a checklist is to make the approach of identifying risks more systematic. Typically risk checklists result from summarizing the lessons learned in regard to risks occurred in previous e-business projects. Risk checklists are usually organized by sources of risks. Typical sources of risks in e-business projects are:

- **Technology**
    - Lack of experience in using cutting edge technology.
    - Complexity of the e-business solution.
    - Uncertain requirements in regard to bandwidths needed.
    - Short project cycle.
- **Client's expectations**
    - Unrealistic time-to-market expectations of the client.
    - Financial health of the client; e.g., faltering Internet start-ups.
    - Wrong understanding on effort required for implementing the solution.
    - Scope creep and high number of change requests.

- **Project team**
  - Lack of skilled e-business resources.
  - Need to involve skills from several disciplines.
- **End-users**
  - Uncertainty about the audience that will visit the e-business solution.
  - Uncertainty about the number of end-users that will visit the site.

7.1.4 Outputs

Risk definition table

The risk definition table summarizes the results of the risk identification and quantification activities. It provides a decision-making input for risk response planning. From the risk definition table you derive which risks warrant a response. Table 9 outlines an example of a risk definition table.

No.	Description	Probability	Consequences	Time frame
1	Client responsibilities: The client is not able to provide content for the prepared HTML templates at the agreed point in time.	40%	The delivery date for integrating the HTML templates in the site can not be met.	Milestone '*Client responsibility 7: delivery of content*'.
2	Project team: The position of the XML programmer is still marked as 'open' in the staffing plan. It might not be filled by the point in time when the coding of the XML pages is scheduled.	30%	The XML pages can not be produced on time.	Start of activity 23: '*coding XML pages*'.
3	Financial health of the client: Due to the dot-com fallout, many customers of the client suffer. This might bring the client into an unhealthy financial situation.	10%	Contracted work can not be reimbursed by the client.	Point in time when the bill is issued and due.
4	Number of end-users: The number of users visiting the web site in parallel can only be estimated. It is uncertain whether the e-business solution is able to handle all users properly if the number exceeds 2000.	30%	Some users will not be able to use the e-business solution; i.e., can not access the server.	Production phase of the project when the number of parallel users exceeds 2000.

Table 9. Example of a risk definition table

7.1.5 Key Success Factors

@ 46 Perform risk analysis throughout the project

Analyzing project risks is not a one-time show. You should perform risk analysis throughout the course of a project. Not surprisingly, most of the risk analysis work has to happen in the project planning phase. At this point in time you are anticipating all potential events that might impact upon the project in the future. However, during project execution the situation is often changing and you are learning more about the project – and more about the project risks.

If you follow an iterative e-business solution implementation approach (see Sect. 1.8), this is an excellent opportunity to review the risks that you had to deal with in a previous implementation cycle before you start the next one. Because here you can benefit from the experience gained in one implementation cycle, i.e., which identified risks really occurred and which did not, and to develop or adjust the risk definition table before you go into the next implementation cycle. Therefore, risk analysis should not be limited to the initial project planning phase; instead you should perform risk analysis throughout the project. By updating the risk definition table on a regular basis, you and the other project stakeholders always have complete and accurate information about the project risks.

7.2 Responding to Project Risks

Responding to project risks is the process of defining for each risk how to respond to it and of determining a procedure for tracking risk occurrence and response (see Fig. 22). In general there are four strategies to respond to a risk:

1. **Avoidance.** Risk avoidance means finding a way for the identified risk not to occur. This can be accomplished by taking appropriate countermeasures or by taking an alternative approach. An alternative approach would be, for example, the use of different technology in the case that the originally planned technology is risk-prone. Consider as one example a situation in which you want to integrate a recently released version of off-the-shelf software into a web site. If you identified as a risk that the new software is highly buggy, a risk avoidance strategy is to decide to build up the e-business solution with an older, proven version of the software and migrate to the new version at a later point in time.
2. **Mitigation.** Risk mitigation means finding a way to reduce the probability that a risk will occur or to reduce the consequences to an acceptable level in the case that the risk occurs. Reducing the consequences can be accomplished by contingency planning. Consider as one example a situation in which you expect the delivery of content for a B2B solution from a client. You identify the timely delivery of the content by the client as a risk. To mitigate the consequences in the case that the client is

really not able to fulfill its commitments by the agreed point in time, you include an adequate contingency buffer between the point in time at which you need the content and the point in time that you agree with the client for delivery. If the client is late in providing the content, the impact on the overall project schedule are minimal to zero, depending on the size of the contingency time buffer and the real delivery date.

3. **Transfer.** Risk transfer means finding a stakeholder outside the project to whom a risk can be transferred. Potential candidates are subcontractors and the client. Consider as one example a situation in which you identified a risk in recruiting an adequate market researcher for your team to perform a competitor analysis. You can transfer the risk by asking a subcontractor, e.g., a market research agency, to perform the job on a firm-fixed-price basis. It is then the responsibility of the agency to find someone expedient for this assignment.
4. **Acceptance.** Risk acceptance means simply to do nothing and accept the consequences if a risk occurs. You choose this alternative in the case the probability of risk occurrence is low or the impact is not severe. The only thing you might do is to put some money aside as a risk reserve. This risk reserve can be used to cope with the consequences in the case that the risk occurs.

The ultimate decision on how to respond to a risk is based in part upon the project manager's opinion and his or her tolerance for risk.

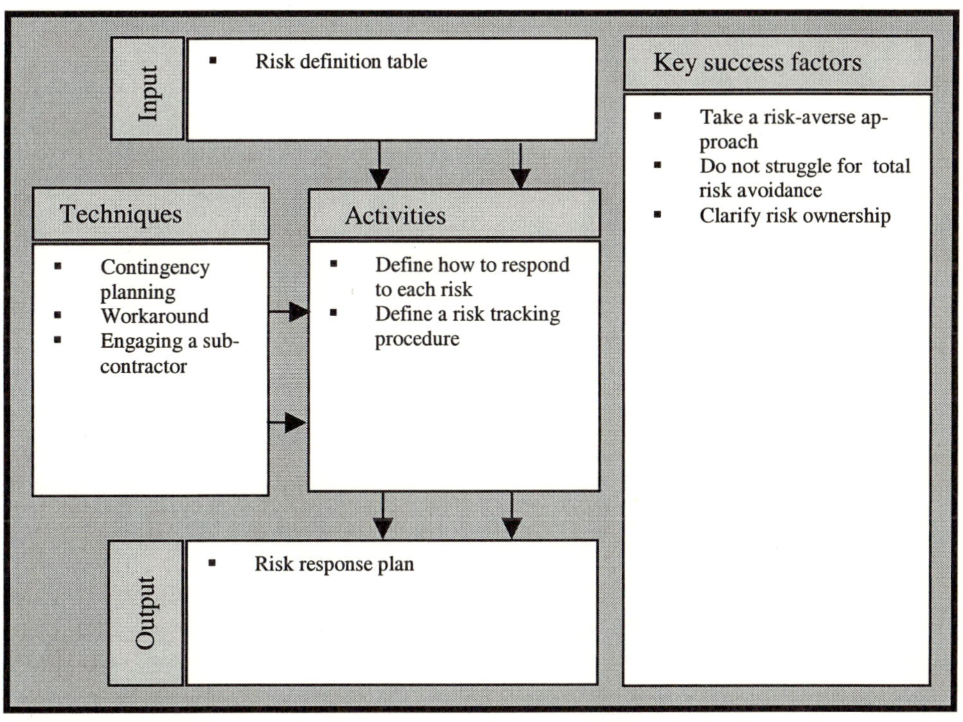

Fig. 22. Responding to project risks

7.2.1 Inputs

Risk definition table

A risk definition table resulting as the output from the risks analysis process serves as the input for response planning.

7.2.2 Activities

Define how to respond to each risk

The objective of this activity is to determine, for each risk, how to respond to it. You take the risk definition table as the input and for each item of the table you identify how to deal with the risk. You outline the response strategy and document a reasoning for choosing the response. The output of this activity is described in form of a *risk response table* (see Sect. 7.2.4).

Define a risk tracking procedure

The objective of this activity is to clarify how risks should be tracked during the project. Tracking involves monitoring whether an identified risk really occurs and in the case that it does occur ensuring that the defined response plan is executed. The risk tracking procedure is described in a *risk response plan* (see Sect. 7.2.4).

7.2.3 Techniques

Contingency planning

Contingency planning is the technique of including a reserve in terms of time or money when setting up the project time plan and project budget respectively. A reserve in terms of time means that you consider some slack time between activities that are dependent on each other. Take for example a situation in which you have to create a couple of HTML pages. A prerequisite for starting the activity 'coding the pages' is that the activity 'producing the storyboard' is completed. The dependency is that the second activity can not be started before the first activity is finalized. Including some slack time as a buffer means that you arrange the activities in the project time plan in such a way that there are a couple of days between the planned completion of the storyboard and the planned coding of the pages. You can use this reserve in terms of time when the finalization of the storyboard is delayed. If the delay is smaller than the buffer, the overall project schedule is not impacted. If the delay is greater than the buffer, the contingency at least reduces the delay of the overall schedule by the buffer time.

A reserve in terms of money means that you include a certain amount of money in the project calculation that is not matched to any specific effort. If an unforeseen event pops up that involves effort that you have not considered in your baseline project calculation, you can use this reserve to cover the additional costs. The amount of reserve that you should include in your planning depends on the risks you identified for your project and your personal tolerance for risk.

Workaround

A workaround is the technique to reduce the impact of a risk to overcome a critical situation. Consider as an example a situation in which you have to integrate a content management system into a B2C solution. You planned to test the integrated solution with content provided by the client. If the client is not able – for whatever reasons – to provide the content by the time the test is planned, you run into a problem. If you postpone the testing activities until the client fulfills its responsibility, the launch has to be postponed. To overcome this situation you can struggle to get alternative content from alternative sources – for example from other projects, or public-domain graphics. Performing the testing activities but with different content is a typical workaround for such a kind of problem.

Engaging a subcontractor

Engaging a subcontractor is one technique for transferring a risk to other stakeholders. Consider for example a situation in which you have to develop a digital brand for your client. You encounter difficulties recruiting a properly skilled digital branding specialist for your team. A solution for this problem is to engage for example an Internet agency specialized in online marketing to take over this work item as a subcontractor.

Selecting an appropriate subcontractor must be considered carefully. You might run into the situation that the original risk (recruiting a properly skilled resource for your team) is transferred to a subcontractor, but that the subcontractor is not be able to perform the contracted work item to your satisfaction with regard to time, quality, or cost. Therefore a new risk comes up. Here is a danger of exchanging one risk for another. You have to ensure that engaging a subcontractor reduces the overall risk level for the project, and does not simply replace a specific risk with a new, more severe one.

7.2.4 Outputs

Risk response plan

A risk response plan is a roadmap that tell the project stakeholders how to deal with the identified risk. The risk response plan contains a risk response table and a description of the procedure used to track risk occurrence and risk response. Table 10 outlines an example of a risk response table.

No.	Description	Response strategy	Reasoning
1	Client responsibilities: The client is not able to provide content for the prepared HTML templates at the agreed point in time.	Mitigation of the impact on the overall schedule by contingency planning.	Occurrence of the risk is outside the control of the project manager.
2	Project team: The position of the XML programmer is still marked as 'open' in the staffing plan. It might not be filled by the time when the coding of the XML pages is scheduled to start.	Transfer of the risk: production of the XML pages is subcontracted.	The XML pages are a central element of the solution. Uncertainty must be minimized.
3	Financial health of the client: Due to the recent dot-com fallout many customers of the client suffer. This might bring the client into an unhealthy financial situation.	Acceptance.	Not very much can be done to avoid or mitigate the risk. The probability of occurrence is low.
4	Number of users: The number of users visiting the web site in parallel can only be estimated. It is uncertain whether the web solution will be able to handle all users properly, if the number is higher than 2000.	Avoiding the risk by planning a second server for load balancing. The second one will be activated if the performance of one server is not acceptable.	Performance and reliability is a key requirement of the client. The risk can neither be accepted nor mitigated, nor transferred.

Table 10. Example of a risk response table

7.2.5 Key Success Factors

@ 47 Take a risk-averse approach

Projects can go awry for many reasons. If you can choose between a risk-prone and a risk-averse approach, take the latter one. This sounds simple and obvious but sometimes does not meet the expectations of all project stakeholders.

Once we were discussing the launching sequence of a highly visible e-business solution in several countries around the world for a well-known client. We were asked by the client to evaluate two alternatives: (1) launching the web sites in the client's bigger markets first and doing the rest of world in a second step; and (2) starting with some smaller markets and launching the sites for the bigger markets in a second run. I voted for the second alternative with the argument that we can take the smaller markets to prove the success of the solution before we venture to the bigger ones. If the solution turn out to be not successful – for whatever reason – the damage to the client's reputation would be significantly lower if this happened in smaller markets. In addition, we could gain experience in the smaller markets. We could benefit from those experiences when rolling the solution out to the bigger markets. My boss run crazy when I stated that this would reduce the risk for us as the contractor for development and launch of the solution. He grumbled "*Of course the risks are higher in the bigger markets, but what happened to you, did you loose your self-confidence? Are you no longer convinced that you can manage the challenge? Are you planning for success or failure? I always plan for success!*" I simple responded "*I plan for both.*" Taking a risk-averse approach is not a sign of weakness or missing self-confidence on the part of the project manager, it is simply an indication of professional e-business project management.

Some people take a risk-prone approach primarily to further their career. They think if they take the risk and the project is successful, they get immediate recognition. If the risk becomes a reality and there are indications that the project will fail, they are looking for a new job. This approach – born from grossly selfish motives – does not serve the betterment of the project and the company, and can not be recommended. From a project management point of view it is best practice to take a risk-averse approach if you have the choice.

@ 48 Do not struggle for total risk avoidance

Philosophically, total risk avoidance is a good idea – but it is not practical. In most cases it is neither feasible nor useful to struggle for an avoidance of all identified risks. In some instances it may pay to watch and wait.

There are several reasons for not eliminating a risk, including: the effort for taking measures to eliminate a risk is higher than the risk's impact, the probability that an identified risk will occur is very low, or a risk mitigation activity would decrease the impact to an acceptable level. So, make sure that your attempt to avoid risks does not shoot beyond the target. You have to evaluate carefully for each risk whether elimination is really meaningful.

@ 49 Clarify risk ownership

Assign someone as the owner of each risk. It does not help you much to develop a detailed risk response plan when no one takes care of this planning. Clarifying the ownership of a risk supports that there is always someone who feels responsible for a risk. The owner of a risk can be someone in the project team, the client, a line manager in the company, or yourself. The risk owner is responsible for monitoring whether the risk shows up and making sure that the response activities are performed according to the defined procedures when the risk occurs. However, assigning someone else as primary owner of a risk does not free you from responsibility. Ultimately, you as the project manager are responsible for managing the project risks. You are accountable for proper risk management.

8 Managing Technology

Although e-business projects are normally more than traditional IT projects, technology still plays an important role. Regardless of the kind of web pages to be developed, or whether the developed solution is for a B2B or a B2C scenario, at the heart of an e-business project is an *e-business solution* represented by a piece of *technology*. This technology – *hardware* and *software* – must be managed [1, 25].

Managing technology is a major challenge in e-business projects. In the e-business environment, technology is changing rapidly. Nearly every day new technology pops up and existing technology is improved, or slandered as outdated. Although e-business projects usually have a short project cycle, it might happen that the relevant technology ages so quickly that the originally planned one can no longer be used. Often clients insist on including the latest technology in their e-business solution in order to obtain a competitive advantage.

The managing technology domain consists of three major processes: (1) planning technology, which is to design an appealing e-business solution and to decide on the kind of technology to be used to build it; (2) implementing the e-business application, which is mainly the software development process to code and integrate the software part of the e-business solution; and (3) deploying the e-business solution, which starts with setting up a production environment and installing the e-business solution so that it is ready for launch and production.

Planning technology, implementing the e-business application, and deploying the e-business solution are not solely project management topics. Instead, these processes represent a major part of the technical work in performing an e-business project. The technical project work is mainly conducted by the people of your team, not by yourself. Nevertheless, performing the technical work requires some project management involvement in the form of planning, controlling, and deciding. This book focuses on the project management aspects of dealing with technology. Technical aspects are discussed briefly when it is necessary to explain the project management context. Details on technical aspects of planning, implementing, and deploying e-business technology can be taken from numerous other excellent books on e-business.

A final word on the term *technology* itself: the term can be used with different meanings. Some people call tools that are utilized to support the management of a project, 'technology'. In fact, tools like databases, project management software and tools, e-mail, workflow management, and others can facilitate project management significantly. Their usage is highly recommended. However, in this book such tools are discussed under the heading 'Techniques' in the respective management domains. When the term 'technology' is referenced in this book, always the technology used to build an e-business solution is addressed and not the tools utilized to manage a project.

8.1 Planning e-business Technology

Planning e-business technology is the process of developing the architecture and design of an e-business solution, and determining the kind of technology used to build it (see Fig. 23). The process covers the hardware as well as the software elements of an e-business solution. The following sections focus on the software elements, the *e-business application*.

The architecture and the design of an e-business application can be structured in two parts. The architecture and the design for the *front-end* – the graphical user interface – and the architecture and the design for the *back-end* – the IT.

Determining the appropriate technology to build the e-business solution is sometimes more of an art than a science. Often there are various alternatives that seem appropriate, but none of which offers clearly superior advantages. The decision for the 'right' alternative can have a dramatic impact on the success of the whole project. A careful evaluation of the alternatives is imperative. However, several alternative technologies do not always exist. Sometimes there is not much choice: the client might mandate a specific technology to be utilized, or technical, economic, or business reasons dictate the usage of specific technology – whether you like it or not.

When you have succeeded in defining the architecture and the design for an e-business application and have decided on the technology to be used, the game is often not over. When new technology appears during the course of the project, you might have to change the original plans to include it. This suggests that although the peak of the technology planning activities can be expected to occur in the project planning phase, in later phases some of the plans may need to be revised to reflect new conditions and circumstances.

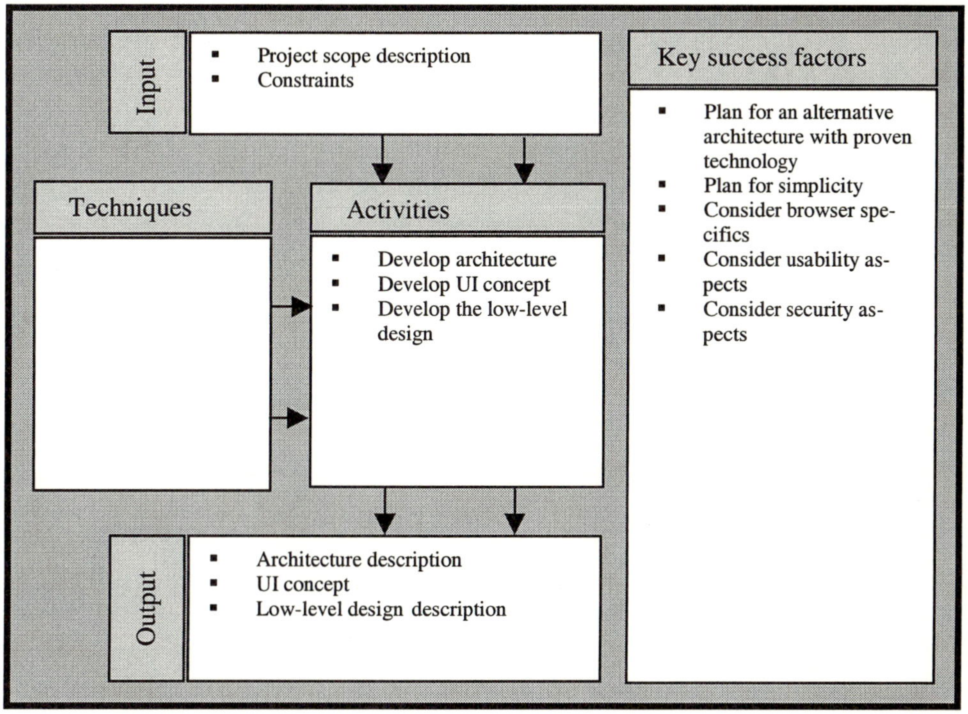

Fig. 23. Planning e-business technology

8.1.1 Input

Project scope

An essential input to the planning e-business technology process is the project scope. The project scope is normally reflected in the statement of work (see Sect. 13.2.1) that is part of the contract between contractor and client. The statement of work defines at a high level the functionality that the e-business solution should provide.

Constraints

Project constraints are all factors that limit your options with regard to the architecture, design, and technology to be used. Project constraints can result from a client's recommendations or dictates, contractor's guidelines and rules, competitor's offers, or from other technical, economic, or political aspects that have to be considered when planning technology for an e-business solution. Often a limited availability or the dubious reliability of the latest technology are project constraints that cut down your options.

8.1.2 Activities

Develop architecture

The *architecture* of an e-business solution can be structured into four elements: (1) The *application* architecture defines how the e-business application as a whole is structured and how the major parts of the solution communicate with each other. (2) The *security* architecture defines how the application satisfies security and privacy requirements, like integrity, authorization, non-repudiation, and authentication [23]. (3) The *hardware* and *network* architecture defines what hardware and infrastructure components are used to operate the application and how the application components are distributed to the infrastructure nodes. (4) The *user interface* architecture defines at a high level how the front-end of the e-business application looks while considering usability requirements.

The architecture is normally documented in an architecture description (see Sect. 8.1.4). Developing an architecture completes with evaluating and selecting the technology to be used to build the solution. This includes the decision as to which kind of technology to exploit and where to get it. A classical *make-or-buy analysis* can support the decision about parts of the solution are implemented by a contractor itself or bought from a vendor and integrated into the solution.

Developing the architecture of an e-business solution is normally performed by IT, hardware, security, and network architects in a phase of a project often called *macro design* (see Sect. 1.8). From a project management point of view, you have to ensure that the developed architecture satisfies the defined functional and non-functional requirements. Evaluating and selecting the technology to be used to build the solution is usually a joint effort between the architects and the project manager, since technical as well as economic and project management factors have to be considered.

Develop UI concept

Developing a screen-based user interface for an e-business application is widely known as 'creative' work. Some people believe that you have to rely on the inspiration of certain individuals, creative geniuses, to get this work done. Those people seem to assume that the outcome of creative work rains down the sky or results from other mystic sources. Consequently, they argue that this type of work can not be planned. I do not share this view.

Although the attractiveness and usability of an e-business application user interface is dependent on the creativity of the people who design it, this creative process can – and in fact *must* – be planned. Creative work appears sometimes to be almost leisurely, but it is real work, hard work. As for each other work item, developing an UI can be broken down into a series of definable steps, from gathering first ideas to the final design.

A fundamental step is the development of a *concept* for the UI. A UI concept usually comprises two parts: (1) a *navigation* concept outlining the navigation structure of web pages and (2) a *content plan* structuring the content information and defining what content will appear in which format on the web pages.

Developing the UI concept is normally an iterative activity. Involving the client in this activity is highly recommended. Often clients expect a specific *look and feel* for the UI of their e-business application. If their expectations are not met by the design, achieving client satisfaction can become difficult.

As project manager you should encourage the client to become embroiled in preparing the concept. Frequent reviews of the concept with the client followed by re-work to take received feedback into account ensures that the client's expectations are achievable. From a project management point of view it is important to insist on a sign off of the final version of the UI concept, because the UI concept serves as the basis for developing the *storyboard* (see next activity) and for coding the web pages. If this basis is not settled, there is a risk that the subsequent activities have to be performed over and over again.

Develop the low-level design

Developing the low-level design of an e-business application is normally performed in a phase of a project often called *micro design* (see Sect. 1.8). The low-level design of an e-business application can be structured into two elements: (1) the *back-end* low-level design specifying in detail which technology is used to build the back-end part of the application and how the application is structured into single modules, and (2) the *user interface* low-level design specifying in detail how the user interface should be build and how it should look.

The low-level design of the back-end part of an e-business application does not differ much from the low-level design of a traditional IT application. The low-level design of the front-end part of an e-business solution is often documented in a *storyboard* (see Sect. 8.1.4). A storyboard describes at a detailed level all web pages of the e-business application. For each web page the definite content – including for example, text, graphics, video, audio, and animation – and its structure is specified.

Developing the storyboard is an iterative activity. It is of advantage to involve the client in preparing the storyboard. The storyboard serves as the basis for coding the web pages. From a project management point of view it is therefore important to obtain a sign off from the client on the final version of the storyboard before coding is started.

8.1.3 Techniques

None.

8.1.4 Outputs

Architecture description

One output of the planning e-business technology process is an architecture description, outlining the application, security, hardware, network, and user interface architecture of the e-business solution. The document is prepared at a level of detail that is appropriate to serve as the input for developing the concept and design of the solution. If the architecture description is a project deliverable that has to be handed over to the client, it is useful to obtain client acceptance before the next steps – concept and design – are started.

The architecture description is normally prepared at a rather early phase of a project. If new technology pops up during the course of the project and needs to be considered, an update of the architecture description is required.

UI concept

The UI concept is a working document that facilitates the design of the user interface. It serves as a discussion basis to agree with a client on the likely design of the user interface. The UI concept lists all pieces of content and serves as a tracking tool for content sourcing and development. It can be presented by any form of descriptive text, mocked-up master screens, flowcharts, graphics, or other elements expedient to give a first impression on how the final user interface will look like. The UI concept is the main point of reference for developing the storyboard.

Low-level design description

A low-level design description is the output of the developing low-level design activity. Normally the description is twofold: it contains a part describing the back-end application design and a part describing the front-end application design. The front-end design description is often called *storyboard.*

8.1.5 Key Success Factors

@ 50 Plan for an alternative architecture with proven technology

e-business solutions are often designed and built using the latest technology. On the one hand new technology can improve the attractiveness and acceptance of a solution. On the other hand new technology is prone to failure. The latest technology has seldom been proven in earlier projects. Due to its short availability experience with proper usage is limited. Sometimes the latest technology is full of bugs and works only under bellwether conditions. Moreover, people with the proper skills to exploit the technology are lacking. All these factors increase the risk that building an e-business solution with new technology will fail. This puts you in an uncomfortable position. When you discover rather late in the project cycle that your team is not able to build the solution with the selected technology, you have hardly a chance to deliver on time.

The risk of not meeting the schedule due to problems with new technology can be mitigated by planning for an alternative architecture with proven technology. In the event that the new technology fails, you have a fallback solution – or at least a plan for it. Planning for an alternative architecture means that the developing architecture activity must be performed twice: ask your architects to develop one architecture with new technology and another architecture with proven technology. To keep the required effort small, the architecture with proven technology can be developed at a high level only.

What is the advantage of this approach? It is rather simple. When you discover that the e-business solution can not be build successfully using latest technology, you can advise your team immediately to follow the alternative architecture. Otherwise, if no alternative was developed previously, this activity must be started from the point at which the flaw is discovered. The consequence is that your team is idle until the alternative architecture is developed. Having an alternative available right away helps to reduce the impact on the overall project schedule.

However, developing an alternative architecture is not always feasible or meaningful. The latest technology might solve a unique problem for which no proven technology is available or your client might insist on using latest technology regardless of the costs and the problems incurred by its exploitation. But these situations are rare exceptions, since normally an alternative is available. Obviously, planning for an alternative architecture with proven technology involves effort. But the effort pays off when the new technology really fails, and unfortunately in e-business projects this does not occur so seldom as you might wish.

@ 51 Plan for simplicity

When the architecture, the concept, and the design of an e-business solution is developed by your staff, you have to ensure that the outcome has a level of complexity and sophistication that is appropriate for the project. You might argue that choosing the right complexity level is up to the technical experts of your team and not a project management issue. This is not the case – project management involvement is urgently required. Otherwise the developed architecture, concept, and design might be too complex. What is the reason for this? It's simple – the mentality and attitude of the involved people.

The architecture, concept, and design for an e-business solution are normally developed by architects and conceptors. The motivation and objectives of these people are often not in line with the motivation and objectives of a project manager. Architects and conceptors find their satisfaction in inventing and planning solutions that are demanding and challenging from a technical point of view. They are proud of designing something that is unique, has never been done before, with technology that has never been used before. The more complex and the more sophisticated a solution, the better.

From a project management point of view the situation looks completely different. The more complex and the more sophisticated a solution, the higher the risk of failure and the higher the costs. For architects and conceptors the feasibility and costs involved to implement a designed solution are second or third priority, at best. It is your job to ensure that the designed solution is simple enough to be implemented within the project budget, on schedule, and with a defined level of quality. This often requires slowing down the enthusiasm and excitement of your team. Acting as a brake has to be performed with sensitivity, otherwise the motivation of your people might suffer. However, planning for simplicity of the e-business solution is one of the decisive factors for project success. It is a necessity.

@ 52 Consider browser specifics

Not only is the technology on the server side continuously evolving, the same holds true for technology used on the end-user side. Normally end-users need a tool called an *Internet browser* to get access to an e-business solution. When designing an e-business solution – especially the front-end part of the application – browser specifics must be considered.

There are only a few Internet browsers that are widely used, but their functionality and capability differ slightly. Often a contractor designs a front-end that is optimized for a specific browser. This can cause problems to users that have a different one – or an earlier version of one. It is sometimes astonishing to see what old versions of browsers are still in use. Acceptance of a developed e-business solution can not be expected to be received from end-users who have problems viewing the web pages due to technical problems caused by their browsers.

When designing the front-end there is a tendency to exploit highly sophisticated features of the latest browser technology. Consider for example the use of 'Flash-films' as part of a web page content. If end-users want to play the film, they need a specific 'plug-in' to be available in their browsers. This puts a prerequisite for the end-users in place: they must have a specific browser, its latest version, and a specific plug-in. For users who are not equipped with the latest version and unable to establish the prerequisites this is a source of frustration. When designing the front-end you should therefore consider that end-users might not have the same browser, exactly the same browser version and all plug-ins available as you. If you want to exploit the latest browser features to make a solution more attractive, include at least a fall-back to display information to users who have other or older browsers.

@ 53 Consider usability aspects

When designing the e-business application – especially the front-end part of it – *usability aspects* should be considered. Usability is a characteristic of an application and determines whether the application is easy to use by its end-users. This is an important aspect, because dissatisfied end-users normally can 'mouse-click' themselves away from an e-business solution at light-speed. Gartner predicts that by 2003, users will be 50 percent more likely to abandon transactions and using Web sites when they encounter usability problems [26]. Normally usability is expressed in terms of *usability attributes*. Usability attributes are features of an application that affect its ease of use from an end-user's point of view.

Four examples of typical usability attributes of an e-business application are: (1) *Navigation:* The navigation hierarchy of the web page tree is less than 4 levels. At any point the end-user is aware of the current position within the navigation structure. The end-user is able to keep in mind a mental map of the navigation structure. (2) *Consistency:* All web pages, operations, and possible actions behave in a common fashion and have a consistent, esthetic look-and-feel that is pleasing to the senses. The layout of portrayal elements is logical, appealing, and distinguishable from the layout of competitor's solutions. (3) *Efficiency:* The web pages and possible actions are structured and organized in such a way that action steps are minimized, crossing web page boundaries is executed automatically, and responses to actions happen quickly, seamlessly, and lead to outcomes that are predictable by the user. (4) *Tailorability*: The portrayal elements can be customized to suit the individual requirements of end-users allowing for work optimization based on experience level, work style, and personal preferences.

Considering usability aspects is usually a three-step endeavor. First, you should define and document usability attributes that serve as *usability goals* for the to-be-developed e-business application. Second, you have to ensure that the usability goals are considered and adhered to when the front-end of the e-business application is designed. Third, you have to verify that the usability goals are meet by the developed application. Defining objective, measurable usability goals simplify their verification.

A prerequisite for a proper consideration of usability aspects is a clear definition of the target audience for which the e-business application is developed. Unfortunately in many e-business projects the client is either not aware who the target audience for the developed e-business application is, or the client does not plan for a direct contact of contractor and intended end-users. It is your job to insist on the identification of the target audience, and that you can contact and communicate with potential end-users directly. Otherwise all measure you take ensuring or improving usability might go into the wrong direction and might be of limited or no value.

Considering usability aspects when the e-business applications is designed and implemented is advantageous to the potential end-users, the client, and finally yourself. The end-users receive an easy-to-use application which increases attractiveness. The more users that a solution attracts the more business the client most probably will receive. Documented and measurable usability goals support getting the application accepted by the client. Because if no usability goals are defined and documented, only the subjective impressions of a client are the basis for evaluating whether or not the client's expectations regarding the user interface design are fulfilled. Obtaining acceptance for a delivered solution based on a client's subjective impressions can be hard for you. An early definition of measurable usability goals and their consideration when designing the front-end application can make your job much easier.

@ 54 Consider security aspects

When designing the e-business solution, *security* aspects should be considered. e-business solutions are prone to 'white-collar-crime' and fraud. A recent survey indicates that 60% of the surveyed companies have suffered from some sort of security breach in the last two years [6]. Nearly daily you can read news headlines reporting on a wide spectrum of security breaches, such as 'viruses attacks', 'denial of service', and 'spamming' to name just a few. Not surprisingly, e-business solutions are a favorite victim to such a kind of attacks. The Web is an inherently insecure technology, because it is a public network that has no 'owner', no central management, and no control. Therefore an e-business solution should be designed in a way that safeguards against fraud and security breaches are included.

Unfortunately some clients do not recognize the necessity for security safeguards. They take a head-in-the-sand attitude and seem not to be worried. "*It will never happen to me*" is a common statement – at least until they become the target of 'hackers'. You should take an active role in advocating the consideration of security aspects.

Designing and implementing security safeguards is normally based on a careful analysis of the security requirements of the e-business solution. Security requirements are usually part of the non-functional requirements (see Sect. 2.1.2). Typical security requirements are *confidentiality*, *integrity*, *authenticity*, and *non-repudiation* [23]. It depends on the sensitivity of the client's data which security requirements apply and which security safeguards are most appropriate to be implemented. Some common security safeguards are *password mechanisms*, the *encryption* of data, the usage of *firewalls*, the installation of *anti-virus scanners*, the implementation of *electronic signatures*, and the use of *SSL*.

When security safeguards are designed to be integrated into the developed e-business solution, they are most effective if they are in line with the *security policy* of the client company. A security policy is a framework that provides a company with a concise and comprehensive strategy to shape its security solutions in relation to business objectives. Unfortunately, not all client companies have a coherent security policy in place. A global information security survey found that in 1998 only 56% of 4300 responders had a security policy in place [8]. If you discover that your client does not have a highly effective security policy, you should recommend to take the current e-business project as a starting point to develop one. The consideration of security aspects reduces the risk that the developed e-business solution will become an easy target for web fraud.

8.2 Implementing the e-business Application

Implementing the e-business application (see Fig. 24) is the process of building the application with defined technology based on the planning activities discussed in the previous sections. Implementing an e-business application mainly comprises coding the web pages that represent the front-end and developing the software that represent the back-end part of the application.

Implementing an e-business application is more like conducting a series of technical work packages than performing project management activities. The implementation activities are performed by members of your team as part of their daily work. Your role in the implementing efforts is limited to giving strategic guidance, controlling the schedule, and resolving problems that are beyond what your team can handle.

Normally a defined approach is followed when implementing an e-business application. Nevertheless, the 'one-and-only' implementation approach applied by everyone for each project is not available. Instead, each contractor utilizes a specific approach that is applied to all its e-business projects – or even multiple approaches exist in parallel in a contractor company.

One possible implementation approach is outlined in Sect. 1.8. However, it is neither the intention of this book to propagate a specific approach nor to give the impression that the outlined approach is a superior one. It serves merely as an example for discussing some project management questions. The following sections concentrate on some implementation aspects that might be useful for you regardless of the specific implementation approach you are using.

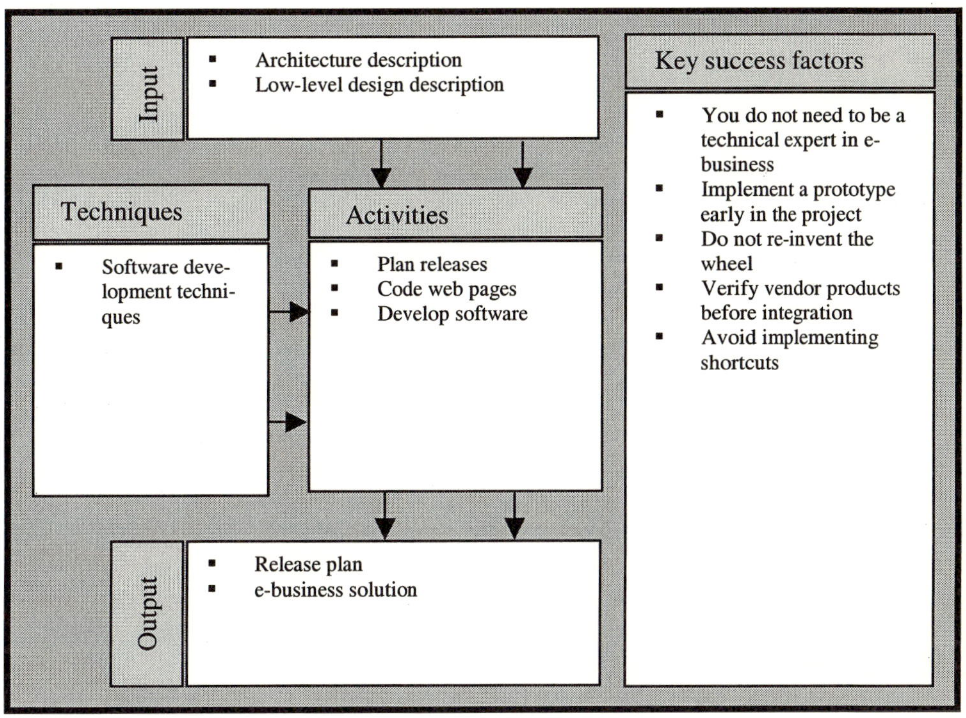

Fig. 24. Implementing the e-business application

8.2.1 Input

Architecture description

One input required to perform the implementing e-business application process is the architecture description.

Low-level design description

The low-level design description specifies in detail how the e-business application must be built. The back-end application design specifies what software components have to be developed while the storyboard prescribes the web pages that have to be coded.

8.2.2 Activities

Plan releases

An e-business application should be implemented *incrementally*. Incrementally means that the total functionality that has to be provided by the e-business application is broken down into *releases*. Each release provides a set of functions and is responsible for achieving defined objectives. Each release – with exception of the first one – is built upon a proceeding release and enriches its functionality. More and more of the application is developed and the last release provides the complete functionality. The advantage of such an incremental approach is that you can review the outcome of every release with your client to ensure that the application is evolving in the 'right' direction.

The number of releases appropriate for a project depends on its nature and the project time frame. Typically an e-business solution is developed in two or three releases. The releases have to be planned, which is a project management activity. You have to select the functions that should be implemented in a release. The outcome of this activity is a *release plan* (see Sect. 8.2.4) identifying when a release is planned to be made available and which functions will be contained.

Code web pages

Coding web pages is the activity of generating the front-end part of the e-business application. The basis for the activity is the storyboard describing the layout and content of each page in detail. The coding itself depends on the coding language (e.g., HTML, DHTML, XHTML, XML, javascript, or Flash) and whether or not a *content management system* is part of the e-business solution. It is a technical activity mainly performed by web developers supported by content designers, text editors, and graphics and sound artists. The web page coding activity is overseen by an art director. As project manager you do not have an active role in this activity.

Develop software

Developing software is the activity to code the back-end part of the e-business application. The basis for the activity is the low-level design description. Developing software for an e-business application does not differ from developing software for a traditional IT application, so classical software development techniques can be applied.

This technical activity is performed by programmers who are skilled in current programming and scripting languages such as Java, JSP, PHB, ASP, C, C++, CGI, and Perl. As project manager your job is limited to ensuring that the activity is performed as scheduled.

8.2.3 Techniques

Software development techniques

The back-end part of an e-business application is represent by a piece of software. Classical software development techniques are applicable to develop the back-end. For e-business projects especially *object-oriented design* (OOD) and *object-oriented programming* (OOP) techniques are favorable. Long shelves of excellent books are available that discuss various software development techniques, and it is not the intention of this book to repeat what can be learned from those books. The important point to remember is that developing software for an e-business application does not differ from developing software for any other IT application.

8.2.4 Outputs

Release plan

A release plan is an internal project deliverable that is used to plan the implementation process. It describes in how many releases an e-business application is planned to be implemented, which functions are contained in which release, and when each release is scheduled to be made available.

e-business solution

Not surprisingly, the output of the implementing the e-business application process is an e-business application. Together with the hardware components necessary to run the application, this represents the *e-business solution*. If an incremental implementation approach is taken to develop the application, the process produces several releases of the application, where each release usually provides more functionality than its predecessor.

The e-business solution is almost always the major external deliverable of an e-business project produced by a contractor. Normally the e-business solution needs to get accepted by the client.

8.2.5 Key Success Factors

@ 55 You do not need to be a technical expert in e-business

When it comes down to implementing e-business technology, one of the most frequently asked questions is on the required technical qualification of the project manager. You might have asked yourself: how much technical expertise is needed to manage an e-business project?

Let me tell you a little story. Once a colleague came up to me: "*I was asked to do an e-business project*" he whispered excitedly and continued: "*I just talked to a screen designer, she showed me what she was doing and talked about breadcrumb navigation, thumbnails, mock-ups and a lots of other things I never have heard before and even can not remember what she called it.*" And with a sheepish grin he informed me: "*You know,*

I have been growing up in an IT world with Pascal, C, and C++ before I developed further to project management. I do not have the technical expertise of a screen designer. Do you believe that I can still do the project?" he asked me. "*No*" I responded briefly.

After a few seconds of silence while he turned pale I continued: "*I do not believe that you can do a screen designer's job. You do not have the technical expertise. To become a professional screen designer you need to study design for some years followed by extensive hands-on training. Given your background, I think you are not properly qualified for a screen designer job.*" A smile came back to his face: "*No, no, this is a misunderstanding, I do not want to join the team as a screen designer, I was asked to care as project manager.*"

I canted: "*Why are you talking about technical expertise for a screen design's job when you are aiming for a project manager's job?*" He responded: "*I want to have at least as much technical knowledge as the people in the team so that I can manage the project successfully.*" I asked a rhetoric question: "*Technical knowledge and expertise in e-business, what does that mean? e-business is more than screen design, it is about content management, HTML/XML programming, branding, media planning, business process consulting, you name it. All these skills are usually required in e-business projects. Do you really believe you can become a technical expert in all those different disciplines? How many decades do you want to spent with studying and training? You are broke or dead by the time you finish.*" He was dismayed.

I continued: "*As a simple matter of fact it is impossible being an expert in all technical disciplines that have to be involved in e-business projects. For managing an e-business project it is not necessary to be a technical genius in all those areas.*" My colleague breathed a sigh of relief and left me in a good mood. He took over the responsibility for the project and did a great job.

Having technical expertise in some e-business areas is obviously an advantage – but it is not a necessity for a project manager. And it is impossible to be a technical expert in all areas that are of relevance for e-business projects. For project managers having served in IT projects before it might take some time to get used to a situation of being the project manager but not the technical expert of the team.

To serve successfully as an e-business project manager, it is essential to be familiar with pertinent e-business topics – but at a high level only. Being familiar with e-business topics on a high level, what does that mean? You must have at least enough understanding of technical e-business topics that you can communicate with the experts in your team comprehending the bottom line of what they are talking about.

To summarize, the only expertise that is really absolutely indispensable for a project manager of an e-business project is expertise in *project management.*

@ 56 Implement a prototype early in the project

The technology risk inherent in every e-business project can be mitigated by implementing a prototype of the e-business application early in the project. What is a *prototype*? A prototype can be viewed as a scale model of the intended application. Do not misunderstand a prototype as the first release of the e-business application. It is more a representation of the intended application used to test or visualize certain aspects.

There are mainly two reasons for implementing a prototype: (1) to test and verify new technology, and (2) to demonstrate and visualize the design of the front-end.

When you are using the latest technology to implement the e-business application, the risk of failure is high. Missing experience, lack of skilled people, or insufficient quality are only a few examples of factors that can cause the implementation effort to fail. You can mitigate the risk by implementing a prototype. Implementing a prototype means developing a small subset of functions – representative of the entire functionality of the application – to verify that the technology is in principle suitable to satisfy the project needs. The earlier in the project you perform this verification the better. If the prototype shows that the selected technology is not suitable, you can look then for alternatives early.

A prototype of the front-end of an e-business application is mainly used to demonstrate and visualize the design of web pages to a client. Some people call such a prototype a *mock-up*. Although the design is planned and described in documents like a UI concept and a storyboard, and those documents are reviewed with a client, sometimes clients are surprised to see how the described design looks on a screen. From reviewing the storyboard they have a different picture in mind and therefore might be not satisfied with the screen design. By building up a front-end prototype with a couple of pages you can visualize the design and discuss it with your client. Client suggestions can be considered before the final production of the web pages is started.

Implementing a prototype is sometimes not applauded by all project stakeholders: senior management might consider the required effort as a "*waste of time and money*". Designers sometimes feel hurt by clients criticizing their proposed screen design. You can weaken some of these arguments by building the prototype in such a way that it can be evolved to the first release of the application. This provides the impression that the work on the prototype was not 'in addition to' the work required to implement the application.

@ 57 Do not re-invent the wheel

For e-business projects a golden strategy proven in many other kinds of projects holds true as well: do not re-invent the wheel. Although each e-business project is unique, the number of distinguishable e-business solutions is limited. When you have to implement a certain e-business application to solve a client's business problem, there is a reasonable chance that there have been one or several previous projects where such an application – or a similar one – has already been implemented. You can not only benefit from experiences gained in these projects, moreover you might benefit from technical work results. Even when the application does not fit your requirements entirely, you might benefit from taking certain elements from it.

Is there any reason for not using available assets and instead implementing again what is already available? If already existing components, elements, or complete applications provide a sufficient level of quality, there is no reason for not using them. The effort involved in integrating or adopting existing components is almost always less than implementing them from scratch. The effort saved might provide relief to your project budget. The project schedule will benefit as well.

A prerequisite for using existing components is of course that copyright and intellectual property rules are respected. A client might insist that a developed application must not be used in other projects for other clients. Or the usage of an application might be restricted to a closed user group so that you can not get access to the corresponding code.

How can you get access to existing components or applications? It should not be a big problem if the components have been developed in another project of your company. Normally a company views the components developed in a project as their *assets*. The free sharing of assets within projects is mostly a matter of company policy. Moreover, a lot of useful components are available on the market free of charge. A surprising amount of so-called 'freeware', 'shareware', 'open source', or 'public domain software', is available for all kinds of e-business problems – often at a sufficient level of quality.

Taking some time to source and evaluate components that can be used and integrated (instead of developing everything from scratch) is often a worthwhile endeavor. Avoiding re-inventing the wheel by using existing assets has prevented some famous and well-recognized e-business projects from failure. Isn't that a strategy for your project?

@ 58 Verify vendor products before integration

Implementing an e-business application often includes the integration of software packages supplied by *vendors*. A vendor is an independent company that offers standard software products, sometimes called 'off-the-shelf' products. Vendor products are available for many typical e-business problems. Often the offered products are 'best-of-breed'. Instead of implementing a certain piece of functionality the integration of a vendor product that provides exactly the required functions is sometimes more appropriate. However, the usage of vendor products is not without risks.

A vendor product must provide the required functionality at a level of quality that is equal to – or better than – the target level of quality that is strived for the whole e-business solution. Otherwise you run into problems when you integrate the vendor product or when you want to obtain the acceptance for the e-business solution from your client.

Whether or not a vendor product provides its functionality at a required level of quality is sometimes not obvious. Do not take certain functionality or an assumed level of quality for granted. It is imperative that you do not rely on statements in vendor marketing brochures, verbal commitments of vendor's personnel, or bellwether demonstration of a product by a vendor only. Too often, vendor sales or marketing people promise you the earth, but after you have signed the check the bubble bursts: you have to discover that promised functionality is missing, incomplete, works differently to what is specified, or does not work at all. At least a commitment in written form of provided product functionality and of a certain level of quality is the minimum you should ask from a vendor. However, even written commitments are no guarantee that the bought product satisfies your needs. Recognizing the flaws only after the integration of a vendor product into the e-business application can result in a disaster. To avoid such a situation, it is good practice to evaluate a vendor product seriously and carefully before you integrate it.

You can ask a vendor to let you have a product for a certain period of time for evaluation and verification before you take the decision whether or not to buy it. This gives you an opportunity to test a product in your environment and to verify whether it meets your requirements with regard to functionality and quality. Dedicating the verification job to those members of your team who are assigned to perform the product integration – if you take the product – offers the benefit that your people already become acquainted with the product. The saved integration effort often compensates the verification effort to a large extent.

@ 59 Avoid implementing shortcuts

e-business applications must often be implemented along a tough project schedule. Time-to-market is key in e-business and clients expect their contractors to work to tight deadlines. As many contractors are not in a position to set their face against client's time pressure, you may have to accept a schedule that is challenging – otherwise a competitor would get the job. If some identified risks occur and a couple of unforeseen problems came up, you may find yourself in a situation in which you encounter difficulties meeting agreed milestones. In such a situation there is a tendency to cut corners by implementing a *shortcut* in order to keep to the schedule.

When implementing an e-business application a shortcut is to implement just 'something' that you can demonstrate to a client pretending that a milestone is achieved. This 'something' differs from the originally planned application. The shortcut looks like the planned application – but only superficially. Your idea is to fix the missing or simplified functionality later when there is less scheduling pressure. The idea looks appealing – at least on the surface: you made the schedule, your senior management as well as your client will praise you. However, the idea of implementing a shortcut has some significant drawbacks.

Implementing a shortcut requires effort. Although the work to implement the shortcut is most probably less than the work required to implement the real application – otherwise you would not have decided for the shortcut, would you? – usually a significant proportion of the effort must be invested. As the shortcut naturally has to be replaced by the real solution sooner or later, the total effort is much higher. You have to spend the effort to implement the shortcut plus the effort to implement the real solution. Normally you end up with nearly twice the originally planned effort – a deep hit for your project costs.

When you decide to implement a shortcut due to scheduling pressure, there is normally not much time for planning and designing the shortcut. Moreover, as the intended life of a shortcut is short – due its nature of being replaced by a real solution – you might shorten the time for planning and designing, or even skip the design completely. This can cause the implemented shortcut to fail. As a consequence you have to skulk back to the original solution.

When the implemented shortcut works from your point of view, there is always the risk that the client discovers that the demonstrated deliverable is what it is – a shortcut and not the real solution. This most probably ruins your credibility. Looking out for a new project – or a new job – is sometimes the only option you can take in such a situation.

Implementing a shortcut often raises more problems – and more severe ones – than the original problem it was intended to solve. In my experience there have been only a few situations where the implementation of a shortcut was advantageous. This suggests that you should avoid the implementation of shortcuts completely.

8.3 Deploying the e-business Solution

Deploying the e-business solution is the process of bringing the developed e-business solution into production (see Fig. 25). Bringing the e-business solution into production means making it available and accessible to its intended end-users. Some people call this the 'launch' or the 'go-live' of the solution. Launching the e-business solution requires a considerable amount of planning and preparation in order to make this event a success.

Deploying the e-business solution is normally a joint effort of contractor and client. While the main responsibility for launching a solution is on the client side, a contractor can contribute with technical support, experience, and consulting.

If the e-business project is performed under a firm-fixed-price contract, the first step of the process is an *acceptance test* (see Sect. 9.2.3) of the delivered solution. The acceptance test is performed by the client. The objective of the acceptance test is to verify whether or not the delivered solution fulfills defined criteria. The role of a contractor is to improve the quality of the solution, if necessary, by fixing errors detected by the client. When the e-business solution provides a satisfactory level of quality, the next step is to prepare the production environment and to install the solution at the client facilities.

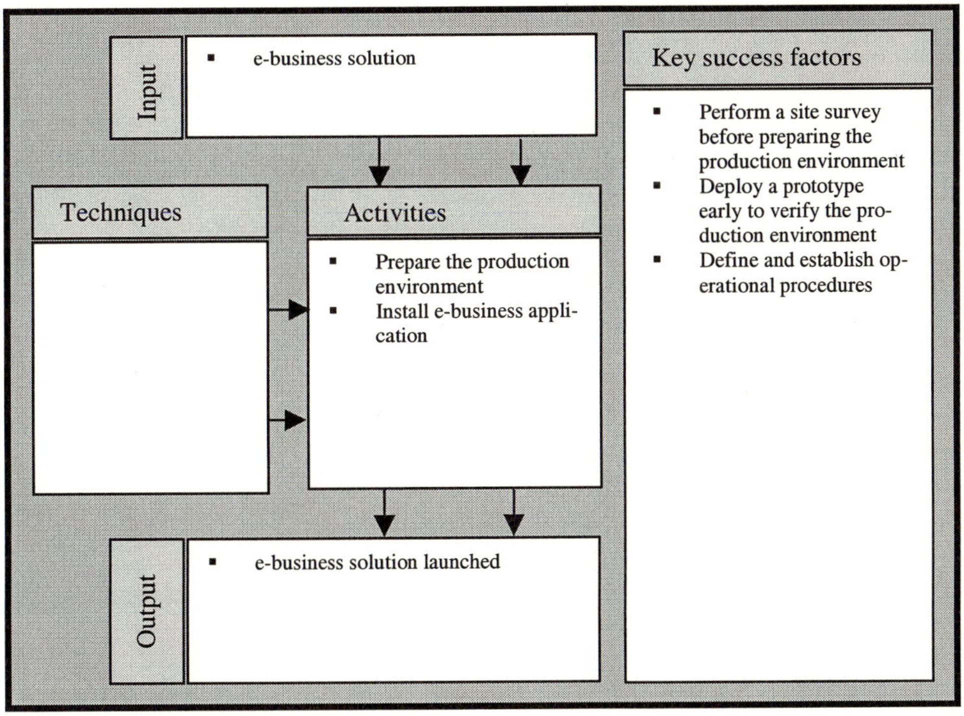

Fig. 25. Deploying the e-business solution

8.3.1 Input

e-business solution

The input for the deploy technology process is the developed e-business solution. An e-business solution normally comprises hardware and software components. In some cases it can be limited to software components when the existing hardware on the client side is used to operate the e-business application.

8.3.2 Activities

Prepare the production environment

Preparing the production environment is the activity of setting up the hardware and the infrastructure required to operate the developed e-business application. Normally the production environment is set up in the facilities of a client. However, there is one exception: *hosting*. Hosting means that a client does not want to operate the e-business solution by itself. Instead another company is contracted to operate the solution on behalf of the client. A decision for the hosting option has to be taken well in advance of deploying the solution. In the following it is assumed that the hosting option is *not* taken.

Setting up the hardware includes installing the machines (e.g., PCs, servers, and mainframes) required to run the e-business application and establishing the network infrastructure (e.g., lines/pipes, routers, switches, and hubs) to connect the machines to the Web. When ordering the lines for connection to the Web from a network service provider, the *bandwidth* requirements have to be evaluated carefully, otherwise the achievable performance might not be satisfying for the end-users. If the e-business solution covers processes critical to the overall client's business, ordering back-up pipes is a good method of improving the reliability and accessibility of the solution.

Install e-business application

The objective of the installing e-business application activity is to cut-over the e-business application from the development environment of a contractor to the production environment of a client. If the e-business solution has to interact with other systems of a client, for example, in order to feed in data or to provide data to back-end systems, the proper integration with those systems must be verified.

The installation activity normally completes with performing a *production readiness test.* The objective of a production readiness test is to verify that all hardware and software components of the solution are working properly so that production can be started. The test is usually performed by a limited number of selected end-users, sometimes called 'friendly customers', who act as representatives for the intended audience for the solution.

If the production readiness test does not detect any major pitfalls, the e-business solution is ready for launch.

8.3.3 Techniques

None.

8.3.4 Outputs

e-business solution launched

The output of the deploying e-business solution process is an e-business solution that is 'live' and accessible to its intended end-users.

8.3.5 Key Success Factors

@ 60 Perform a site survey before preparing the production environment

Visiting the client's facilities to perform a site survey avoids unpleasant surprises that might otherwise happen when attempting to set up the production environment, because often there is a big difference between plans and reality.

As an example, once a client wanted to use a specific machine to operate the developed e-business application. The machine was originally planned for a different project and as such ordered and installed in a machine room of the client a few months previously. The client wanted to protect its investment and decided to use the existing machine for the current project. A careful review of the machine's technical specification was performed. All technical details on CPU power, disk space, memory space, etc. were checked seriously and it fitted perfectly the requirements of the current project. The big surprise came at the date when the installation of the e-business application was planned. The 'machine' was not much more than an empty box – it had been salvaged completely during the few months it has been idle. All useful parts had been extracted and were scattered around various other projects.

The list of problems that can hamper preparing the production environment is long and inexhaustible: salvaged or disappeared machines, insufficient air conditioning, or lines installed by a network service provider ending hundreds of yards from the respective modems are only a few examples of problems that a site survey can discover. Performing such a survey well in advance of preparing the production environment gives you a fair chance to resolve discovered problems – if any – in time.

@ 61 Deploy a prototype early to verify the production environment

A site survey is a good starting point to inspect the production environment, but this measure is normally not sufficient In addition, another measure should be taken to verify whether or not the planned environment is ready for production. This is the deployment of a prototype or a first release of the developed e-business solution early in the target production environment. Only the actual deployment of the developed e-business application in the production environment is a definite test whether or not all required prerequisites are fulfilled. If the deployment of the prototype or a first release fails – for whatever reason – you can benefit from the experiences gained. If you deploy the prototype early in the project you have the opportunity to re-work what went wrong in order to be better prepared when the final release – or the release that is planned to be launched to the public – will have to be deployed.

@ 62 Define and establish operational procedures

Too often clients are unaware of the activities required to operate an e-business solution or underestimate the effort needed to perform them. Supporting a client to define and establish *operational procedures* is a worthwhile endeavor. Operational procedures are guidelines and rules for operating an e-business solution.

Operational procedures should cover at least four aspects: (1) *Technical procedures*, outlining which – and how – technical work items required to keep the solution alive have to be performed. Technical work items are, for example, backup and recovery of e-business solution data, monitoring network traffic and performance, maintaining disk space, administrating databases, and controlling log files. (2) *Content maintenance procedures*, describing how the content of the e-business solution is maintained. The content of web pages needs continuous maintenance in order to keep it up-to-date. Outdated content information is a major drawback to the attractiveness of an e-business solution. Updating content must be performed in a controlled and defined manner. The usage of a content management system can facilitate content maintenance. (3) *Administrative procedures*, describing when and how administrative work items are performed. Administrative work items are, for example, creating, changing, and deleting end-user profiles, administrating passwords, and maintaining access lists. (4) *Roles and responsibilities*, defining who is responsible and accountable on the client side for performing which operational work items.

It is good practice to document the operational procedures in an *operational handbook.* This document can be communicated on the client side to all relevant individuals who are involved in operating an e-business solution.

9 Managing Quality

The main purpose of managing quality is to ensure that a project satisfies the needs of its stakeholders. Managing quality covers two quality perspectives: the quality of the *management of a project* and the quality of the *e-business solution* developed by a project.

What is *quality* in general? According to the International Organization for Standardization *quality* is basically "*The totality of characteristics of an entity that bear on its ability to satisfy stated or implied needs*" [19]. The interesting question is: what is the meaning of *quality* in e-business projects?

The area of traditional quality management and quality assurance can look back on a long history of research and experience. Buzzwords like 'total quality management (TQM)', 'ISO 9000', and 'Kaizen' [18] have kept thousands of engineers and researchers busy for decades. These quality subjects have been debated in hundreds of conferences and long shelves of books discussing all aspects of quality are available. In most of these efforts quality management and quality assurance is viewed from the perspective of the production industry. A major characteristic of this industry is that normally a high number of identical entities is produced. Unfortunately, in a project environment the situation is quite different. By its very definition a project is a non-recurring endeavor to create a unique solution. As a consequence, a lot of well-known traditional techniques for improving the quality in a production environment are not applicable to the context of a project.

In the last couple of years a considerable amount of research work has been undertaken in the IT software industry to improve the quality of both the *software development process* and *software products*. The procedures and techniques invented here can be applied to e-business projects as well. However, due to the mostly rather short e-business project cycle, some of the procedures and techniques have to be adapted slightly to fulfill the specific needs of e-business projects.

The managing-quality domain consists of two major processes: (1) planning the quality management efforts for a project and (2) assuring quality in a project.

9.1 Planning Quality

Planning quality is the process of arranging the quality assurance efforts necessary for a project to keep or to achieve a defined level of quality for both the management of the project and the developed e-business solution. The main purpose is to define appropriate quality assurance procedures and activities for improving or maintaining the quality in a particular project (see Fig. 26).

Planning quality must be based on the *quality policy* of the contractor company. The quality policy is a set of overall company business rules that must be adhered to when conducting a project. Planning quality is the responsibility of the project manager. It is mainly performed at an early project stage. However, initially defined quality assurance procedures must be reviewed regularly during the execution of a project for possible revisions or expansions.

An important point to remember is that quality assurance activities are not free of charge – they incur costs and take time. Consequently, these activities must be considered when estimating project costs and when developing the project schedule. The fundamental assumption is that the benefits received from conducting the quality assurance activities outweigh the costs of its implementation.

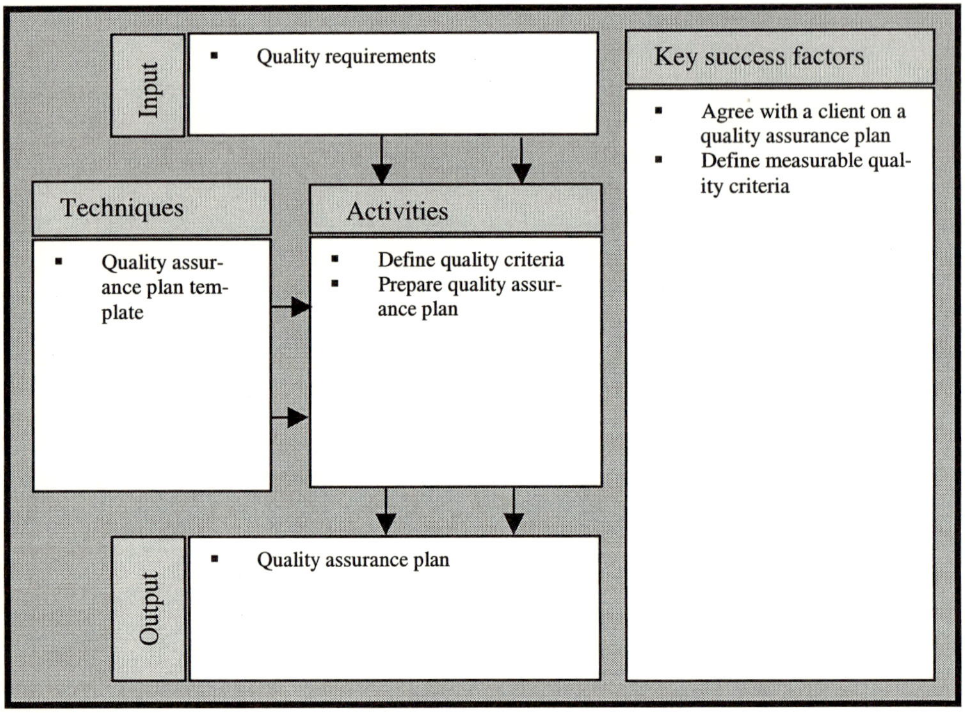

Fig. 26. Planning quality

9.1.1 Input

Quality requirements

The input for the quality planning process are *quality requirements*. Quality requirements for a project can sprout from various sources. The *contract* might contain quality requirements of the client with regard to the e-business solution – for example, compliance to ISO quality standards [18, 19]. *Project stakeholders* might have implicit expectations regarding the quality of both the management of the project and the quality of the e-business solution. The contractor might have to adhere to *quality guidelines* and to consider the *quality policy* of the company. A *project management system* or defined *project procedures* might stipulate specific quality assurance measures or tools [39].

9.1.2 Activities

Define quality criteria

The objective of the define quality criteria activity is to transform quality requirements, that are often only abstractly or implicitly expressed, into tangible and measurable *quality criteria*. Quality criteria are a set of attributes by which the quality of a given technical or services deliverable can be described and evaluated. Quality criteria are usually divided into categories. What are typical quality criteria categories in e-business projects? Some generic criteria are listed in Table 11. Concrete quality targets for an Internet portal solution are given as example.

Quality criteria category	Example of quality target
Reliability	During the first three months of production not more than two severity-1 errors and not more than ten severity-2 errors should be detected by a client and its end-users in the delivered e-business application.
Functionality	All functions specified in the functional specification must be implemented in the e-business application.
Usability	Ordering an item via the online shop must not require more than two 'clicks' for a registered end-user after an item was placed successfully into the shopping box.
Performance	The transaction response time for receiving an information page hosted on the web server should be less than one second on average when less than 200 end-users are simultaneously accessing the web server.

Table 11. Quality criteria

Installability	The developed online shopping application must be installable by an experienced developer of the client on a UNIX web server in less than three hours when adhering to the provided installation instructions.
Visibility	More than 300 end-users should be attracted by the online promotion campaign planned to introduce the online shopping solution to the end-users in the first three weeks after its launch.
Maintainability	Replacing specific content on a designed web page should be possible without programming, e.g., changing any XML scripts.

Table 11 (cont.)

The quality criteria and the examples above address the quality of an e-business solution. A typical quality criteria for managing a project is, for example, 'adherence to defined project procedures and processes by the project team'. A possible quality target is that an independent project audit does not discover more than one violation.

Quality criteria often serve as the *acceptance criteria* for a project. Acceptance criteria represent a set of specified conditions that must be fulfilled by a project deliverable in order to be officially accepted by a client. Acceptance criteria can be assigned to a whole deliverable or to parts of a deliverable. Normally it is agreed that only a subset of the deliverables has to be officially accepted by a client. Usually, acceptance is limited to those deliverables that are critical to the overall project success. To ease the acceptance process it is good practice to define quality criteria in an objective and measurable manner.

Prepare quality assurance plan

The defined quality criteria are an important element of the quality assurance plan (QAP). Preparing a QAP is the activity of documenting the quality-related aspects of a project. The QAP describes the quality assurance activities that are planned to be performed in a project to ensure that defined quality criteria are met. An initial QAP is usually prepared at an early stage of a project. When new conditions or new information become known during the course of a project, the QAP has to be expanded or revised. The QAP should be written at the level of detail required to ensure that quality criteria can be met within the effort estimated for managing the project and building the e-business solution.

9.1.3 Techniques

Quality assurance plan template

Although each e-business project is different, the quality requirements are often quite similar. As a consequence, the quality assurance procedures, techniques, and methods used in one e-business project may be widely applicable to other projects. A QAP usually contains many elements common to all e-business projects. When preparing a QAP there is no need to start from scratch in each project. Instead, a generic QAP template should be used as the basis for preparing a specific QAP (see Sect. 9.1.4).

9.1.4 Outputs

Quality assurance plan

The output of the managing quality process is a QAP for the project. A QAP describes quality targets and the activities that should be performed throughout a project to achieve the defined targets. What are the main elements of a QAP? A typical QAP for an e-business project covers the following quality areas:

- *Quality strategy* and *quality policy* describing the overall quality management approach and the overall quality goals of the contractor company.
- *Quality criteria* for *managing the project* by applying defined project procedures and processes. Normally the quality criteria are listed by category and a measurable target is defined for each quality criterion.
- *Quality criteria* for *the e-business solution* developed in the project and for the e-business services required for solution development. Specifying measurable quality targets is in particular important for those quality criteria that serve as acceptance criteria.
- *Quality assurance measures* planned to be performed in order to fulfill the defined quality criteria. Typical quality assurance measures in an e-business projects are:
    - *Reviews* to inspect technical deliverables produced in the project.
    - *Testing* to validate the developed e-business solution.
    - *Audits* to verify that the project is managed according to defined project procedures and methods.

  For each quality assurance measure the following should be described: what the measure is, what the objectives of the measure are, when it is planned to be performed, any prerequisites (if any) that must be fulfilled before it can be performed, who performs it and who is responsible for it, and exit criteria for finishing the measure.
- *Quality assurance tools* – such as error reporting and tracking systems or automated test tools – suggested to be applied in a project to support the quality assurance activities.

- A description of the process for *error handling* and a definition of *error classes* to clarify how and with what priority errors discovered by the contractor and by the client should be handled.

9.1.5 Key Success Factors

@ 63 Agree with a client on a quality assurance plan

When a contractor requests from a client the final acceptance of a delivered solution, the quality of the e-business solution is sometimes a source of dispute. While contractors may believe that the achieved level of quality is sufficient to fulfill their contractual obligations, this level of quality may be viewed by clients as not acceptable to satisfy their needs. The discrepancy often results from a different understanding of the term 'quality', and what it means in the context of a specific e-business project. Such a misunderstanding can be avoided by involving the client in the quality planning of the e-business solution.

As outlined in Sect. 9.1.2, a cornerstone of quality planning is the QAP. If you develop the QAP together with the client, quality criteria and quality targets as well as the quality assurance activities defined to achieve the targets are well known to the client. If you agree with a client on a QAP, the client's expectations are set and documented. When you duly apply the defined quality measures during the project lifetime, and when you achieve the defined quality targets, quality should not be a source of trouble in the acceptance phase. You can always refer to the QAP in the case that the client is grumbling about the quality level. When the quality criteria are met, complaints about low quality can be discussed coolly.

@ 64 Define measurable quality criteria

When defining quality criteria, especially those that serve as acceptance criteria for an e-business solution, keep in mind to define them in such a way that they are 'measurable'. What does 'measurable' mean in this context? Measurable means that a quality criterion is defined in terms of quantifiable attributes or characteristics when applied to a specific object. Consider for example a situation in which you want to define a quality criterion regarding the performance of a web server. Take a look at two definitions: (1) "*the web server should have a sufficient performance*" and (2) "*the response time for accessing pages hosted on the web server should be less than two seconds on average when 100 users are simultaneously accessing the server*". The first option is rather vague, and it is up to the reader to interpret what 'sufficient' is. Even the general term 'performance' leaves room for misunderstandings. In the second option it is clarified that 'performance' is viewed as the time required to access web pages and a metric (< 2 s.) is specified. In addition, the context and the condition under which the quality criterion should be measured (100 simultaneous users) is given. Defining measurable quality criteria ensures that you can identify without ambiguity whether or not a criterion is fulfilled. This makes discussions on solution acceptance with a client much easier than when the decision on fulfillment of a criterion is left to the personal interpretation of individuals.If you specify not only a quality target but also the technique for measuring the accomplishment of the target, the room for client complaints on the achieved level of quality decreases further.

However, I have to admit that defining quality criteria in a measurable form is not always possible. There might be specific circumstances that do not allow measurable quality criteria. Take for example the UI concept (see Sect. 8.2.4). How can you 'measure' the quality of a UI concept? What are measurable quality criteria? It is hard to find one. For these situations my recommendation is to define quality criteria as precisely as possible when they are not 'measurable'. For the UI concept you can, for example, at least define some usability criteria that can be verified with a usability test. The general recommendation for defining quality criteria is: the less room that is left for interpretation, the easier the negotiations on whether or not a criterion is fulfilled will probably be.

9.2 Assuring Quality

Assuring quality is the process of performing the defined quality assurance activities necessary for a project to achieve or to keep to a defined level of quality for both the management of the project and the e-business solution (see Fig. 27). Quality assurance is not limited to technical issues. Quality assurance is the responsibility of the project manager. However, there are specific activities (e.g., *audits*) that may be initialized by other stakeholders like senior management or people from a separate quality assurance department. Quality assurance activities have to be performed throughout the life of a project – it has to start with the first day of a project and continues until its last day.

The common element of quality assurance activities is that they involve some sort of *control*. 'Controlling' in the context of quality assurance means verifying and validating that project deliverables or project management activities comply with defined quality targets. The result of a controlling activity might be the uncovering of deviations between the current level of quality and a defined target. A quality improvement is achieved by eliminating detected deviations.

Many quality assurance methods and techniques for improving quality are known. A proven principle for improving quality is the concept of *prevention* over *correction*. Usually it is less costly to avoid errors than to correct them. In the event that error prevention is not achievable, a second principle should be considered: correcting an error is more costly when it is discovered later in the life of a project.

A common objective of quality assurance activities is attempting to prevent the occurrence of errors or trying to detect them as early as possible. Three quality assurance techniques that are appropriate for applying in e-business projects are *tests*, *reviews*, and *audits*.

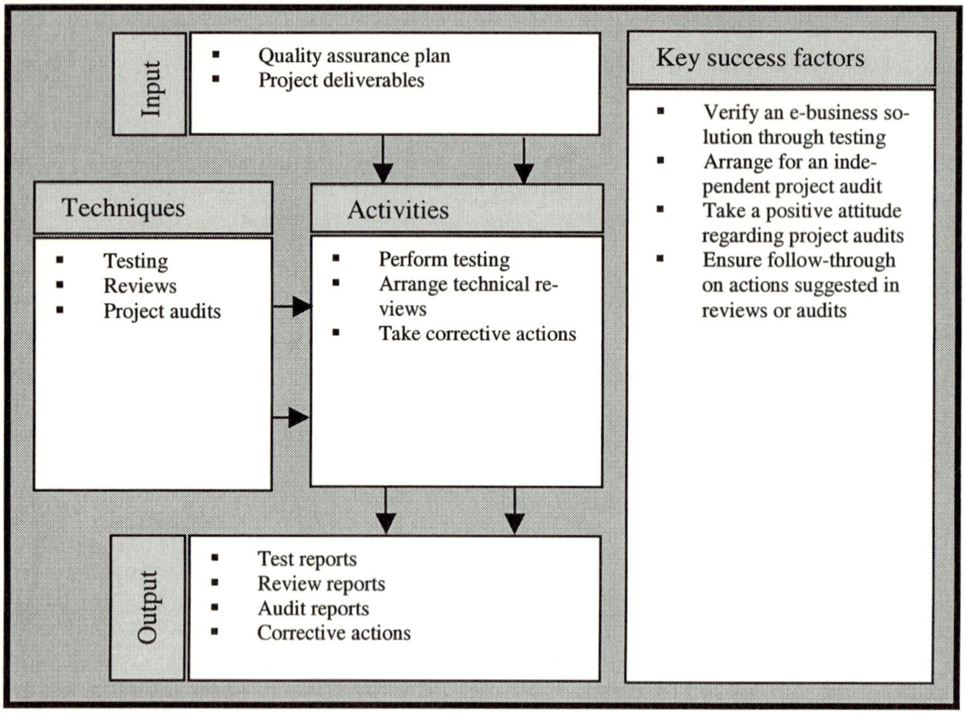

Fig. 27. Assuring quality

9.2.1 Input

Quality assurance plan
The input for the quality assurance activities is the QAP. The QAP describes what quality assurance activities should be applied and what quality targets should be achieved.

Project deliverables
All kinds of project deliverables such as documentation, code, or services are subject to inspection by quality assurance activities. Although the focus of quality assurance activities is on improving the quality of external deliverables that have to be handed over to a client, some activities might address the quality of internal project deliverables.

9.2.2 Activities

Perform testing
The objective of testing is to assess and improve the level of quality of the software of a developed e-business application (see Sect.9.2.3). The area of software testing is complex and can not be described in detail here. However, since an e-business solution consists of software, the experience and knowledge gained in traditional software development can

be exploited when testing e-business solutions. Many excellent books dealing with software testing are available. Therefore, here only a short overview on testing is given. Testing usually follows a three-step approach:

1. **Test preparation.** This step consists of planning the testing activities, preparing a test environment, and developing test cases. The planning activities are usually documented in a *test plan.* Test cases can be specified as formal, informal, detailed, or high level. The format and level of detail depends on the *test methodology* and the *test tools* used.
2. **Test Execution.** The execution of test cases can be performed manually or with the support of test tools. Normally the outcome of executing any single test case is logged. When the test execution discovers an error, it is usually documented in an *error report.* Detected errors can be categorized in terms of *severity.* A severity classification is used to prioritize the error-fixing efforts.
3. **Test reporting.** The results of the testing activities are usually documented in a *test report.* A test report provides information on the test cases, their execution, and the errors detected.

A quality improvement is achieved by fixing the errors detected by the testing activities. Error fixing is a corrective action (see Sect. 9.2.2). Although the activities 'perform testing' and 'take corrective actions' are described here as discrete elements, in practice they usually overlap and are not performed separately.

Arrange technical reviews

The objective of arranging technical reviews (see Sect.9.2.3) is to verify whether technical project deliverables fulfill defined quality criteria. The verification is usually performed via a structured manual inspection of the deliverables by individuals acting as 'reviewers'. The technical deliverables are either elements of the developed e-business solution or elements that support its development. The deliverables can be internal deliverables that are used only within the contractor company or external deliverables that have to be handed over to the client. What are typical deliverables in an e-business project that should be reviewed? You should arrange reviews for the following *external* deliverables: design specification, storyboard, and navigation concept; architecture description; produced code, scripts, and HTML/XML pages; and documentation (user /administrator handbook). You should arrange reviews for the following *internal* deliverables: project planning documentation; UI concept; and test plan, test cases, and test data.

When several individuals act as reviewers it is often useful to organize a review in the form of a meeting. Who should take part in such a review? You as the project manager have to initiate the review and to select appropriate participants. Naturally you should involve subject matter experts as reviewers. For reviewing internal deliverables you will probably find the experts in your team. For external deliverables it might be useful to involve client staff in addition to your own people. Involving client staff in a review has the advantage that the client gets a good insight into the quality of a deliverable. This might ease the acceptance of an external deliverable by a client. Often a joint review can be used to obtain a sign-off from the client.

Arranging and conducting a review consists of three major steps: (1) Preparing a review. This step comprises making available the deliverables to be reviewed, selecting the participants, and organizing the review logistics. (2) Conducting a review. This step depends heavily on the nature of the deliverables to be inspected and on the individuals acting as reviewers. A common element in conducting a review is that the reviewers are attempting to verify whether quality criteria defined in the QAP are met. When deviations are detected, corrective actions are determined that might be expedient to eliminating discovered deviations. (3) Documenting the results of a review in a report. The review results are mainly the detected deviations – often called 'findings' – and the corrective actions determined.

Reviews can be arranged at any point during the course of a project. Obviously a good date to conduct a review is when the final version of a deliverable is available. Nevertheless, sometimes it is useful to review an intermediate version of a deliverable. The advantage of this approach is that if significant quality deviations are discovered, corrective actions can be taken rather early. This might save effort.

Take corrective actions

Taking corrective actions is the attempt to lift the current level of quality to the target defined in the QAP. Not surprisingly, this activity is only necessary when the current quality level falls short of a defined target. The corrective actions taken depend heavily on the reason and nature of the difference between current and target quality levels. One corrective action that you will find in nearly every e-business project is the fixing of errors detected by testing activities. It is important to organize the error fixing and regression testing effort in a systematic and structured way. The use of a *defect tracking tool* might help the handling and controlling of the fixing activities.

9.2.3 Techniques

Testing

Testing is a widely accepted technique for verifying in particular the software components of an e-business solution. Too often, the intention of 'testing' is misunderstood: many people believe that "*testing is the process of demonstrating that a software component is correct*", while defining 'correct' as the 'absence of errors'. In fact, the absence of errors can not be demonstrated via testing. The fundamental objective of testing is exactly the contrary. A more appropriate definition is: "*Testing is the process of executing a program with the intention of finding errors*" [28]. This objective of testing may initially seem surprising. You may ask: "*Why should I demonstrate that the developed software contains errors, i.e., that it does not work?*" The answer is simple when you take the overall objective of quality assurance activities into account. The basic idea is to improve the level of quality of the developed software. The fewer errors that a piece of software contains, the higher the level of quality. Improving the level of quality can therefore be achieved by reducing the number of errors. The obvious prerequisite for fixing an error is that it is known, and this closes the loop. A quality improvement of the developed e-business solution can be achieved by first detecting errors (testing) and then fixing them.

Testing can be performed at various levels. In traditional software development the following tests are applied:

1. **Unit Test.** Unit testing is performed by the developer of a module or an object. Unit testing focuses on basic functionality and the exercising of program logic and flow of execution through the program code.
2. **Integration Test.** Integration testing is used to evaluate the integration of single modules to a bigger component or into the complete solution. Integration testing is performed incrementally as modules and objects are completed and successfully unit tested. Integration testing mainly focuses on reliability and functionality of components and of the complete solution.
3. **System Test.** System testing is used to evaluate the complete solution and its integration into the environment of a client. A system test is an 'end-to-end' test. System testing is conducted after integration testing is completed. Due to the incremental integration test approach, the final integration test often serves as a system test. While unit and integration tests are mostly performed by the developers of the modules, system tests are often conducted by different people who have not been embroiled in the development efforts. What is the background behind this strategy? It is a psychological one: it can be assumed that an individual who was involved in development will not detect as many errors than an individual who is independent. Besides functionality and reliability, other quality criteria such as performance, usability, and maintainability are evaluated in a system test. Often formal test cases are generated and executed to ensure that adequate end-to-end testing of the system is accomplished. The results of a system test are usually documented in a formal system test report.
4. **Acceptance Test.** While unit, integration, and acceptance tests are usually performed by a contractor, acceptance testing is normally performed by a client. The objective of an acceptance test is to verify whether the level of quality of a solution delivered to a client is sufficient from a client's perspective. Normally quality criteria are specified in terms of acceptance criteria defining measurable quality targets in order to base an acceptance decision on quantitative data.

The outlined tests, usually conducted in traditional software development, can be applied to e-business solutions as well – with two adjustments: (1) The outlined tests are applied in traditional software development only once. When developing an e-business solution the development process typically follows an iterative implementation approach where several releases of the application are developed (see Sect. 1.8). (2) Due to the iterative implementation approach, in e-business projects usually no distinction is made between integration and system test. Normally only one test, called either the 'integration' or 'system' test, is performed.

Testing to detect errors is only the first step for improving quality. The second step – fixing the detected errors – must follow. Usually regression tests are performed after fixes have been applied to verify that the initially detected errors do longer occur.

Reviews

A review is a structured manual inspection of a deliverable prepared by a project. The objective of a review is to determine whether the characteristics of a deliverable fulfill defined quality criteria. A quality improvement can be reached by taking corrective actions in the event of the discovery of a difference between current and target quality levels. Reviews may be conducted at any level. They can address a single deliverable or only parts of it, as well as a whole e-business solution or the overall project management efforts. Dependent on the deliverables to be inspected, a specific review might be called an 'audit', a 'walk-through', 'proof-reading', or an 'inspection'.

The common element of reviews is that there are one or more objects that have to be inspected and one or more individuals who act as 'reviewers'. A reviewer is usually a subject matter expert in the field of the object that should be inspected. Naturally a reviewer is not identical to the person who produced the to-be-inspected object. The basic idea of not asking the originator of an object to perform a review is that other persons might have a more 'objective' view on the deliverable than the originator. However, often it is useful that the originator of a deliverable participates in a review meeting. There is a strong case for having the originator available: the reviewers can address upcoming questions or clarify misunderstandings directly with the person who probably has the best knowledge of the object inspected. The result of a review is normally documented in a *review report* (see Sect. 9.2.4).

Project audits

A project audit is a special form of a review. What are the specifics of an audit? While a technical review is used to evaluate the quality of the e-business solution developed by a project, an audit is used to evaluate the management of a project. An audit is performed internally by a contractor company without the involvement of a client. The results of an internal project audit are naturally not shared with a client. The objectives of an internal project audit are: (1) ensuring that the procedures and quality assurance activities defined in the QAP are followed by the project team and (2) evaluating the benefit and effectiveness of the defined procedures and quality assurance activities, and identifying possible improvements.

While reviews of technical deliverables are normally arranged by the project manager, projects audits are often called or conducted by senior management. In a project audit the project manager usually plays the role of the project representative who 'is reviewed', while the other participants are the 'reviewers'. The reviewers are often senior managers or peer project managers who are not involved in the project. Taking reviewers who are not stakeholders of a project helps to achieve an 'independent' view on a project.

Conducting an audit usually consists of three steps: (1) verifying whether the defined procedures and activities are followed by the project team and identifying deviations, if any; (2) in the case of deviations, investigating the reason why the project team is not adhering to defined procedures or is not performing defined quality assurance activities; and (3) determining either which corrective actions should be taken to encourage the team to adhere to the defined procedures and activities, or in which way procedures and activities need to be changed or improved so that a higher quality level is achievable. The result of an audit is normally documented in an *audit report* (see Sect. 9.2.4).

9.2.4 Outputs

Test reports
Test reports are an outcome from testing activities. A test report usually provides information on the testing activities applied throughout the project and its results. It documents the test environment, test cases, test execution, and the errors detected.

Review reports
Review reports are an outcome from technical reviews. A review report usually provides information on objectives, performance, and the results of a review. It documents the version of the deliverable that was subject of a review, the findings (deviations between current and target quality level), and suggested corrective actions.

Audit reports
Audit reports are an outcome from project audits. An audit report usually provides information on objectives, performance, and the results of an audit. It documents who took part in the audit, the findings, and the suggested corrective actions. If a project audit was arranged by senior management, usually a *management summary* is included in it.

Corrective actions
Corrective actions are all measures taken to improve the level of quality in order to bring it in line with the quality target defined in the QAP.

9.2.5 Key Success Factors

@ 65 Verify an e-business solution through testing

Client and end-user expectations regarding quality are increasing. In the early days of the computer age when only a few specialists were using computer programs, quality criteria such as reliability were of little importance. If a program 'crashed', this situation was recognized as a 'normality' and simply solved by a 'restart'. Severe errors were reported to the supplier of the software and fixed in a later release. In those days end-users often served as the 'testers' of a solution. In the Internet age this situation is no longer tolerated. End-users expect an e-business solution as reliable and as stable as possible. Not meeting reliability expectations can mean the death of an e-business solution. The attention and visibility when unreliable software is published can be overwhelming.

Testing an e-business application is an effective quality assurance activity to increase the reliability of its associated software. However, often this important activity is either not considered properly in planning, or planned but not performed. The latter is often the case when the project falls behind schedule. As software testing is usually performed in a late phase of the project, there is a tendency to have testing fall by the wayside in order to keep to a defined delivery date for the solution. Too often companies emphasize making the shipment, regardless of whether the solution is right or just close to right. My recommendation is not to shorten or skip testing even if this would cause a slippage in the hand-over date of the solution to the client. The negative consequences of insufficient quality are almost always harder to tolerate than a slippage in the project schedule. There is no excuse for not verifying an e-business solution through testing – it is an absolute must.

@ 66 Arrange for an independent project audit

One trigger for a project audit might be a request from senior management to review your project management efforts performed for a project. There is another situation in which a project audit is reasonable: that is when you are asked to take over the project management position for a project that is already underway but has been managed by another project manager. There can be many reasons for the replacement of a project manager. One common reason is that senior management is not satisfied with the performance of a project manager and there is a lack of trust that he or she will manage the project successfully in the future.

If senior management wants to replace a project manager – and the replacement is you – you should be very careful. The most important point for you in such a situation is to gain a true understanding on the real status of the project. Such an understanding is a fundamental necessity for you to decide on the next steps to take. To gain an understanding on the project status you can review the project planning documentation and talk with the project stakeholders. You might discover that the original plans regarding cost, schedule, and quality are no longer valid and have to be revised. As such a revision usually causes some disappointment on the side of the project stakeholders, this puts you in a tickler, because it is you, the new project manager, who comes up with disappointing news. As bearer of such a message you will probably not be applauded and loved – you may be a victim of the typical 'shoot the messenger' culture. Some people might suspect that you rate the project status worse than it is in reality, in order to appear as the 'white knight' who rescues the project.

What can you do to avoid such an assumption? The answer is quite simple: arrange for an independent project audit. 'Independent' means that the audit is performed by people who are not involved in the project. However, the individuals should be from the contractor's company. Such people can be peer project managers or individuals from the quality assurance department. The important condition is that those individuals should be viewed by the project stakeholder as objective in rating the project status. It can be expected that the result of such an independent audit regarding the project status is much more accepted by senior management than when you came up with the result. Having the results from an independent project audit available puts you in a much better starting position when you take over the project management responsibility.

@ 67 Take a positive attitude regarding project audits

If senior management or an internal quality assurance department arranges for a project audit sometimes project managers are not pleased to be invited to such an event. Often project managers view a project audit as control of their project management efforts and as meddling into their sphere of influence. Project managers might anticipate negative consequences for a project or their personal career when deviations between current and target quality are discovered by the reviewers. This might lead to a negative attitude of a project manager regarding project audits. Such a negative attitude might degenerate even to a situation in which a project manager tries to deceive the reviewers regarding the true status of project quality. The project quality is presented in a brighter light than it is in reality, or quality flaws are simple camouflaged. In the long term this is neither to the benefit of the company nor to the benefit of the project manager. Almost always insufficient quality will become transparent sooner or later. If it becomes obvious in an audit that a project manager pretends to have achieved a higher quality level, he or she might probably undergo tough times.

Taking a positive attitude regarding project audits is the better option. Only when quality flaws are uncovered, corrective actions to improve the quality can be planned and taken. A project audit is an opportunity to obtain an independent assessment on the project. Such an assessment might discover quality problems that you overlooked due to your involvement in the day-to-day work. Although it is true that the disclosure of quality problems that might result from wrong decisions you took is not enjoyable for you, it is good to have the problems on the table. No one is perfect and always takes the correct decision. In an open atmosphere when you can trust your senior management the disclosure of mistakes – also in project management activities – is an opportunity to change something in the future. A project audit is an excellent opportunity to learn and to improve your project management capabilities. Do not waste this opportunity by taking a negative attitude.

@ 68 Ensure follow-through on actions suggested in reviews or audits

The results of reviews and audits are usually documented in reports. Many reports contain a list of suggested actions to be taken to improve quality. Ensure that those actions are really arranged and taken. Too often appropriate corrective actions are identified in a review or an audit, but a project manager fails to follow-through on them. It is always a disappointing situation when proper actions for improving quality are known but not followed – for whatever reason.

Follow-through on suggested actions can be supported by assigning each action to a dedicated member of your team. Make the assigned individuals feel responsible for performing the defined actions. Setting a planned date for completion of an action or for achievement of first intermediate enhancements is an obvious but useful measure. Remember, even if you assign actions to members of your team, finally you, the project manager, are accountable for successful execution. If a review is one out of a series, it is good practice to report at the beginning of a follow-on review on the status of actions defined in the preceding review.

10 Managing Change

In e-business projects there is a high propensity for change. Unforeseen changes will inevitably arise during the course of a project. Nearly all project elements can be subject to change. Changes may occur to requirements, scope, contract, schedule, quality, code, team members, technology, deliverables, and documentations, to name just a few. It is the project manager's responsibility to deal with all these changes.

Managing change is a critical factor in the success of a project. Some changes can be handled internally by the contractor without involvement of the client. Typical examples of such changes are replacing a team member or changing the code of the e-business application. In dealing with these changes the client need not be involved – and most clients are not even interested in knowing about them. Other changes can not be handled without client involvement. These need to be agreed on between the contractor and the client prior to implementation. Typical examples are changes to the project scope, the contract, or the project schedule. A change in this category can not be implemented without prior agreement and approval and they require special attention and are the primary focus of the change management domain examined in this chapter.

Before we jump into discussing change management in detail, we have to differentiate this topic from two others that are sometimes not distinguished clearly. The first topic is *configuration management*. Configuration management is concerned with controlling different versions of project deliverables or outcomes produced in the project (see Sect. 13.1.3). Configuration management is distinct from change management. Configuration management is performed by a contractor to control its internal work.

The second topic that is distinct from change management is the *management of change on the client side*. An e-business project often implies that certain elements must be changed on the client side in order to fully exploit the value added by a project. This might include changes to the organizational structure of the client's company, changes to internal business processes, changes to the 'culture' of the client's company, and many other changes. An objective and a work package of the e-business project might be to support the client in performing those changes or to give recommendations on what needs to be changed and in what way. Nonetheless, the management of changes to the client organization and environment is distinct from change management within the project, and is outside the scope of this chapter.

Change management within a project needs the involvement of two parties. One party – either client or contractor – requests a change, and the other party provides or denies approval. In most of the cases requests for changes in this category are introduced by the client. Nevertheless, in some situations requests for a change might be initiated by the contractor. Regardless of who the initiator is, all changes in this category must be handled according to a defined change management procedure. The primary purpose of a well-defined change management procedure is to ensure that requested changes that would be of benefit to the project are implemented, while proposed changes that would add little or no value are not incorporated.

The change management domain consists of three major processes: (1) defining a change management procedure, (2) issuing change requests, and (3) analyzing and responding to change requests.

10.1 Defining the Change Management Procedure

Changes to a project that have to be agreed on between contractor and client prior to implementation must be handled in a well-defined manner (see Fig. 28). A change management procedure, describing the way of dealing with changes must be defined and approved by both parties – client and contractor. A documented change management procedure ensures that all project stakeholders have a common understanding how changes to a project are handled.

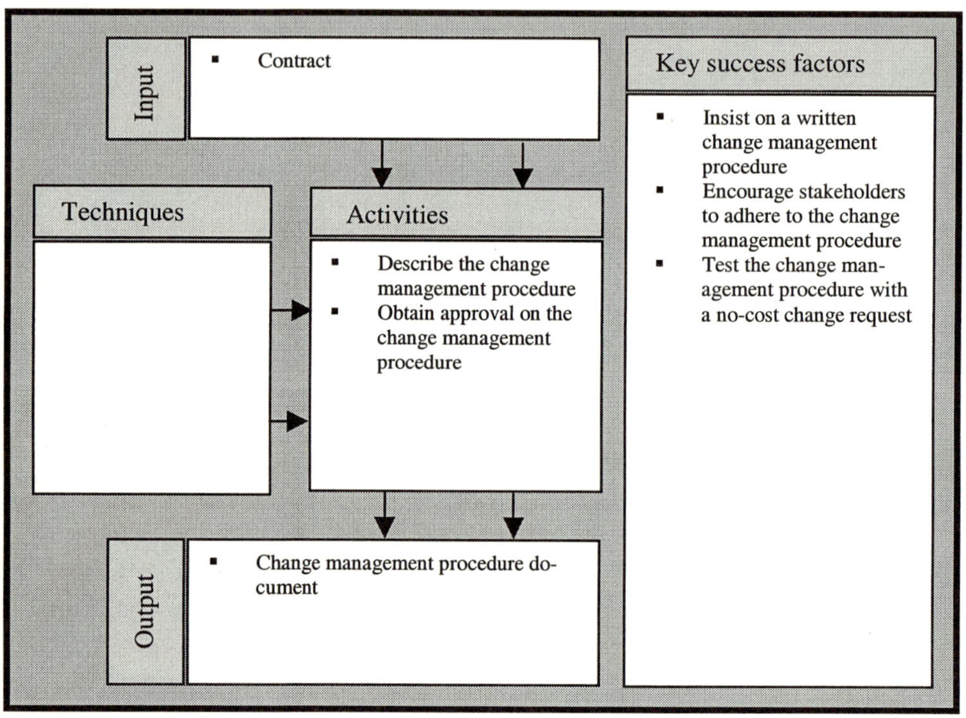

Fig. 28. Defining the change management procedure

10.1.1 Inputs

Contract

The contract for a project signed by contractor and client can sometimes be taken as the input for defining a change management procedure. Often a contract includes a high-level view of the handling of changes which can be taken as a framework for defining a detailed procedure.

10.1.2 Activities

Describe the change management procedure

The change management procedure applied in a project must be defined and documented. Typically this activity is performed rather early in the project by the project manager of the contractor. The output of this activity is a *change management procedure document* (see Sect. 10.1.4).

Obtain approval on the change management procedure

The defined and documented change management procedure must be approved by the contractor and the client. As the contractor's project manager usually prepares a proposal for the procedure, this proposal must be discussed with the client's project manager. The objective is to obtain the approval of both parties. Good practice is to have the document describing the procedure signed by the project manager of the contractor and the project manager of the client.

10.1.3 Techniques

None.

10.1.4 Outputs

Change management procedure document

A change management procedure document describes the change management procedure to be applied for a project. A change management procedure document usually covers the following aspects:

- The format in which a change is communicated. Usually this is performed with a *change request* (see Sect. 10.2.2). Often a change request template is designed.
- The elements of change requests with a short description of the elements and its meanings.
- An indication of who is authorized to issue a change request and a contact to whom change requests must be submitted. Usually the contact points are the project managers on client and contractor sides.

- The technique used to administer and store change requests, e.g., using a central repository.
- The procedure of how a change request is handled by the receiving party. This may include a time frame by which a response to the issuing party should be given, an indication of who is authorized to respond to a change request, and a description of possible response types.
- An indication of who is authorized and who drives the decision-making process. Usually the decision makers are the project managers on client and contractor sides. In big projects a change management board consisting of representatives from client and contractor can be established.
- A description of an escalation path in the case that the two defined decision makers are unable to agree whether or not a change is implemented.
- The way of updating the project planning documentation to incorporate accepted change requests.

Normally the document is approved and signed by the contractor's and the client's project managers.

10.1.5 Key Success Factors

@ 69 Insist on a written change management procedure

Changes are a major risk to project success. Standish Group research into failing IT projects ranks changes to the project's requirements and scope as one of the top three reasons for project failure [37]. To cite an IT director of a company: "*Changes, that's the biggest issue I have: changes, changes, changes; they're the real killers.*" In order to avoid changes delivering the death-blow to a project, changes have to be handled according to a well-defined procedure.

A defined change management procedure is a solid basis for handling changes. It is good practice to document the defined procedure in written form. The advantage of having the procedure available in written form is twofold: (1) you can better achieve a common understanding on the change management procedure with the client if you have the details on paper, and (2) you can use the document to make the agreed procedure known to the project stakeholders.

Sometimes clients have reservations about agreeing on a procedure in written form. They believe that it is 'too formal' or 'overkill' for a rather small e-business project. They tend to stress the 'good relationship' with a contractor arguing that insisting on a written format would be a sign of lacking trust. They often believe that an informal procedure is sufficient. Even if the project is small, a well-defined and documented change management procedure is useful. And a 'good relationship' might change over the time – for what ever reason. It is therefore important that you insist on having a expedient change management procedure defined and documented in written form.

@ 70 Encourage stakeholders to adhere to the change management procedure

Defining a change management procedure is one thing, applying it is a different ballgame. Too often, a procedure is described in detail, but the project stakeholders do not adhere to the defined procedure. The people – especially the project manager of the client and his or her team – need some time to become familiar with the procedure.

When the situation for a change request comes up, the client project manager often confronts you with a question like: "*Can we do this change outside the defined procedure? You know it is only a little one, the defined procedure is complex and we are not yet familiar with it. We can do the next upcoming change in accordance with the formal procedure. I swear to you that this is definitely the last change request that is handled outside the procedure*". If you accept such a request, there is a high likelihood that there is always a 'definitely last one' and the procedure is never applied.

Another characteristic of change requests in e-business projects is that many of the requested changes are rather small. 'Small' means that the effort required to implement them is not significant. A typical example is changing the color of a button on a screen. Often a client asks for processing such a change outside the agreed change management procedure. "*Can't we just advice the screen designer to do it?*" is a typical question you will receive. There is only one valid answer: "*No*". Because there are often interdependencies with other work items – a change on the GUI might influence the back-end part of the e-business application. If you do not document and communicate such a change, the developers of the back-end part of the e-business solution might never get aware of it. This can lead to inconsistencies between front-end and back-end part of the application that can result into serious errors. Therefore, be very rigid in applying the defined procedure. The earlier in the project that you use the procedure, the better. If the people involved have already handled a few change requests according to the procedure, they often recognize the value of a formal procedure and stick to it throughout the life of the project without grumbling.

Sometimes not only the client team members need encouragement in adhering to the defined change management procedure – often the same holds true for your team members. When working closely together with client team members, some people tend to forget about formal procedures. Once I had an IT architect in my team who met with an architect of the customer to clarify a few tiny technical questions. When they showed up around 24 hours later they had designed a completely different architectural approach for the solution. The two guys were happy and in total agreement on the change. My architect was so excited about the technical advantage of the new approach that he already informed the programmers and the web developers who started to work towards the new architecture. In fact, the new approach was impressive from a technical point of view. But the impact in terms of additional effort that could not be covered without postponing major milestones was impressive as well. The client project manager could neither share the excitement of his architect nor afford the additional costs the new architecture would introduce. As a consequence the original architecture remained. I learned from this experience that it is sometimes necessary to hold up your own people. It is important to encourage them to introduce changes only via the defined change management procedure.

@ 71 Test the change management procedure with a no-cost change request
Most of the changes requested by a client cause additional effort for the contractor. This effort must be reimbursed by the client, resulting in additional costs for a project. There is a special type of change request that does not result in a price increase. Two typical examples of changes of this type are:

1. Small modifications to the scope are requested at a very early stage of a project when neither a detailed planning of the project work packages has been performed nor any activities started. This means that you can consider the small change without an increase in effort.
2. Project planning documentation or the contract is proposed to be changed to correct deficiencies, to fill gaps, or to adjust deadlines, and the proposed change neither influences the way you are approaching the project nor causes additional effort.

Although the processing of this type of change involves administrative effort you can offer to implement these changes for no cost.

No-cost change requests are an excellent opportunity to test the change management procedure. Clients are much more happy to process and to agree on changes that do not cost them anything. By processing a no-cost change in accordance with the defined change management procedure, you set a precedent as to how changes have to be handled. This precedent will pay off later when you have to process change requests that result in a price increase, due to the fact that the client is then already used to the procedure.

10.2 Issuing Change Requests

When one party believes that there is a need to change something in a project area, and the change can not be implemented without prior approval of the other party, a *change request* has to be issued (see Fig. 29). In most cases a change causes an impact on costs, schedule, or quality. Issuing a change request must be considered carefully. In principle, any project stakeholder may initiate a change request. In order to avoid that the project team is flooded with unnecessary change requests, usually only one individual on each of the contractor and client sides is named who is responsible and authorized to issue change requests. This individual collects the potential change requests from the team members and verifies the necessity of a change before a request is raised. A change request normally comprises a definition of the proposed change and a description of the rational behind the request. Examples of situations that may lead to a change request are:

- New requirements came up and the client wants to modify or enhance the scope of the project.
- New technology pops up and is exploited in an e-business solution of a client's competitor. The design and the architecture of the e-business solution is adopted to make use of this latest technology.
- Contradictions, gaps, or other deficiencies are detected in the contract defining the relationship between contractor and client from a legal point of view.
- A variance between planned and actual progress indicates that a major milestone or a deadline can not be achieved and the project time plan must be adjusted.

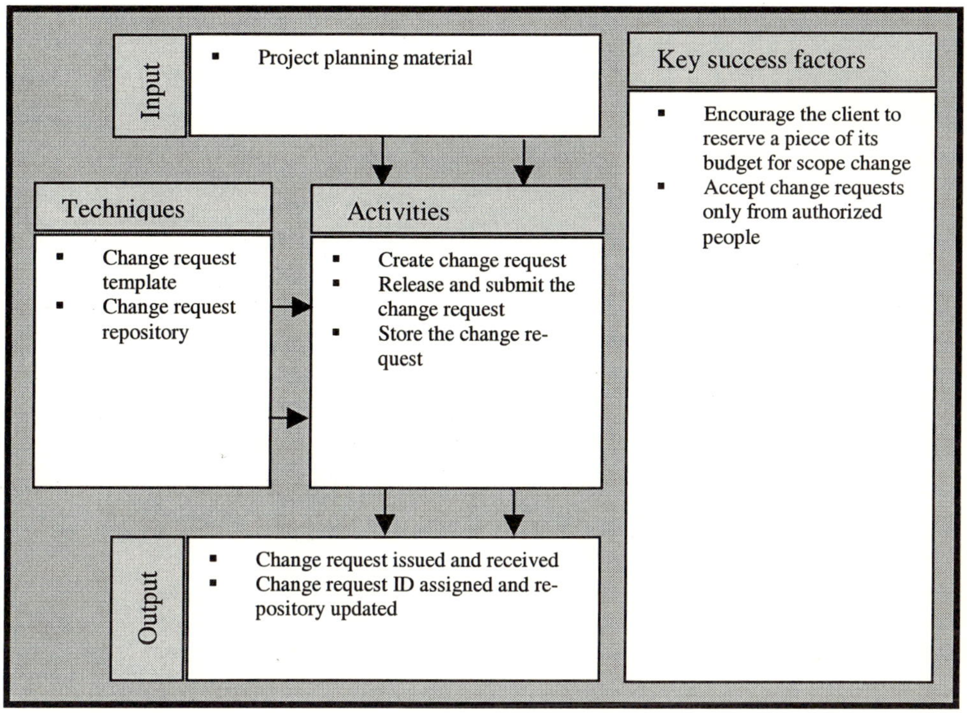

Fig. 29. Issuing change requests

10.2.1 Inputs

Project planning material

The input to a change request is the material defining the object that is subject to change. Consider, for example, the following situations: if the request is to change the contractual agreement between client and contractor, the contract would be the input to the change request; if the scope should be changed, normally the project scope description, the functional specification and the WBS would be the input; if the overall schedule should be changed, the project time plan is the input; and if technology should be changed, design or architecture documents would be the input.

10.2.2 Activities

Create change request

A change request should contain all the information necessary to decide whether the proposed change is implemented. In addition, if the decision is to implement the change, the change requests should allow tracking of its implementation.

The usage of a *template for a change request* (see Sect.10.2.3), with fields for the relevant elements, supports structure and homogeneity of proposed change requests. The activity of creating a change request is simply to fill in the fields of the template with the required information. It is important to note that the activity to create a change request does not cover the filling of all fields; only the information necessary to decide on the implementation of a change is covered. The outcome of the decision and further information needed to track the implementation are filled in by the party who has to implement the change.

Release and submit the change request

Submitting a change request is the activity of conveying a created change request to the named contact point of the other party. In order to avoid duplicated change requests, usually only one individual on the client and contractor sides is authorized to release and submit change requests. This individual verifies the need for the change and the presence of all required information to decide on a change request before it is released and submitted to the other party. The media used for submission is defined in the change management procedure. In most cases the change requests are submitted in electronic form via e-mail.

Store the change request

When a change request is released, it is good practice to store the change request form in a *change request repository* (see Sect. 10.2.4). There should only be one central repository for all change requests, regardless whether they have been issued by the client or the contractor. As most change requests are usually issued by the client, it seems reasonable to establish the repository on the contractor side.

10.2.3 Techniques

Change request template

A template for a change request form is outlined in Table 12.

No.	Element	Comment
1	Change request ID	A unique identification of the change request. Usually change requests of a project are identified by consecutive numbers.
2	Abstract	A short description characterizing the subject of the proposed change.
3	Status	One of the following: OPEN: the default status when a change request is created. APPROVED or REJECTED: the state after a decision was taken. CLOSED: the state when a change is implemented
4	Description	A detailed description of the proposed change.
5	Priority	An indication of how important the originator rates the urgency to decide on the proposed change.
6	Date	The date at which the change request is released and submitted.
7	Impact	A description of the impact that the implementation of the change would cause to the project.
8	Effort	An estimate of the effort required to implement the proposed change.
9	Costs	An estimate of the resulting costs if the change is implemented.
10	Delivery date	A planned date when the change can be implemented.
11	Decision	The outcome of the decision as to whether the proposed change will be implemented or not, and a brief reason for the decision.

Table 12. Change request template

Remark: In a real change request the 'comment section' of the form shown in Table 12) contains the fields where the information on the proposed change is to be filled in. Here only a brief explanation of the meaning of the fields is provided. Fields 2–6 are filled by the originator of the change request and fields 1–7 to 10 are filled by the individual responsible for analyzing and responding to a proposed change. Field 11 is filled in after both parties agree on whether or not a change is implemented.

Change request repository
A change request repository is a database used to maintain change requests. The change request repository is usually administered by the contractor. For better convenience and easy sharing of information, the client gets access to the repository as well – at least in a 'read' access mode. Logging and storing all change requests in a central repository supports controlled and easy handling of all change requests.

10.2.4 Outputs

Change request issued and received
The output of the process is a released change request form describing a proposed change issued by an authorized individual of one party and successfully received by an authorized individual of the other party.

Change request ID assigned and repository updated
For any released and received change request, a unique identifier is assigned and the 'Change request ID' field of the change request form is updated accordingly. The change request form is stored in the change request repository.

10.2.5 Key Success Factors

@ 72 Encourage the client to reserve a piece of its budget for scope changes
In most cases a client request to change the project scope will result in additional effort for the contractor. The costs incurred by the effort must be reimbursed by the client resulting in a cost increase for the project. If many scope changes are requested, the additional effort can be significant. In my own experience in many e-business projects, the additional effort introduced by scope changes was between 20% and 30% of the total project implementation effort. Too often clients plan a fixed project budget for the contractor's work, which is exactly equal to the total value of the contract signed. Change requests that increase the costs exceed the budget and force the client into a dilemma. On the one hand the client feels a strong need for changing the scope, on the other hand the client does not have the money to afford the effort triggered by the change. As most scope changes are meaningful and of benefit to the overall project, this situation is a back-stroke for the contractor as well.

This awkward situation can be avoided if part of the client's project budget is reserved for changes. Of course this sounds simpler than it might turn out in reality. Often a client has to struggle very hard with its senior management to get a budget of a size that equals the total contract value. However, experience shows that it is often easier to ask senior management for a little more money once rather than coming back later asking for more money when the changes come up. Too often clients are not aware of the fact that there is a high tendency in e-business projects for scope changes. It is therefore good practice to make a client aware of this fact so that the client project manager can prepare an appropriate strategy for getting a project budget of sufficient size.

@ 73 Accept change requests only from authorized people

The document describing the change management procedure usually names two individuals – one on the client and one on the contractor side – who are the only ones authorized to release change requests. In most projects the authorized persons are the project managers.

Frequently you find on the client side a complete team dealing with project affairs. The members of the client team are often eager to contribute to the project with good ideas resulting in proposed changes to the scope. With great enthusiasm they create change requests. Too often, in their belief and commitment in project execution speed, they submit change requests directly to you, skipping the person on the client side authorized to release change requests. If this happens, you should acknowledge the commitment of the people, but not accept such change requests. Encourage the client team members to adhere to the defined change management procedure. Otherwise you can end up in a situation where you are busy with responding to change requests that have never been released 'officially' by the client. When the client project manager becomes aware of the situation, many of those changes might be cancelled. This means that the time you and other key members of your team invested in analyzing and responding to those unauthorized change requests is wasted. You do not run into this situation if you accept change requests from authorized people only.

10.3 Analyzing and Responding to Change Requests

The purpose of analyzing and of responding to a change request is to find out what needs to be done to implement a proposed change and to determine its impact in terms of benefits, effort, and costs (see Fig. 30). The result of the analysis supports an informed decision on whether or not to implement the change. For change requests issued by the client, the analysis is performed by the project manager of the contractor. For changes issued by the contractor it is the other way round. However, these changes are infrequent and usually do not involve efforts or costs. Therefore, the description in the next sections neglects changes issued by contractors and focuses on those issued by clients.

Changes have different degrees of impact on a project. In general, the impact caused by a potential change is twofold: (1) the project planning material (e.g., project time plan, human resource plan, or risk management plan) must be adjusted to reflect the change; and (2) project activities to implement the proposed change from a technical point of view have to be performed. The impact in terms of effort and cost is estimated and the value added to the project is determined. The result of the analysis is documented in the change request form and conveyed back to the client. Finally, a decision is taken whether the proposed change is implemented or not.

A vote for implementing a change must be supported by both parties, contractor and client. The contractor must approve that the resources and capabilities for implementing the change are available and that the work can be performed within the defined project time frame. The client must approve the increased costs – if any – incurred by the additional effort. If one of the parties is not willing or able to approve the change, it will not be implemented. Often, if one party is voting against implementation while the other is heavily interested in it, some negotiation between the two project managers take place. If those negotiations do not lead to an agreement, the escalation path defined in the change management procedure must be followed.

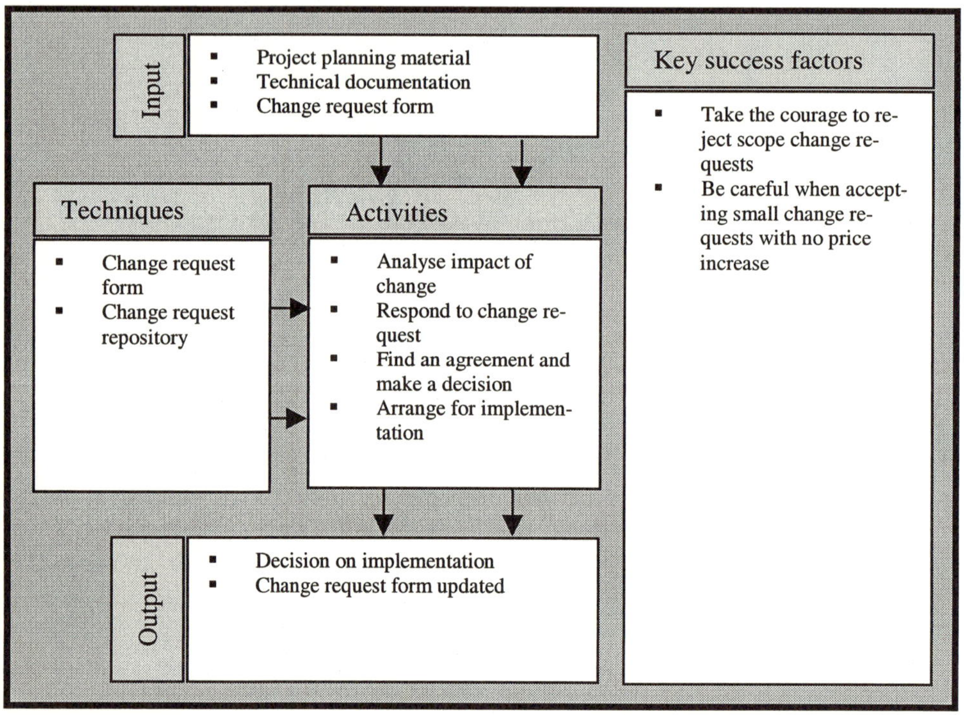

Fig. 30. Analyzing and responding to change requests

10.3.1 Inputs

Project planning material

For analyzing the impact that a proposed change would evoke, the project planning material such as the WBS, project time plan, human resource plan, and risk management plan is required as input. An important factor determining the effort required to implement a change is the status of the work packages that are affected, because the effort is usually significantly different when a work package that should be changed has already started or is even completed compared to the status when the work has not yet been started. Another important project planning material to be considered in impact analysis is therefore the project status reports documenting the project status and past performance.

Technical documentation

Another input required for analyzing a proposed change is the technical project documentation that is relevant to change. To illustrate, consider for example a scope change request. The technical documentation that must be taken as input is the project scope description defining the scope of the project. By comparing the original project scope with the proposed new scope, the functionality that has to be changed can be identified. If a scope change request arrives when a design specification and a UI concept for the e-business application is already available, this documentation can support the estimation of the impact in terms of the effort required.

Change request form

Essential input to the analyzing process is of course the change request form (see Sect. 10.2.4) describing the proposed change.

10.3.2 Activities

Analyze impact of change request

A change request can impact upon many project elements. Depending on the characteristics of the change, it may have an impact on project implementation approach, WBS, schedule, effort, quality, risks, human resource requirements, project organization, subcontractors, architecture, and design of the e-business solution.

Who is performing the impact analysis? Typically this is a contractor project manager's job. However, if an in-depth technical evaluation is required to determine the impact of a requested change, you might consult some of your team members for assistance. You might delegate the analysis activity or parts of it to certain team members, like architects, consultants, or art directors. However, finally you are accountable for the impact analysis. You must ensure that all stakeholders who might be impacted are involved prior to responding to a change request.

Respond to change request

Responding to a change request is the activity of communicating the result of the impact analysis and the vote of the contractor about its implementation decision to the client. Typically, this activity is performed by the contractor project manager. In general there are two types of responses. One type of response is simply to reject the proposed change. This means that the contractor votes for not implementing it. Typical reasons for such a vote are:

- The change request is invalid. This is for example the case if the received change request is simply a duplicate of one that has already been processed, or if the change request was due to a misunderstanding or a mistake on the part of the originator.
- Implementing the change would impact the project schedule in such a way that major milestones that could not be postponed would be missed.
- The effort evoked by the change would be too high to be covered by the available team, and you do not see any chance of obtaining adequate resources on board in time for implementing the change.
- The change would raise a significant risk that could not be avoided, mitigated, or accepted.

There might be numerous other reasons that suggest voting for not implementing the change. A common practice for dealing with change requests that are valid and meaningful but must be rejected due to missing resources or risk of not meeting deadlines is to defer those changes to later releases. This means that a change is rejected to be implemented in the current release, but it will be considered in a later phase or a follow-on project.

The other type of response is to endorse the change. This is achieved by documenting the expected impact on the project, especially in terms of effort, costs, and benefits.

Find an agreement and make a decision

In the event of the contractor endorsing the proposed change, the client takes the estimates on effort and costs incurred as input for its decision to approve or reject the change request. If the client is not willing or able to approve the change, the decision is clear and the change will not be implemented. If the client approves the change, there is no obstacle to implementing it. Often the decision is not so easy, for example, the client is not happy about the estimated costs but still wants the change to be implemented. Disputes between the contractor's and client's project manager on change requests are frequently a major source of trouble in e-business projects. However, in most cases negotiations between the parties lead to an agreement and a final decision. If the final decision on whether the change is implemented is taken, this decision is documented in the change request form. The status of the change request is moved forward – either to 'APPROVED' or 'REJECTED'.

Arrange for implementation

The decision to implement a change is only the first step. In a second step you have to ensure that the approved change is implemented. This starts with revising the project planning documentation to incorporate the change in the project planning. The next step is to communicate effectively the implementation decision to those project stakeholders who need to know about. After this point the day-to-day tracking of proper implementation of the change is performed using the same methods and techniques as for all other project activities. When the implementation activities for a change request are completed, the status in the change request form is moved forward to 'CLOSED'.

10.3.3 Techniques

Change request form

The change request form (see Sect. 10.2.4) is the basic tool for all activities on handling changes.

Change request repository

A change request repository (see Sect.10.2.3) is a tool to store change request forms. It supports the administration and controlled access to the change requests.

10.3.4 Outputs

Decision on implementation

One major output from the analyzing and responding to change request process is the decision on whether or not a proposed change is implemented.

Change request form updated

The change request form is updated, including the response on the change request and the decision taken. The updated change request form is stored in the change request repository.

Project planning documentation revised

The project planning documentation is revised to reflect the change – obviously only in the event that the decision was to implement it.

10.3.5 Key Success Factors

@ 74 Take the courage to reject scope change requests

In e-business projects the majority of change requests that you will receive from your client probably ask for modifying or enlarging the original scope. When an e-business project ignites, there is often a climate of excitement and creativity around the project on the client side. The client team is eager to contribute and to add good ideas. Everyone wants to leave their mark showing creativity and expertise in the e-business field. These contributions usually result in numerous change requests asking for a modification or an enlargement of the original project scope. At first sight you might be happy about this situation, viewing the change requests as an opportunity to get more funding from the client for the overall project. However, change requests asking to alter or to add functionality will add complexity to the project. Before you are aware of it, you and your team have to tackle a project that is two to three times more complex than when it started – with a potential to become unmanageable. And moreover, the client often expects the complete functionality including the changes to be delivered at the originally planned deadline. In order to avoid that heavy scope changes could be the kiss of death for your project, you have to reject many of these change requests.

You might realize that rejecting scope change requests is an unpopular decision. You disappoint at least two project stakeholders: the client is disappointed that you are discarding its 'brilliant' and 'innovative' ideas out of hand. Your senior management is disappointed that you miss the opportunity to generate more revenue for the company. However, accepting all scope change requests is often a recipe for disaster. So, how many change requests can you accept? The two extreme answers to this question are: (1) none – pretend that nothing can be changed and reject all change requests, and (2) all – accept all or the majority of change requests issued. Depending upon the specifics of your project, you have to find the right balance between these two extreme positions.

However, you are responsible for overall project success. If you recognize that accepting additional scope changes would endanger the overall project success, you should be rigid and reject them. It is almost always better to take this unpopular and sometimes painful decision than to jeopardize the whole project.

@ 75 Be careful when accepting small change requests with no price increase

Some change requests you will receive might be rather 'small' – small in terms of effort that is required to implement the change. If such a small change requests come up, you will often be confronted with a statement from the client's project manager such as: "*Look, that's a real small change, the effort involved is not worth mentioning, just a few hours for your team. Let's do it without talking about money. I just awarded a multi-million contract to you, so come on, I do not want to deal with peanuts. Implement it as a no-cost change!*" In principle, the client project manager is correct with regard to the effort. If you compare the costs of the few hours needed to implement a small change with the total contract value, it is really nothing. Nevertheless, you have to think carefully about accepting a change with no price increase, especially the very first one.

Keep in mind that a few hours are needed for one single change, but if you receive 10 such small ones, it sums up to a few days. If you receive 100, it is a few months. Even more might sum up to person-years of effort you have to perform – free of charge for the client. And for sure you will receive a lot of them, so when you accept the very first one you are opening the door for 100 or more that will follow. Accepting a first change request with no price increase is often seen by the client as an invitation for more to follow. You will be snowed under with change requests, keeping you and key members of your team busy. Other project activities will suffer and the overall project is jeopardized.

What can you do to avoid this woefully situation? The answer is simple: do not accept any no-cost change request! Not appealing enough to you? Sometimes this answer is really too simple. If you rigorously reject those changes the relationship with your project management counterpart on the client side might 'cool down' a little bit. What other alternatives do you have? You can put a price tag on any of the small changes, a few hundreds dollars only, more a symbolic value than an exact reimbursement of the real costs. The effect of this strategy is that the client project manager has to approve each small change and to evaluate whether the assigned price tag is adequate. In other words, this puts a lot of work on the shoulders of your counterpart. To be sure, this will calm down significantly the enthusiasm for requesting a lot of small changes.

Another alternative is to encourage the client to collect a bunch of small changes and to put them in one bigger change request. This would give you a better opportunity to calculate a fair price, and to reduce the administrative work on both sides for handling the changes. To summarize: think about the consequences carefully before accepting a small change request with no price increase, especially the very first one.

11 Managing the Subcontractor

The managing subcontractor domain focuses on the management of the relationship between a contractor and its subcontractors. What is a *subcontractor*? A subcontractor is a company that prepares one or several project deliverables on behalf of a contractor. The deliverables are used by a contractor to fulfill its project responsibilities against a client. Normally there is neither a direct relationship nor direct contract between a subcontractor and the client for a project. The subcontractor provides pieces of work that have to be performed in order to deliver a project, but the work is performed on behalf of the contractor. The relationship between contractor, subcontractor, and client is outlined in Fig. 31.

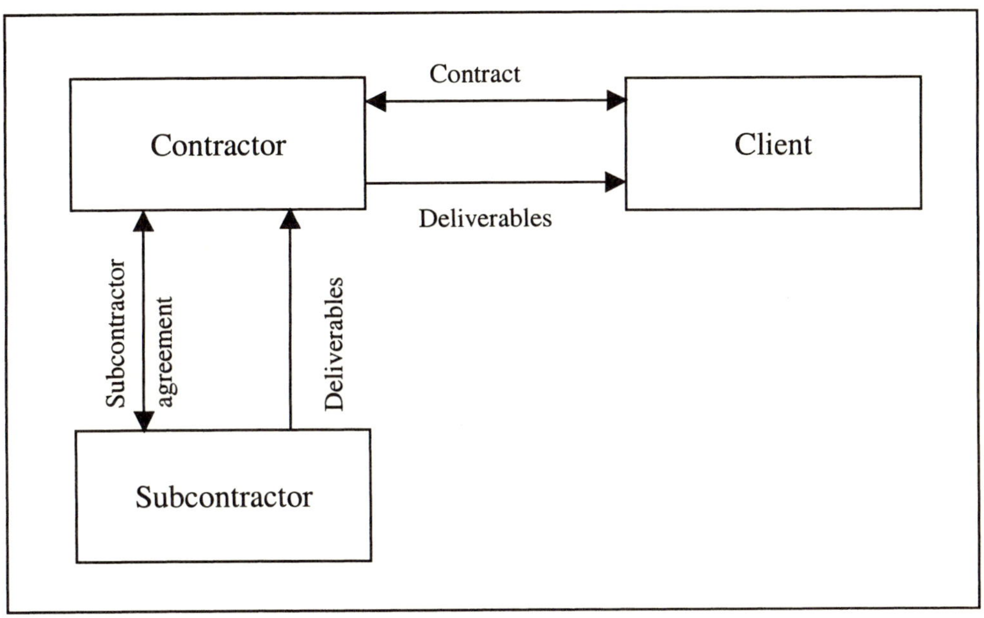

Fig. 31. Contractor, subcontractor, and client relationship

The legal relationship between a contractor and a subcontractor is normally defined in a *subcontractor agreement*. The subcontractor agreement is distinct from the contract that specifies the legal relationship between a contractor and a client. Deliverables produced by a subcontractor are normally delivered to the contractor. The contractor either forwards the deliverables over-the-counter to its client or integrates those with other deliverables to an integrated e-business solution.

In Fig. 31 only a single subcontractor is depicted for the sake of brevity; in an e-business project more than one subcontractor might be assigned by a contractor. In this case the activities, techniques, and recommendations described in the following have to be applied to each of them.

A major characteristics of 'subcontracted work' is that assigned deliverables are provided under the full responsibility of the subcontractor. But the subcontractor is accountable to the contractor and not to the client of a project. To compensate for preparing the deliverables, a subcontractor usually receives a fixed amount of money from the contractor.

A subcontractor has to be distinguished from three other types of suppliers who might also contribute to a project:

1. **Vendor.** A vendor supplies standard software, hardware, or services that are used by a contractor to develop an e-business solution. The main difference between a vendor and a subcontractor is that a vendor offers standard components – often called off-the-shelf products – that are not produced specifically for a specific project. Anyone can buy any number of the standard product from a vendor.
2. **Staff Provider.** A staff provider is a company that places human resources at the disposal of a project to perform project work. The individuals provided are usually integrated into the project staff of the contractor as members of the contractor's project team. While both staff provider and subcontractor have their employees working on a project there is a decisive difference: the people of a staff provider are managed by the contractor while the people of a subcontractor are managed by the subcontractor itself.
3. **Consortium Partner.** A contractor might form with another contractor a *consortium* to deliver a project for a client. In this case each consortium partner performs a part of the total project work. The main difference between a consortium partner and a subcontractor is that a consortium partner is accountable to the client while a subcontractor is accountable to the contractor for performing project work. Moreover, the legal relationship is usually based on a contract between a client and each of the consortium partners. Whereas a subcontractor does not have a contract with a client but instead with the contractor.

Subcontracting work means that a part of the total project work is not performed by a contractor itself but instead given away to someone else. What are typical reasons for a contractor to subcontract work in an e-business environment? Here are just a few:

- **Missing skills.** e-business technology is evolving at a breathtaking speed – nearly every day new technology is invented. If a contractor wants to include a specific e-business technology, the people with specialized skills required to exploit it can neither be found internally nor externally via staff providers. The expert skills are limited to a few companies in which the new technology was invented or developed. As time-to-market is key in e-business, no time for building up the skills in the new technology is available. Or building up skills in this specific technology does not fit into the overall strategy of a contractor. Subcontracting the piece of work to a company in which appropriate know-how is available is sometimes the only solution for this problem.

- **Capabilities shortage.** As the e-business market is booming the order books of many contractors are running over. They are short in capabilities and encounter problems performing all the projects awarded to them. Often they are eager to increase their capabilities but this is a long and tedious effort: people with specific e-business skills are rare and difficult to source. Subcontracting work can be used to overcome capabilities shortages temporarily until the contractor's capabilities are increased to a sufficient level.
- **Single source.** A specific technology that is required for building an e-business solution is provided only by a single supplier. This supplier has a *monopoly* and is not interested in licensing its technology. The only opportunity to exploit the technology in the project is to subcontract the supplier.
- **Lower costs.** Another company is able to provide a piece of work at lower costs than the contractor company – for whatever reason. Subcontracting this piece of work increases the profit of the contractor compared to the situation in which the work would be performed by the contractor itself.
- **Specific tools.** Specific tools (e.g., for creating audio or videos) are required to build an e-business solution and those tools are not available on the contractor side. Purchasing the tools for a single project is an investment that does not pay off for a contractor, and renting, leasing, or licensing the tools is not feasible. Subcontracting a company that has those tools available is the only solution.
- **Shorter project duration.** A particular company is able to provide a piece of work faster than the contractor. Reasons for this might be experience gained in similar projects, access to special focus groups, or specific industry know-how. Subcontracting this company shortens the total project duration.
- **Risk transfer.** Subcontracting a piece of work transfers the risk for delivery to the subcontractor. A contractor can take this approach to reduce its overall project risks.
- **Client request.** A client mandates or dictates that a particular subcontractor must participate in delivering the project. The client might be driven by economic, legal, or political reasons.

However, whether or not to subcontract pieces of project work has to be evaluated carefully by a contractor. Sometimes even the client had to be involved. Some clients insist that all the project work is performed by the contractor itself; other clients want to approve the deployment of subcontractors.

If the decision for subcontracting is taken, two main processes have to be performed: (1) selecting an appropriate subcontractor and agreeing on the terms and conditions under which the subcontracted work is performed, and (2) monitoring a subcontractor in order to ensure that the subcontracted work is performed to the satisfaction of the contractor.

11.1 Selecting a Subcontractor

The main purpose of the selecting a subcontractor process is to source and select a company that is most appropriate for performing the piece of project work that you have decided to subcontract (see Fig. 32). Although selecting a subcontractor is primarily the responsibility of the project manager, normally the procurement department of the contractor company also needs to be involved.

The techniques and procedures for subcontractor selection are often dictated by rules, guidelines, and policies of the procurement department. Selecting a subcontractor works best if it is performed as a joint effort between the project manager and the procurement department, so that the experiences and strengths of both parties are exploited to their best advantage.

The activities and techniques described in the following are based on a commonly performed approach. You may have to adjust the approach to fulfill the requirements of your procurement department or the particular needs of your specific e-business project environment.

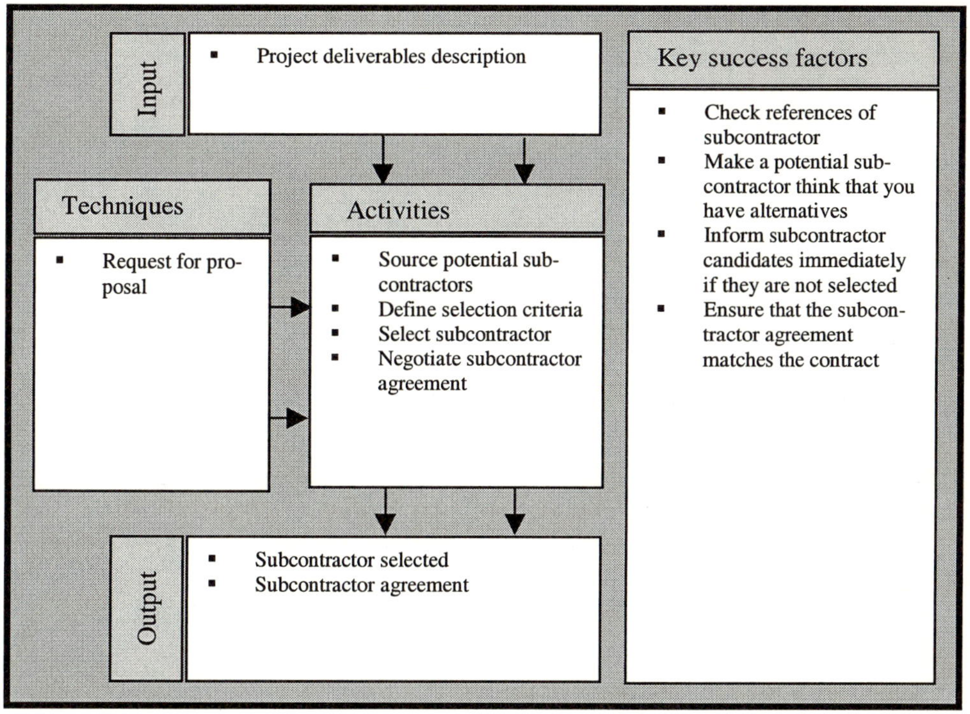

Fig. 32. Selecting a subcontractor

11.1.1 Inputs

Project deliverables description

The input to the selecting a subcontractor process is a description of the pieces of work that a contractor wants to hand over to a subcontractor. Knowing and defining precisely what a subcontractor should deliver is a basic prerequisite for both contractor and potential subcontractor.

For a contractor, the project deliverables description serves as a source for the requirements a potential subcontractor has to fulfill in terms of skills, capabilities, and qualifications. For a potential subcontractor, a deliverables description outlines the pieces of work that have to be performed and delivered to a contractor. Based on this description, a potential subcontractor can identify and evaluate whether or not it is prepared and willing to provide the work on behalf of the contractor.

What pieces of work can be subcontracted? In principle, work can be subcontracted to prepare technical project deliverables as well as to deliver services for a project. But you have to consider that services to be provided are difficult to describe and to control. Therefore, subcontracting is mostly limited to preparing technical deliverables. However, in principle any piece of project work can be handed over to be performed by a subcontractor, with one exception – project management. Project management must remain in the hand of the contractor.

11.1.2 Activities

Source potential subcontractors

Sourcing potential subcontractors is the activity of identifying companies that are both willing and able to perform the work you want to subcontract. The number of potential subcontractors that you can identify heavily depends on the nature of the work to be subcontracted, and might vary from only one to several hundreds. In order to limit the sourcing effort you may stop the activity when you have identified four or five. If you managed to identify at least five potential subcontractors, you have a valid basis for a competitive selection.

What are typical options for obtaining information on where to source appropriate candidates? Here are just a few suggestions:

- **Purchasing department.** Often the purchasing department maintains a short list of companies that have served as subcontractors for your company in previous projects.
- **Experience.** You or members of your team may have experience with adequate subcontractors used in previous projects.
- **Client.** The client can suggest – or sometimes dictate – a particular company to be assigned as subcontractor due to economic, political, or legal reasons.
- **Request for proposal.** A contractor can publish a formal *request for proposal* (see Sect. 11.1.3) and use received proposals as a source for subcontractor selection.

Define selection criteria

If you succeeded in identifying several potential subcontractors, you have to select one of the candidates. To support the selection of the most appropriate candidate, it is good practice to define a set of *selection criteria.* Selection criteria are usually attributes, characteristics, or requirements that are used to evaluate and rate the identified subcontractors. Using objective selection criteria obviously makes the selection process less subjective. In an e-business environment typical selection criteria are:

- **Skills.** The level of skills required to perform the subcontracted work that is available on the subcontractor side. The skills criterion might include but is not limited to technological, management, methodological, or industry specific aspects.
- **Experience.** Whether or not a subcontractor has performed any work packages similar to the current one. Experience from previous, similar projects is a good reference and a valuable indication that a subcontractor is able to perform the kind of work.
- **Price.** The total amount of money a potential subcontractor requests as compensation for taking over the subcontracted work. Normally, subcontracted work is performed on a firm-fixed-price basis.

- **Availability.** The ability of a potential subcontractor to start with the subcontracted work at a point in time that is viewed by the contractor as adequate to complete the work packages in a timely fashion.
- **Working mentality.** The 'mentality' of the subcontractor in terms of working style, atmosphere, methodology, tools, etc., should fit with those of the contractor. A similar working mentality of contractor and subcontractor is often a key factor for successfully working together on a project.
- **Financial health.** The financial health of a potential subcontractor. The financial health of a subcontractor is particularly important if it is a startup company. Given the recent dot-com fallout, there is a high risk that a company without a sound financial position will break, and as a consequence be unable to deliver the subcontracted work.
- **Client preference.** Often a client prefers a particular subcontractor for participation in a project. If a contractor follows the preferences of a client, getting acceptance of project deliverables prepared by the preferred subcontractor might be easier.

The final step in defining selection criteria is to specify the weighting of the criteria in relation to each other, because normally the importance of the defined selection criteria differs from a contractor's perspective.

Select subcontractor

Selecting a subcontractor is the activity of choosing one of the identified subcontractor candidates to perform the project work that you wish to subcontract out. As preparation for taking a decision, you evaluate the subcontractor candidates against the selection criteria. Applying a numeric weighting systems introduces a degree of objectivity into the evaluation procedure: you can identify the subcontractor that best meets the selection criteria.

When a numeric weighting system is not used the evaluation might not be straightforward, but instead iterative. With an iterative approach you reduce the total number of candidates to a short-list of perhaps two or three. In a second step you rate the remaining ones against each other or you establish a ranking order. Requesting additional information from subcontractor candidates, conducting further discussions with the subcontractor's personnel, or visiting the subcontractor facilities are common measures used to support the final selection. It is important that you conduct the selection process in a fair and equitable manner in order to give all competing subcontractor candidates equal chances of winning.

Negotiate subcontractor agreement

When you have selected one of the subcontractor candidates as the one whom you want to assign the subcontracted work, you have to agree on a *subcontractor agreement.* A subcontractor agreement is a formal document that defines the responsibilities of contractor and subcontractor (see Sect. 11.1.4).

Negotiating a subcontractor agreement is the activity of discussing a proposed document until both contractor and subcontractor are willing to sign it in order to approve it formally. In some companies the negotiation activity is primarily performed by the procurement or legal department, and the project manager only supports the activity. However, it is important that you are involved in this discussion, otherwise your colleagues from the procurement or legal departments might accept terms and conditions for performing the work that are not appropriate for successful project execution from your point of view.

The output of the negotiation effort is an approved subcontractor agreement that is a legally binding contract between contractor and subcontractor.

11.1.3 Techniques

Request for proposal

Issuing a RfP is a formal method to source and identify subcontractor candidates. What is a *request for proposal*? An RfP is a procurement document that invites potential subcontractors to register their interest in performing the work to be subcontracted. Usually the RfP is submitted directly to companies that are on the subcontractor short-list of your procurement department. Another option is to publish the RfP in appropriate journals, databases, news groups, or discussion forums in order to achieve a broad circulation.

The format and structure of an RfP is normally defined by the procurement department. A typical RfP contains the following elements:

- The *deliverables description* (see Sect. 11.1.1) of the work to be subcontracted.
- Details on the *terms and conditions* under which the work is expected to be performed.
- A request on *company information* of the potential subcontractor. This may include but is not limited to financial data, skills, experience with similar projects, tools, techniques, methodology, and availability.
- A request on the total *amount of money* that a potential subcontractor expects as compensation for performing the work.
- A specification on the *desired structure and content* of a subcontractor's response to the RfP.

The RfP documentation should on the one hand be rigid and detailed enough to ensure consistent and competitive responses, but on the other hand be flexible enough to allow creative responses that might bring up new aspects that a contractor had not thought of.

Preparing an RfP involves a considerable amount of effort. The same holds true for evaluating the proposals received in response to an RfP. Sourcing potential subcontractors via an RfP is therefore particularly meaningful for e-business projects that are rather big or have a long duration. For smaller e-business projects with a short project cycle, informal sourcing techniques are often the better option.

11.1.4 Outputs

Subcontractor selected
Not surprisingly, one output of the subcontractor selection process is that a subcontractor for performing the work has been selected. Besides deciding on one subcontractor to whom you want to hand over project work, it is important that you can agree with the identified candidate on the terms and conditions under which the work is performed. If you can not achieve a subcontractor agreement you have to enter the selection process again until you find a candidate with whom an agreement can be reached.

Subcontractor agreement
A subcontractor agreement is the outcome of the negotiating subcontractor agreement activity. The subcontractor agreement defines the mutual commitments of contractor and subcontractor and their responsibilities. It is the formal and legal basis for the contractor-subcontractor relationship. Usually a subcontractor agreement contains two main elements:

1. **Statement of work (SoW):** A SoW is composed of a description of the deliverables that have to be provided by the subcontractor, a specification of requirements – for example, level of quality – that have to be met by the prepared deliverables, and a time table when the deliverables have to be handed over to the contractor.
2. **Terms and conditions (Ts & Cs):** Ts & Cs specify mostly legal and administrative aspects of the relationship between contractor and subcontractor. Typical examples of terms and conditions are: payment schedule, copyrights and intellectual properties on deliverables, acceptance procedure and criteria for deliverables, escalation procedure in the case of conflicts, confidentiality in regard to project data, agreement on liquidated damages in the case of non-fulfillment of responsibilities, liability, and warranty.

When a subcontractor agreement is signed and approved by both contractor and subcontractor, it is a legally binding contract.

11.1.5 Key Success Factors

@ 76 Check references of subcontractor

Letting a part of the project work be performed by a subcontractor requires a certain level of confidence that the subcontractor is able to provide the defined deliverables on time and at an acceptable level of quality. If a subcontractor fails to fulfill its responsibilities, normally no financial damages have to be encountered – in this case you simply will not pay the bill. Nevertheless, non-performance or untimely delivery of subcontracted work usually impacts the ability to fulfill your responsibilities to the client of the project.

When selecting a subcontractor, its ability to deliver successfully requires special attention. How can you establish trust that a subcontractor is able to perform a piece of work to your satisfaction? An important indication for a subcontractor's capabilities is when a subcontractor has already performed a similar type of work for your company or for other companies. If a subcontractor was able to complete a similar type of job successfully in the past, there is a reasonable likelihood that it is able to do the same in the future. It is therefore good practice to check the references of a subcontractor before the final selection.

Checking references is easy in the event that the subcontractor has performed similar work for your company. You can simply contact the colleague who was in charge of the respective project and ask how the subcontractor performed. Checking references is a little more complicated and sensitive if the subcontractor performed the work for a competitor of your company. Receiving true and honest statements on subcontractor performance in such a case requires a solid portion of instinct from you.

An alternative to asking a competitor for references might be to take a direct look at previous subcontractor deliverables. For example, if building the front-end of an e-business application was performed by a subcontractor in a previous project, and the e-business solution was launched to the Web, you can simply visit the corresponding web site to get an impression of the subcontractor's work.

@ 77 Make a potential subcontractor think that you have alternatives

When you have succeeded in sourcing several subcontractor candidates, you are in a comfortable position: you can select the best candidate and negotiate a subcontractor agreement. The subcontractor candidates are in a competitive situation and you can compare and rank the candidates to decide upon the most appropriate one. When you – for whatever reason – can not come to an arrangement with the selected company on a subcontractor agreement, you always have the chance to fall-back to the second best candidate and contract this one instead. Having alternatives puts you in a very strong negotiating position.

If you sourced only a single potential subcontractor your position is much weaker – in this situation the subcontractor knows that you do not have any alternative. In this case a subcontractor might offer to perform the work packages on a much higher price and under less comfortable terms and conditions compared to a competitive situation. If a subcontractor knows that you have to arrange with it, the balance of power is clearly on subcontractor side. This situation might force you to accept terms and conditions in the subcontractor agreement that are not balanced in your favor.

In the case that it is really not possible to source more than one potential subcontractor, you should try to avoid that the single subcontractor becomes aware of this fact. If a subcontractor thinks that you have alternatives, the subcontractor might be more inclined to accept compromises when discussing financial, technical, or legal aspects.

However, this is not an invitation for telling lies! Not telling the truth is completely unacceptable and irreconcilable with professional project management behavior. If really no other potential subcontractor can be sourced, there is always a final alternative – doing the work yourself. Normally no one can force you to subcontract work. A contractor always has the opportunity to perform all the work without subcontracting. When negotiating with a potential subcontractor you can mention at least this option.

@ 78 Inform subcontractor candidates immediately if they are not selected

If you have succeeded in sourcing more than one potential subcontractor, you can select one of the candidates to perform the work for a project. As consequence of selecting one candidate the others are not needed for this project. For the candidates who have not been selected this is most probably bad news: they lose potential business.

It is fair business practice to inform the candidates that they have not been chosen immediately after you have taken the selection decision. This allows the not-selected subcontractors to free resources they might have blocked for the opportunity that you offered to them.

In order to have a fall-back alternative available in case you can not come to an arrangement with the selected subcontractor when negotiating the subcontractor arrangement you might keep the second best candidate in a 'hold' position. This means that you tell the subcontractor candidate that it is not your first choice and that the business was awarded to someone else, but that you might come back in case that the negotiations with the selected one fail.

Most potential subcontractors appreciate to be informed about a non-selection as early as possible. This allows them to look out earlier for other business. Some contractors tend to keep potential subcontractors waiting unnecessarily long after the selection decision is taken. They might want to keep all options available until the subcontractor agreement negotiations with the selected subcontractor are finalized – or they are simple too shady to inform the not-selected ones. This is not a fair business behavior, but it still happens. Do not act in such a way! You might not only damage other companies, you might harm yourself. When your practice becomes known in the market – and be sure it will get known if you frequently act in such a way – you will encounter difficulties sourcing qualified subcontractors in the future; they simply will refuse to do business with you. Currently the demand for qualified subcontractors outstrips supply in the e-business market. Despite the tough competition of subcontractors, you can not risk to lose your reputation as a serious business partner. Therefore, inform the not-selected subcontractors immediately.

@ 79 Ensure that the subcontractor agreement matches the contract
Both the subcontractor agreement and contract define work that has to be performed for a project and the conditions under which work results have to be delivered. While the contract specifies the responsibilities a contractor has to fulfill against a client, the subcontractor agreement specifies the responsibilities a subcontractor has to fulfill against a contractor. Ensure that the subcontractor agreement matches exactly with the contract. What does that mean?

To illustrate, consider a situation in which the contract between you and the client contains acceptance criteria for a specific project deliverable. To achieve acceptance from the client on this project deliverable, it has to fulfill the defined acceptance criteria. If you decide to subcontract this project deliverable, it is useful to specify exactly the same acceptance criteria in the subcontractor agreement. This means that you accept the deliverable prepared by your subcontractor only if it fulfills the acceptance criteria. When the subcontractor is able to fulfill the criteria, you accept the deliverable. In this case the deliverable will most probably be accepted by your client when you forward it. If there would be a difference between the acceptance criteria specified in the contract and those specified in the subcontractor agreement, this might result in a situation in which you accept the deliverable from your subcontractor but you do not get the acceptance from your client. In this case you have a serious problem.

To avoid trouble it is good practice to match the subcontractor agreement with the contract. This holds true for all contract elements that are of interest. In particular, the deliverables description, quality and acceptance criteria, and the terms and conditions of the contract should match those specified in the subcontractor agreement. A simple but effective measure to ensure such a matching is to copy the relevant text passages from the contract to the subcontractor agreement.

One aspect deserves special attention: if you agree to deliver a project to a client under a firm-fixed-price contract, you should subcontract work only under the same type of contract. Never arrange for a delivery of subcontracted work on a time-and-material contract while you have to deliver to your client on a firm-fixed-price basis, you might damage your project profit dramatically or even encounter a loss with the project under this contractual circumstance.

11.2 Monitoring a Subcontractor

Selecting a subcontractor and then approving a subcontractor agreement are only the starting points of a contractor–subcontractor relationship. After this a contractor has to ensure that the subcontractor fulfills its defined commitments. Especially the timely delivery of the defined subcontractor deliverables is essential for a contractor, otherwise a contractor might not be able to fulfill its responsibilities specified in the contract with the client. In order to ensure that a subcontractor delivers to the satisfaction of a contractor, the subcontractor has to be monitored and controlled (see Fig. 33).

The degree of control and the effort expended on monitoring a subcontractor depends on the nature of the subcontracted work and the contractor–subcontractor relationship. Influencing factors are, for example, the size and complexity of the subcontracted work, the importance of the subcontracted work to the overall project success, whether or not a subcontractor has performed previous business with a contractor, and the track record of a subcontractor in performing similar work packages.

Many of the project management methods and techniques – described in other chapters of this book – used to monitor and to control the internal project work by a contractor can be applied to monitoring and controlling a subcontractor. However, pay special attention to the fact that the subcontractor staff is not under your direct control. You can not use exactly the same techniques used to monitor the progress of your project team to monitor a subcontractor. A subcontractor performs its work under its own responsibility. Some subcontractors bristle when monitored too tightly. Nevertheless, leaving a subcontractor alone and only contacting it when the deliverables are due is also not the silver bullet.

You have to find the right balance between too much and not enough control. A specific level of uncertainty on the subcontractor progress and its ability to deliver successfully always exists. You should monitor and control the work of a subcontractor at such a level of detail that the remaining risk of subcontractor failure is tolerable to you.

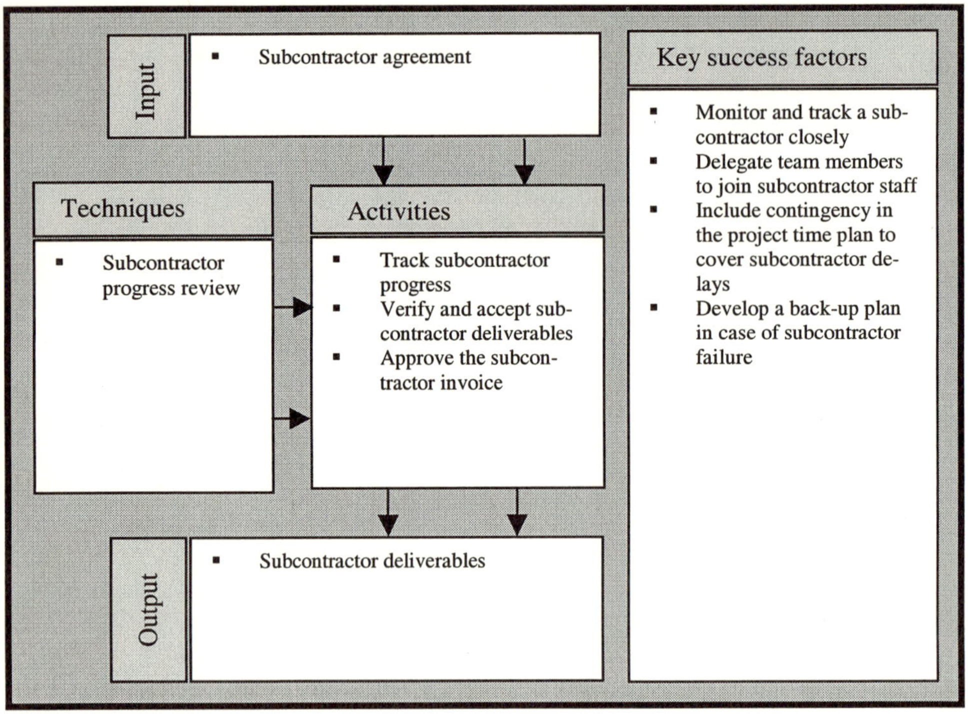

Fig. 33. Monitoring a subcontractor

11.2.1 Inputs

Subcontractor agreement

The fundamental input for the monitoring subcontractor process is the subcontractor agreement. The subcontractor agreement defines the deliverables a subcontractor has to provide, the delivery time, and other aspects that are of relevance for the contractor–subcontractor relationship.

11.2.2 Activities

Track subcontractor progress

A subcontractor prepares the defined deliverables under its own responsibility. Nonetheless, you as the 'client' of the subcontractor can expect to be informed by the subcontractor on its progress. Tracking the subcontractor progress is to assess whether or not a subcontractor will be able to provide the agreed deliverables on time and to the specified level of quality. Continuous tracking reduces the risk that a subcontractor does not fulfill its commitments which might impact upon your ability to deliver the overall project successfully to your client.

How can you track the subcontractor progress? A fundamental prerequisite for effective progress tracking is that you agree with your subcontractor on a detailed work plan along which the subcontracted work should be performed. When preparing the subcontractor work plan, insist on including measurable milestones. Tracking the subcontractor progress can be supported in particular by two measures:

1. You ask the subcontractor to provide you with a regular *status report*. The elements of a report can be rather similar to the elements of the project status report that you submit to your client to report on the overall project progress (see Sect. 12.2.3). The report should be submitted on a weekly or bi-weekly basis to you. It should include a comparison of the planned and achieved progress.
2. You conduct a *subcontractor progress review* meeting (see Sect. 11.2.3) with appropriate subcontractor representatives on a regular basis.

When tracking the subcontractor progress, focusing on time only is not sufficient. Timely delivery is important but the quality of the deliverables must not be neglected. You have to verify that both the process of producing the deliverables and the deliverables itself satisfy your quality expectations.

If you detect a variance between the planned and the achieved subcontractor progress or quality, discuss with the subcontractor how to come back on track.

Verify and accept subcontractor deliverables

After handover of deliverables produced by a subcontractor you have in a first step to verify that those satisfy your needs. You can apply some of the standard quality assurance techniques, such as testing or technical reviews discussed in Sect. 9.2.3, to verify the level of quality of the deliverables. If the deliverables have to be integrated with components that your team prepared, perform or test this integration.

The next step is the formal acceptance of subcontractor deliverables. Evaluate the deliverables carefully against the acceptance criteria defined in the subcontractor agreement. If the acceptance criteria are met, declare and document the acceptance of the subcontractor deliverables formally. Otherwise request the subcontractor to rework the deliverables until the acceptance criteria are met.

Approve the subcontractor invoice

The final activity in a successful contractor–subcontractor relationship is the approval of the subcontractor invoice. When all subcontracted work items have been performed and the deliverables are accepted by a contractor, the subcontractor will probably issue an invoice to the contractor to obtain the agreed compensation for the work.

It is your job to approve the invoice and to authorize your accounts department to pay the agreed amount of money to the subcontractor. Before approval you should verify that all work specified in the subcontractor agreement is successfully completed, the amount of money requested by the subcontractor is identical to the agreed compensation, and that no open issues between you and the subcontractor remain.

11.2.3 Techniques

Subcontractor progress review

A subcontractor progress review is a technique used to ensure that a subcontractor fulfills its responsibility in accordance with a defined work plan. Typically a subcontractor progress review is performed in the form of a meeting at which you discuss the progress with appropriate representatives of the subcontractor. Conducting such meetings regularly – for example weekly – provides you with good information as to whether or not a subcontractor is performing as planned. In addition, you can use such meetings to take a look at intermediate work results and draft versions of deliverables. Moreover, you can ask the subcontractor to demonstrate some of the deliverables to you. Demonstrating tangible deliverables allows a look 'under the surface', thereby avoiding that the subcontractor presents the progress in a brighter light than it is in reality.

Progress review meetings with subcontractor personnel are an excellent opportunity to determine how honest and reliable a subcontractor is.

11.2.4 Outputs

Subcontractor deliverables

The output of the monitoring subcontractor process are accepted subcontractor deliverables that fulfill the quality requirements of a contractor.

11.2.5 Key Success Factors

@ 80 Monitor and track a subcontractor closely

Although a subcontractor normally performs the subcontracted work under its own responsibility, you should monitor and track the subcontractor's progress closely. This is because usually you are highly dependent on a subcontractor – in particular, that you receive its deliverables on time and at the defined level of quality. If a subcontractor is unable to fulfill its responsibilities, this might impact upon your ability to fulfill your project responsibilities to the client. Ensuring that a subcontractor performs as planned is therefore essential. If the planned performance can not be achieved, it is advantageous to become aware of the problem as soon as possible.

Early discovery of problems in delivery of subcontracted work might put you in a position to take appropriate countermeasures to minimize or even eliminate the impact on the overall project. The earlier you discover a problem the better. A close monitoring and tracking of a subcontractor is therefore essential.

@ 81 Delegate team members to join subcontractor staff

If the successful delivery of subcontracted work is absolutely critical to the overall project success, you should not rely on the tracking techniques of regular status reports and subcontractor progress reviews only. Reports and review meetings are only as reliable as the person who prepares the reports and provides you with information in meetings. In the event that you do not fully trust the information conveyed via these media, there is another option: you can delegate one or several of your team members to join the subcontractor staff.

Joining the subcontractor staff means that members of your team work together with subcontractor staff, normally in the facilities of the subcontractor. By working together with the subcontractor team, your people obtain direct insights on status and progress of the subcontracted work. This measure is often taken in a final phase, for example, a few weeks before the date a subcontractor delivery is due.

Nevertheless, you have to select members of your team with adequate skills – technical as well as interpersonal – for this job. Their role is not limited to a 'passive observer'. Instead they should be able to contribute actively to the subcontractor progress. The basic idea is that the subcontractor accepts your people as valuable supporters to bring its work forward and does not view them as 'controllers'.

As a positive side effect this measure is an excellent opportunity for the delegated team members become familiar with the subcontractor deliverables. Know-how can be transferred from the subcontractor staff to your staff. This helps especially in the case that the subcontractor deliverables are not forwarded directly from you to your client, but instead an integration with components that you produce takes place. This might to some extent compensate the costs incurred on your side associated with delegating members of your team to join the subcontractor staff, because usually a subcontractor will object to reimbursing the costs incurred by this measure.

@ 82 Include contingency in the project time plan to cover subcontractor delays

When building up the overall project time plan (see Sect. 3.1.4) it is good practice to include some contingency to cover potential subcontractor delivery delays.

Despite careful monitoring and tracking of a subcontractor, it can happen that a subcontractor is unable to provide its deliverables by the agreed point in time. When you schedule follow-on activities to subcontractor deliveries in the overall project time plan in such a way that those follow the planned subcontractor delivery immediately, a delayed subcontractor delivery impacts the overall project schedule.

An impact can be lessened, or even completely avoided, if you include an appropriate contingency in the overall project schedule. Contingency in this context means that you include a buffer in terms of slack time between the planned date of a subcontractor delivery and the start date of a dependent activity. In the event that the subcontractor delivery is really delayed, the impact on the overall project schedule is minimal or null. The magnitude of the impact depends on the size of the buffer and the dimension of the encountered delay.

Determining the size of the buffer is more an art than a science. A general recommendation for the amount of slack time can not be given. Influencing factors might be the level of trust you have in the subcontractor's capabilities and the importance of the subcontractor deliverables to the overall project success.

@ 83 Develop a back-up plan for subcontractor failure

Subcontracting work implies always a certain level of uncertainty. You can never be sure whether a subcontractor delivers in time – or delivers at all. The impact caused by a late delivery can be lessened by appropriate contingency planning. Contingency planning does not help much in the event that a subcontractor fails completely to perform the subcontracted work. Although such a situation does not happen very often, it does happen. In order to be prepared for such a situation, it is good practice to develop a back-up plan.

A back-up plan identifies options that can be taken in the event that a subcontractor fails. Possible options are, for example, handing over the defined work to another subcontractor, performing the work within your team, or negotiating with the client to reduce the project scope by the subcontracted deliverables. However, you have to be aware of that an appropriate back-up plan can support minimizing the impacts on the overall project. But normally a subcontractor fallout is such a significant event that a complete avoidance of the impact is seldom possible. Here the same principle as for other project problems holds true: the earlier you recognize that a subcontractor is likely to fail and the earlier you can implement the measures of the back-up plan, the smaller that the overall consequences to the project most probably will be.

12 Managing Communications

Communication is a critical success factor for e-business projects. According to PMI, project managers spent about 90% of their time acquiring and communicating information [32]. In an e-business project you have to communicate throughout the day. You have to spend many hours in meetings with your team, the client, subcontractors (if any), and senior management, to name just a few. You have to inform the stakeholders on project status and progress. You have to send and respond to e-mails and written reports. You give and receive phone calls and you take part in conference calls. You might do a good job in all other management domains, such as motivating the team, delivering good results, making the schedule, but poor communication – especially to the outside stakeholders – can negate all the things you are doing right. If you are not able to convey the right information in a proper form to the right people at the correct point in time, you simply lose.

Managing communications consists of the processes *planning communications* and *performing communications*. Performing communications is mainly requesting information and delivering information to the project stakeholders. This includes all activities that ensure the timely and proper generation, preparation, dissemination, and storage of information. A prerequisite for proper delivery of information *to* the stakeholders are adequate requests for input information *from* the stakeholders.

Another aspect that must be considered in disseminating information is the proper receipt of information. According to Robert Fulmer [11], one of the most common pitfalls of communications is the assumption that because a message was sent, a message must have been received. Moreover, communications is more than getting a single message across. Managing communications includes building and maintaining communication paths with all project stakeholders.

12.1 Planning Communications

The purpose of planning communications is defining and specifying how the communications requirements of the project stakeholders can be satisfied. This includes identifying who needs what information, when the information is required, and the form in which the information is delivered (see Fig. 34). While in all e-business projects a need for communicating information exists, the communications requirements of stakeholders and the methods and techniques to convey information vary widely.

Identifying the project stakeholders, analyzing their communications requirements, and determining the best way to deliver information are important project management activities. The result of this identification, analysis, and determination should be documented in a *project communications plan*. The project communications plan (see Sect. 12.1.4) supports you in the following way:

- Identifying and understanding the communications requirements of the project stakeholders.
- Achieving a clear understanding among the stakeholders when, how, and in which form they are provided with information.
- Determining your activities and your effort necessary to satisfy the communications requirements of the project stakeholders.

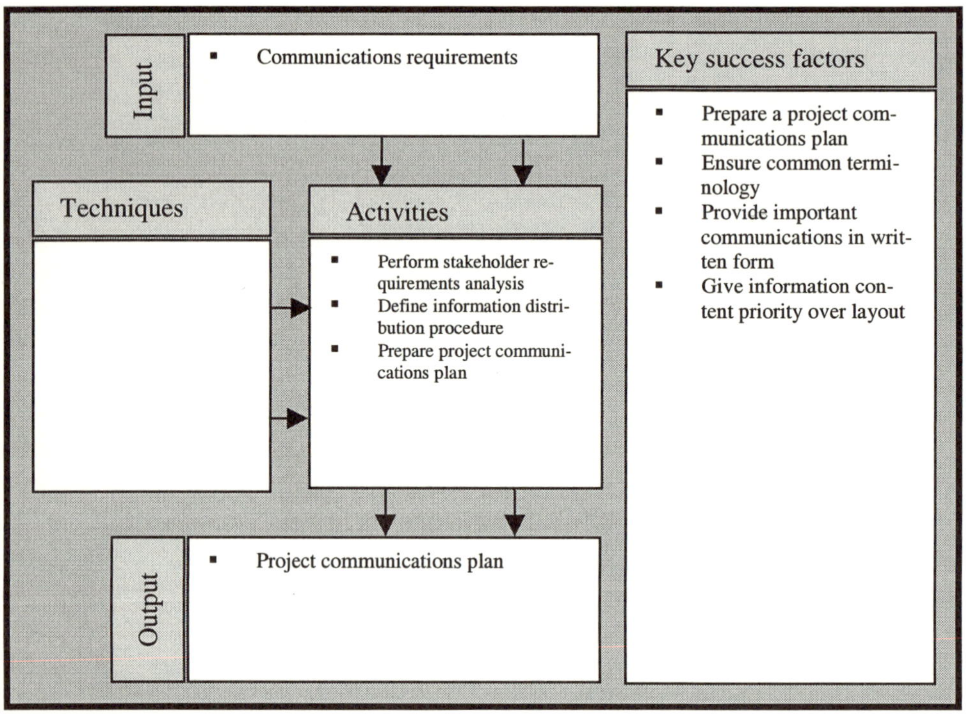

Fig. 34. Planning communications

12.1.1 Inputs

Communications requirements

Communications requirements are the entirety of the information requirements of the project stakeholders. Some communications requirements might already be determined by other project planning material like the WBS, project time plan, staffing plan, the contract with the client, or subcontractor agreements. Some communications requirements might be obvious and can be derived from the defined project organization structure. Other communications requirements might be not so obvious. They must be determined as part of the communications planning process by analyzing the needs of the project stakeholders. The communications requirements are the input for defining the *information distribution procedure*.

12.1.2 Activities

Perform stakeholder requirements analysis
The communications requirements of all project stakeholders should be analyzed systematically in order to define an appropriate information distribution procedure that satisfies their communications needs. What are project stakeholders? Project stakeholders are individuals or organizations who are involved in the project or who might be affected positively or negatively as a result of project execution. What are the major stakeholders of an e-business project? Besides yourself, you typically find the following stakeholders:

- **Project team.** The people you recruited and assigned to a project to perform the defined work.
- **Client.** The organization or company that contracted your company to perform a project. The key person on the client side is the *client project manager*.
- **Senior management.** High-level managers in the company for which you serve as project manager.
- **Subcontractor (if any).** The organization you contracted to perform pieces of work.

In addition to those four key stakeholders their might be several others. It is important to identify all of them and to analyze carefully their requirements. When the stakeholder requirements are analyzed, for each stakeholder communications objectives are defined as target that should be accomplished by proper communications.

Define information distribution procedure
Define for the project stakeholder an *information distribution procedure*. The information distribution procedure should cover:

- What information (including level of detail) is distributed to whom.
- When the information is distributed and who is responsible for the distribution.
- Which distribution media is used. Examples of typical distribution media for conveying information in e-business projects includes but are not limited to e-mail, face-to-face, meeting, facsimile, phone call (individual and conference), voice mail, project site, team room, database, online chat facility, pager, SMS, and video conferencing.

Prepare project communications plan

Preparing a project communications plan (see Sect. 12.1.4) is the activity of documenting the results of the stakeholder communications requirements analysis and the procedure of distributing information. The produced project communications plan should be discussed and agreed on with all relevant project stakeholders, especially the external ones. Every stakeholder must understand how the communications that he or she is involved in as an individual impacts or contributes to the project success.

Preparing the project communications plan is usually performed at an early stage of a project. However, things might change during the course of a project: therefore it is good practice to review the project communications plan from time to time, and to revise it if necessary.

12.1.3 Techniques

None.

12.1.4 Outputs

Project communications plan

The project communications plan resulting from the communications planning activities might be formal or informal, high-level or detailed, and based on the specific characteristics of the e-business project. A project communications plan is a document that typically provides the following information:

- A brief description on the general project communications objectives and strategy.
- A list of assumptions about project factors that are uncertain but have been considered as true or certain for planning purposes.
- Definition and clarification of specific terms that will be used in distributing information to ensure that all stakeholders have a common understanding regarding terminology.
- A list of the stakeholders that are of relevance for information distribution, and a summary of their communications requirements and communications objectives.
- Prerequisites with regard to technology that must be available on the stakeholders side in order to receive distributed information efficiently, e.g., specific conference software, links to project web site, access to project team room, e-mail software, and network access.
- The information distribution procedure (see Sect. 12.1.2) detailing which information is distributed to whom, when, and via which distribution media.
- A description of the information to be distributed in terms of format, structure, content, level of detail, and conventions used. Templates for typical communications documentation, such as meeting minutes, agendas for meetings, and project status reports might be included.

- A description of the responsibility of the project stakeholders when they receive project information. For example, meeting minutes should be approved and signed by the client project manager, sensitive project information should be kept confidential, etc.
- A description of what distributed information is stored or archived for later use, including conventions for structure and naming, the location, and the media where and in which format different types of information are stored or archived.
- A description of information that must be provided, produced, or collected by stakeholders: e.g., labor reports by team members and status reports by subcontractors. Appropriate templates for those reports might be included.
- The method for updating the project communications plan if it must be changed during the course of the project, including an indication on who is authorized to perform such updates.

12.1.5 Key Success Factors

@ 84 Prepare a project communications plan

Prepare a project communications plan – this sounds obvious and the entire section of this book provides you with guidance how you can master it. However, I have seen many e-business projects where a project communications plan was not prepared. I have heard arguments such as: "*The project is too short*", "*The project is too small*", "*It's administrative overhead*", and "*It's obvious how we communicate, there is no need for writing it down*". In fact, most e-business projects are short, many are small, preparing a project communications plan involves effort, and some communications items might be obvious, but are those valid reasons for objecting to a plan? Effective communications is essential and must be planned – also in short and small e-business projects. It might not be obvious to all stakeholders in every situation how communications in a project is performed.

What are compelling reasons for preparing a project communications plan? I see three major ones. First, all project stakeholders can obtain a clear understanding on the communications topic by reading the plan. Under ordinary circumstances this is more efficient than briefing each stakeholder about communications individually. Second, having a communications plan available in written form is a solid basis for negotiating and agreeing with outside stakeholders (client, subcontractor) on the information flow. Third, preparing the communications plan supports you in clarifying and understanding the communications requirements of the stakeholders so that you can, on the one hand, perform the communications activities in a proper manner and, on the other hand, calculate the effort required for these activities. Preparing a project communications plan really pays off, even if your project is small and short.

@ 85 Ensure common terminology

e-business projects normally involve stakeholders from a variety of disciplines. This starts with your team that is usually composed of people from creative, IT, consulting, and marketing disciplines. It continues with the client where often several business units or departments such as IT, marketing, accounting, production, and sales are involved. And you might have software vendors, marketing companies, Internet agencies, or others as subcontractors. Every discipline has its own specific language and terminology.

When communicating with different stakeholders you have to ensure that they understand you and that you understand them. It is essential that information is not disseminated only to the stakeholders – it must be received as well. Sometimes the same term is used by people of different disciplines, but the term has a different meaning for them – often the recipe for trouble. You can reduce misunderstandings in communicating with the stakeholders by ensuring a common terminology and clarifying the meaning of terms.

A project communications plan is an excellent place for defining critical terms that might have a different meaning for stakeholders. By defining terms you can ensure a common terminology for the project. This will probably ease communications significantly. If a common terminology can not be achieved in your project, make sure at least that all people mean the same thing regardless of what words they use.

@ 86 Provide important communications in written form

Communications can be formal or informal, written or verbal. For certain communications – the important ones – you should prefer the written form. What is the benefit of the written form? It is rather simple: you can prove that the communications have taken place and you can verify what was communicated. Both aspects can be hard to achieve when the communication is performed verbally. However, that does not mean that you should perform *all* communications in written form. There are many situations in which the verbal form is of advantage. The art and challenge is to decide which communications to do in written and which in verbal form.

Not surprisingly, the written form should be preferred in the case of important communications. But what is important communications? There is not always a perfect answer; it depends heavily on the specific characteristics of your project at to what communications is important. In general you should prefer written communications in the following situations: (1) when you have to inform your client or your senior management on aspects that have major consequences for the project, e.g., schedule slippage, quality problem, and costs overrun; (2) to remind a client or a subcontractor about fulfillment of its responsibilities; and (3) to document major decisions or agreements. There are numerous other situations where it is good practice to perform communications in written form or to protocol afterwards what was communicated verbally previously. If you are in any doubt about whether to communicate in written or verbal form, choose the written form.

@ 87 Give information content priority over layout

In e-business projects a lot of project management-related aspects have to be documented or presented in written form. Project status reports, notes, memos, meeting minutes, and presentation slides are only a few examples where you have to put down information in written form. To prepare information in written form consists of producing the information content and of arranging the content in terms of format and style: i.e., doing the 'layout'. Often people put too much emphasis on the second part – the layout – in written communications. This holds true especially for presentation slides.

Some people believe that they have to present slides of the same level of layout quality as the screens they design for the e-business solution. Once a project manager told me when I saw him preparing slides: "*We spent a lot of time to design the screens for the site of the e-business solution. We are dealing with fancy graphics the whole day. I can not present the status of the project using a presentation with a clumsy layout. This might give a wrong impression on our capabilities. I have to show and prove the creativity and e-business competence of the team and myself by producing slides that look as professional as the designed screens.*" In preparing the presentation he spent about 10% of the time thinking about the content and 90% designing the layout.

My recommendation is to give information content priority over layout in written communications. Otherwise, what might be the consequences when you emphasize on layout – format and style – instead of content? First, arranging the content is a time-consuming activity. You can spent days making a document or a presentation really fancy looking – days that are no longer available for other project management activities. Getting bogged down in layout details will distract you from more important work. Second, if you put a lot of effort in preparing a nice looking document or presentation once, the audience expects that you will keep this level in the future. If you are short in time when you prepare the next documents and presentations, your audience most probably will be disappointed by the outcome; you are not able to meet their high expectations. Third, people who read the documentation and slides might become suspicious about you and the project. They may think "*What's going on in this project, does the project manager have not enough serious work to do so that he or she can spent so much time in preparing fancy documents and slides?*" It is better to spend more time in thinking about the content of the information than in arranging the layout. However, this does not mean that the information layout can be neglected completely. Some effort must be invested to present information in a proper format and style, but this effort should have a healthy relationship with the effort invested in preparing the information content. It is up to you to find a balanced approach that is adequate for your project.

12.2 Performing Communications

The main purpose of performing communications is to keep the project stakeholders informed in a timely manner (see Fig. 35). A lack of proper project communications is often the cause of unsuccessful or abandoned projects. A recent survey indicates that nearly one-third of all IT projects in major companies are abandoned before completion, and of those that are completed nearly two-third suffer from project schedule slippage and cost overruns [31]. Poor communications among project stakeholders was identified as the main cause of the problems.

The techniques and tools for communications in e-business projects do not differ much from those used in other projects. The important point to mention here is that e-business projects require an extra portion of communications. When planning the project activities you should keep in mind that a lot of time needs to be retained for communications – especially your time, because performing communications is mainly a project manager's job.

Performing communications can be divided in two categories: *formal* and *informal* communications. Formal communications mostly takes place in written form in terms of project status reports, formal letters, and change requests. But it can also be performed verbally, for example, in meetings or phone calls. Formal communications is often used when exchanging information with clients and subcontractors. Informal communications takes place throughout the project and includes face-to-face talks, conversations before or after formal meetings, maintaining an 'open-door-policy', walking around in the project area, informal phone calls, etc. Informal communications is mostly used when communicating with the project team. Informal communications might provide you with insights about the project that you might otherwise not recognize.

Formal as well as informal communications can happen *planned* or *event-driven*. Examples of planned communications are project status meeting with the client on a regular basis, biweekly status reports, regular conference calls to brief senior management, etc. Event-driven communications is 'ad hoc' in nature and is triggered by unexpected project events. The characteristics of event-driven communications is that it can not be planned when this type of communications takes place. Events that trigger this type of communications are situations like: the client can not fulfill its responsibility, a severe bug is detected in the code of the e-business application, interpersonal conflicts in the project team came up, a change request is received, etc.

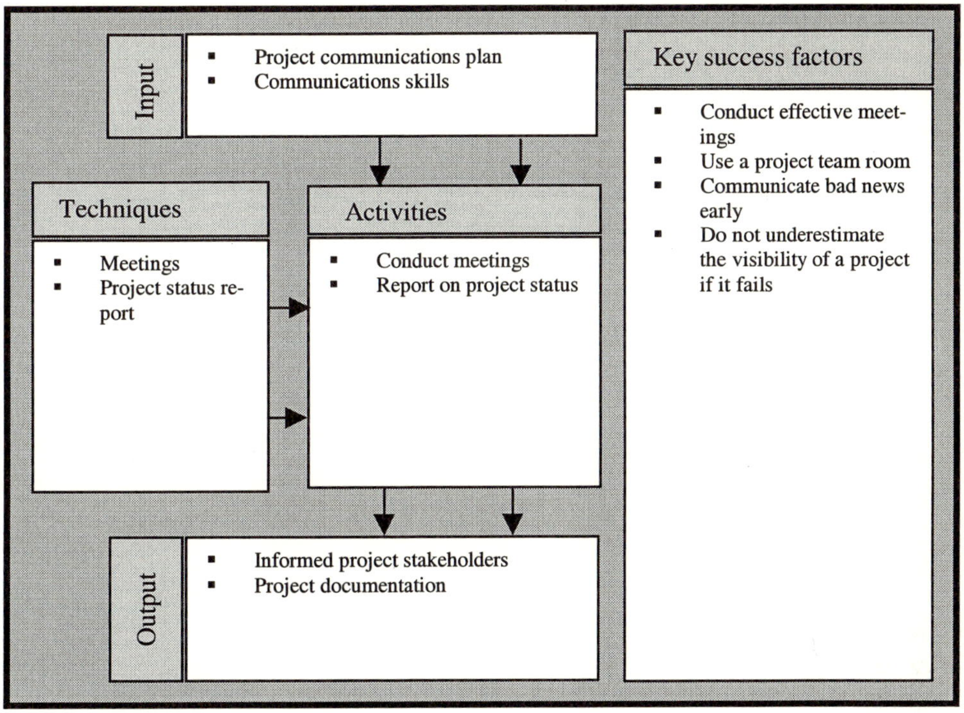

Fig. 35. Performing communications

12.2.1 Inputs

Project communications plan

The project communications plan provides you with the framework for performing communications. However, it is an outline only that you can use as input to support your activities. There might be situations or circumstances where sticking to the plan is the wrong approach. Communications has a lot to do with common sense and the right 'feeling' for a situation. The project communications plan is a good way of informing the project stakeholders about the way communications are planned to happen in the project. The plan is the basis for communications activities, but it is not a replacement for performing the communications.

Communications skills

Good communications skills are essential for e-business project managers. Communications skills are the entirety of a person's ability and capability to exchange information. Some people possess excellent interpersonal communications skills by nature, others need to be trained or learn by themselves to become effective communicators. In general it is the project manager's job to act as a communications expediter by bringing people together and initiating relationships for informal communications. Communications between people from different disciplines – IT, marketing, consulting, or creative – often needs extra encouragement. Improving your communications skills is a valuable investment that will pay off.

12.2.2 Activities

Conduct meetings

Conducting effective meetings has been recognized as one of the cornerstones of successful project management for many years. This recognition holds true for e-business projects as well. What are the critical factors for conducting an effective meeting? First, a meeting must be prepared. This includes but is not limited to arranging the meetings logistics (e.g., room, accommodation, and technology), developing a meeting agenda, inviting the participants and providing them with documentation, and preparing the material to be distributed, presented, or discussed during the course of the meeting. Second, the meeting itself should be conducted in an effective manner. This can be supported by establishing a meeting policy, assigning meeting roles, managing the meeting in the allotted time, and keeping the conversation relevant to the meeting topic and objectives. Third, the main discussion points, results, and decisions taken or achieved in the meeting should be documented in the meeting minutes. This ensures that all participants later have the same understanding on the discussed topics, and people who could not attend the meeting have the chance to get information about the meeting's outcome by reading the minutes.

Report on project status

Another important communications activity is reporting on project status and progress. The purpose of the reporting is to inform the relevant project stakeholders on project performance. The reporting usually includes information on the current status, indicating where the project stands now, describing what has been accomplished, and giving a forecast of the future.

Often the reporting is performed via written *project status reports* (see Sect. 12.2.3), but it can also be performed verbally, for example using a presentation. The form, the information content, and the frequency of reporting varies depending on the nature of the project, its characteristics, and the audience for which the reporting is intended. Often reporting is performed on a regular basis: weekly or monthly. The main audience for written status reports are the client and your senior management.

12.2.3 Techniques

Meetings

Meetings are one of the major techniques used by a project manager to receive and distribute information. The participants of meetings can be internal or external stakeholders.

Besides you, a meeting can involve only one, a few, or many persons, depending on the characteristics and objectives of a meeting. Meetings can be categorized by their objectives. *Information* meetings deal with collecting and distributing information. They are mainly used to update the project team, the client, or senior management on project status and progress. The very first meeting with the project team is normally called the 'kick-off' meeting (see Sect. 4.3.3). *Technical* meetings are used to discuss technical questions mainly internally with the team or externally with the client, where 'technical' topics are not limited to IT topics. In these meetings all project-related topics from the marketing, creative, and consultant areas are addressed. These meetings are used to resolve technical problems or to take technical decisions. *Interpersonal* meetings are mainly used for team-building purposes to motivate and praise the project team, to ensure the personal commitment of the project staff.

Sometimes meetings can have multiple objectives. Meetings can be scheduled on a regular basis, for example, having a project status meeting with the client on a weekly basis, or spontaneously triggered by a specific event, for example, when a technical problem is discovered or a change request is received.

Project status report

A project status report is a written document describing the actual status of a whole project or parts of it. Often it includes information on achievements accomplished within a certain reporting period and an outlook to the future. Project status reports are usually created by the contractor project manager for its senior management or for the client. But preparing a report is only one side of the coin. You can also request your subcontractors, if any, to provide you with information on their work via status reports. In this case you are the receiver and reader of status reports. The content and form of project status reports depends on the specifics of a project. Normally the following information is included in a project status report:

1. Information on scope, schedule, costs, quality, and risks. Typically the report covers the past with a comparison of plan versus actuals, including an explanation for deviations, if any, and an outlook to the future. The information on costs can be in form of graphs, in order to show trends clearly.
2. Major accomplishments achieved during the reporting period in terms of milestones, deliverables, issues resolved, actions taken, and risks handled.
3. Project statistics regarding risks, change requests, errors, and issues that have been raised, resolved, or fixed. Usually the statistical data is provided for a specific reporting period as well as the cumulative project-to-date.
4. An overall status rating to summarize the status of the project, for example, in the form of a 'green', 'yellow', and 'red' light color scale.

The level of detail in which a report is written depends on the audience of the report. For senior management often a short summary report is preferable. A more detailed report can be provided as an appendix for those who are interested to more detail.

12.2.4 Outputs

Informed project stakeholders

The output of the communications efforts are well-informed project stakeholders. However, communications activities are not a one time event – communications must be performed throughout the course of a project. The aim is that all project stakeholders are continuously well informed about all aspects of a project that are of relevance to them. Well-informed project stakeholders are a prerequisite to project success.

Project documentation

Project communications in written form is an important element of project management documentation in terms of project records. Archiving the relevant project communications, for example, project status reports, meeting minutes, presentations, letters, notes, and memos allows others to trace the history of the project also long after its completion. A clean and complete set of project records is a good indication of professionalism and operational excellence of a project manager.

12.2.5 Key Success Factors

@ 88 Conduct effective meetings

Conduct effective meetings! This is easier said than done. According to a PMI survey an average of 25% of meeting time is spent on non-productive items [32]. What can you do to make a meeting effective and productive? First, you should call for a meeting only when there is a need to. Too often meetings are held only because a regular meeting schedule was set up, but nothing substantial has to be communicated. Such meetings are a waste of time – they simply should not take place. Second, it is important that the right people are invited and that they attend the meeting. Often, too many people are participating who can neither contribute something valuable nor need to get informed via a meeting. Do not invite those people. A meeting is more productive and effective when less people are attending. Nonetheless, there is another extreme, when people who are required to contribute or receive information are not invited, or do not attend a meeting when they are invited. When inviting people to a meeting obtain a commitment from the key persons that they will attend. Otherwise it is better to cancel or postpone the meeting.

A critical factor for effectiveness is meeting preparation. Ensure that an agenda is distributed in advance, that meeting documentation is disseminated prior to the meeting, and that the meeting logistics in terms of room availability, required technology (e.g., pointer, overhead projector, and Internet connection), and accommodation is organized. Frequently not all attending people arrive on time; do not wait for people. It is absolutely unproductive for a big group of people to wait for a few that arrive late – for whatever reason. Begin the meeting on time, and the missing participants can drop in later. During the meeting it is important to follow the agenda. Too often, an agenda is distributed prior to the meeting or agreed on at the beginning but during the course of the meeting the discussion is driving in different directions. It is your responsibility to keep the meeting on track.

Sometimes action items or issues can not be resolved within a meeting. They are documented in meeting minutes as open points or actions that should be resolved or performed at a later point. Too often, no one acts upon the documented items. It is good practice to assign each such item to a responsible person and to fix a plan date for completion or resolution. This supports you in following-up on these items and verifying that they are handled afterwards.

@ 89 Use a project team room

Use a project team room to boost communications with your team members. What is a *project team room*? A project team room is a piece of project management software that supports asynchronous communications. A lot of companies are now offering software that allows you to interact with team members. Usually this kind of software is called 'groupware'. A team room is simply a single centralized location where information in electronic form can be published and accessed. This is an excellent technique to share information with your team members at different times but through a common medium. The project team room can serve as a centralized data repository, discussion forum, or knowledge database.

Usually a project manager puts information into a team room while the team members read it. However, this is not a strict rule. When a sufficient level of discipline can be assured, there is no reason why team members should not also add information. What information should you put into a team room? Generally, all project management information that you would like to share with the team can be placed here. Project status reports, meeting minutes, project time plans, action lists, achievements, team recognitions, and news to name just a few are expedient candidates for storage in a team room.

When using a team room for communications you should keep two aspects in mind. First, a team room needs a structure. Especially in big and long projects, a lot of information comes up and is expedient for storing in a team room. If the team room is not well structured, you can put in a lot of information but the team members might have problems finding what is relevant for them. Second, establishing and maintaining a team room involves effort. As most of the information is put in by yourself, especially you need to reserve some time for maintaining the information in the team room. Remember, a team room is only as good as the information in it. However this investment in effort pays off.

What are the main advantages of using a team room? First, it is its asynchronous communications capability – the team members can access information whenever it is most convenient for them. This is one major advantage compared to synchronous communications media like meetings and phone calls. Second, on the assumption that the team room is well structured, the people can select and read only the information they are interested in. This is an advantage compared to communications media like e-mail. Team members are often buried with e-mails whether or not they like to receive them. Of course one can skip reading an e-mail, but to recognize whether it contains something of interest one has to take at least a look at it. In addition, a team room decreases your effort, because you have to send fewer e-mails. Information such as project status reports, meeting minutes, and action lists that you normally would have sent via e-mail to your team members can now be made known to the them by putting it in the team room.

@ 90 Communicate bad news early

Communicating good news is an easy job. Normally, the receivers of the information appreciate getting positive news and you, as delivering the information, will be loved. When you have to communicate bad news, the situation is completely different. 'Bad news' here is seen as information about a situation in a project that has a significant negative consequence or impact on the project success. Typical situations are cost overruns, schedule slippage, subcontractor failures, promotion fallout, or quality problems. You have to inform the client and your senior management about such situations. What is the best point in time for communicating bad news? It is as early as possible – do not delay the delivery of bad news. You might think about postponing the communications based on the assumption or hope that the situation will improve – it seldom does. The 'head-in-the-sand' attitude does not help you much in such a situation. Also countermeasures or recovery plans are rarely successful.

The principle of communicating bad news as early as possible holds true for internal as well as external stakeholders. Neither the client nor your senior management likes to receive bad news. However, there is only one thing they dislike more: when they are not informed or informed with a delay! After delivery of the information you might have tough times. And some people like to 'shoot the messenger'. Nevertheless, it is absolutely your job to deliver the bad news. You should never delegate this job to a team member or let the information spread around as rumors. Rumors are often worse than the actual situation.

You should communicate bad news in an open, honest, and clear manner. When both internal and external stakeholders need to be informed, it is good practice to inform the internal ones (like senior management) first and external ones (like the client) second. This helps to avoid the woeful situation that the client's senior management calls yours – and your bosses do not know anything about what is going on. They are ambushed by a client and hear that there seems to be a major problem in your project. Surprising your senior managers is another example of a situation that is better avoided.

What is the best form to communicate bad news – written or verbal? I recommend to deliver bad news verbally whenever possible. From my perspective it is better to provide such information in a face-to-face talk or in a phone call rather than to write a formal note, letter, or memo about it. Communicating bad news verbally has the advantage that the receiver has a chance to ask questions about the situation which you can address immediately. This can help the receiver to get a better understanding on the real criticality of the situation. And giving the information in verbal form does not prevent you to from providing it in written form afterwards.

@ 91 Do not underestimate the visibility of a project if it fails

When you manage an e-business project you will of course struggle to make it a success. However, the Gartner Group forecasts that through 2002, 75% of all e-business projects will fail [12]. I hope that by considering the key success factors discussed in this book you will not find your project on the list of unsuccessful ones. Nevertheless, there is no absolute guarantee that a project will be successful. It might happen – for whatever reason – that your project fail.

If an e-business project fails, the visibility might be overwhelming. What are reasons for this extreme visibility? First, e-business projects usually involve many departments and organizations on the client side. While traditional IT projects are normally known only to a few people in the IT department, e-business projects are often recognized at the executive management level. If such a project fails, the whole client company might be affected and many people on the client side are aware of the failure. Second, e-business projects, especially those building B2C solutions, can have an extremely large number of end-users as audience. If the e-business solution produced by a project is launched on the Web and afterwards the solution turned out not to meet the end-users expectations, a lot of people will be disappointed. You can expect a similar level of awareness if an announced launch date can not be met and the start of production must be postponed. Be sure that you will have a large audience commenting on the failure. In particular, competitors of the client love to draw attention to failed projects and the media publishes those situations with great passion. Many failed e-business projects get into the news headlines.

In the case of failure often no one is really asking for the reason. The client will simply blame the contractor, making it responsible for the failure. Clear, open, and honest communications with all stakeholders – especially the client and the media – will help you to overcome or lower the negative impression.

13 Managing Documentation

Managing documentation is a domain that is often neglected in modern project management – especially in an e-business environment. Many people view documentation as an unnecessary left-over from brick-and-mortar businesses. From their perspective dealing with documentation – often dismissed as 'paper' – is a waste of time and money and no longer useful in an 'e-world'. Taking a look at modern work places and office desks gives a different impression: more paper is produced and used than ever before – the latest statistics on paper consumption prove this fact. We are still far from the idea of a 'paperless office', propagated in the early eighties. Moreover, 'paper' is not the only format for documentation – documentation might come also in electronic format.

Documentation is still an essential communication medium in the day-to-day business of a project manager – also in e-business projects. What is *project documentation*? Project documentation is any information available in written form that is required or supports to perform a project.

Managing documentation is the process to deal with all kinds of project documentation in a proper way. Specific project planning documentation – for example, the project time plan, change management procedure, risk management plan, and communications plan – are explicitly discussed in other chapters of this book. The remaining documentation can be divided in two categories: (1) *technical* project documentation and (2) *legal* project documentation. For each category a separate process is discussed in the following.

13.1 Managing Technical Documentation

Managing technical documentation is the process of dealing with project documents that do not address the legal relationship of a contractor with its client or with its subcontractors. What is *technical* project documentation?

Based on the origin and the purpose it has to serve technical project documentation can be structured in three classes: (1) Documentation that serves as input to perform a project. Usually those documents are supplied by a client to a contractor. Examples are technical specifications, standards, description of e-business strategy, business process description, and marketing brochures. (2) Documentation that is produced by a project as a deliverable that has to be handed over to a client. Typical examples are the administrator handbook, style guide, installation manual, and training material. (3) Documentation that is produced by a project and used internally by a contractor to perform the project work.

Typical examples are the internal design description, navigation concept, content plan, and lessons learned.

Objective of the managing technical documentation process is to ensure that all classes of technical project documentation are handled in a proper way in the interest of the project (see Fig. 36). Managing technical documentation is a process that has to be performed continuously throughout the course of a project.

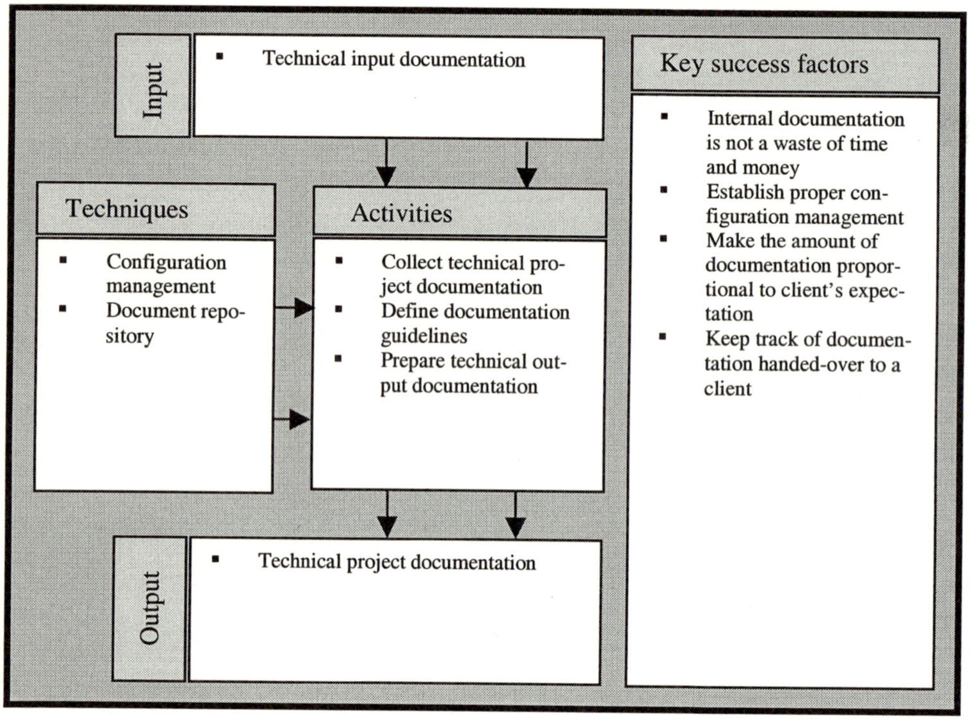

Fig. 36. Managing technical documentation

13.1.1 Inputs

Technical input documentation

The inputs to the managing technical project documentation process are all kinds of technical input documents that have to be considered, applied, adhered to, or used by a contractor to perform the defined project work. Typically those documents are handed over by external stakeholders to the contractor. The hand over might take place at the beginning of a project or at defined times during the course of a project.

13.1.2 Activities

Collect technical project documentation

Technical project documentation that is provided as input to a project by external project stakeholders needs special attention. First, you have to ensure that all documents which have to be considered from the perspective of external project stakeholders are known and available to you, and available at the point at which they are needed. Second, you have to ensure that the project activities are performed with the correct version of technical input documentation. Often technical documents, such as style guides, corporate design, and corporate e-business guidelines, are changed by a client during a project. For each document you should agree on the exact version that should be used in the project. A document repository, listing the version and the date of receipt, can ease the collection of technical project documentation. Third, you should agree with external stakeholders on a procedure for providing technical input documentation to your project. It is especially important to dedicate a member of your team who serves as a single contact point for receiving documents. Otherwise external stakeholders might submit documentation to somebody in your team with the assumption that the document will reach the intended receiver. Often those documents remain in the e-mail or paper inbox of single individuals and never reach the intended audience.

Define documentation guidelines

Normally, technical project documentation is produced by an author for one or more readers. The primary purpose of technical project documentation is to share information among project stakeholders. Sharing information in the form of technical documentation can be made more efficient by defining *documentation guidelines*. Documentation guidelines are rules that have to be adhered to when technical documents are prepared for both internal and external use. Documentation guidelines should cover at least four aspects:

1. **Document format.** The format of a document is mainly determined by the tools used to prepare or view it. Today documents are created almost always in electronic form. Only a few different types of text editor, graphics tool, presentation tool and document viewer are used. Although most tools include converters for transforming documents from one format to another, the conversion often mutilates the layout. Working with a document in different formats by several parties often results in additional effort or causes misunderstandings. Defining a set of tools – including the exact version of the tools – that have to be used by the project stakeholders to prepare and view technical documentation is an imperative cornerstone for smooth information sharing via documentation.
2. **Document structure.** Although the content and the nature of technical project documentation varies, there are some elements that most documents have in common. Capturing some basic requirements on the structure and the layout of documents supports a more cohesive look of all documents prepared in a project and

facilitates the reading of them. For specific types of documents the usage of templates with a defined document structure is another measure to make document preparation more efficient.

3. **Document identification.** Initially created documents are often updated during the course of a project. When creating a document in electronic form, usually a name has to be assigned to it. Including unique document identifiers in the document name supports searching and identifying a document The unique document identification may consist of a version identifier and the date at which a document was created or modified. Including a version identifier and the creation date allows for several versions of a document. This gives you the chance to refer back to older versions in order to trace the history of a document. Controlling different versions of documents is often supported by using *configuration management* (see Sect. 13.1.3) .
4. **Document storage structure.** Most technical project documents are available in electronic form. They have to be stored somewhere. For document storage a *document repository* (see Sect. 13.1.3) is a useful tool. Searching and sourcing technical project documents can be supported by defining a document storage structure. A document storage is usually organized in the form of a hierarchical directory structure.

After defining the documentation guidelines you have to communicate them to the relevant project stakeholders. Obtain a commitment from all project stakeholders that they will adhere to the defined guidelines. Act as a shining example for your team when you prepare technical project documentation and ensure that the other project stakeholders follow the defined guidelines.

Prepare technical output documentation

A significant part of the documentation that is produced in a project is of a technical nature. This kind of documentation is either prepared for internal or external purposes.

Internal technical project documentation is used internally by a contractor to perform the project work. This kind of documentation is only distributed and used by internal project stakeholders. Internal technical project documentation might contain confidential information that is not intended to be communicated outside the contractor company. Such confidential information may include intellectual capital generated in a project, specific techniques or methodologies that serve as a competitive advantage for a contractor, or internal design or architecture information on a developed e-business solution. In order to ensure that internal technical project documentation is not distributed mistakenly to outside project stakeholders, it is widespread practice to mark the respective documents as ‘internal’ or ‘confidential’.

External technical project documentation is prepared for external project stakeholders, usually the client of a project. The external technical project documentation can be part of the project deliverables that a contractor has to prepare for a client. Typical examples for such documents are user manuals, training materials, brochures, and administrator handbooks. As these documents are part of the project deliverables their acceptance is often bound to defined acceptance criteria. When preparing those documents you have to keep in mind that they have to fulfill the defined quality criteria. Assigning the preparation of such documents to subject matter experts, like technical writers, will probably result in a higher level of document quality.

Another category of external project documentation are documents that are not part of the official project deliverables but are used to share information with external project stakeholders during the course of a project. A typical example of such a document is a *storyboard*. A storyboard is a document that describes the layout, structure, and content of web pages that will be part of the e-business solution developed for a project. The storyboard is usually prepared before coding of the web pages is started. Reviewing and discussing the storyboard in detail with a client is an excellent opportunity of obtaining agreement on layout, structure, and content of the web pages before development starts. This provides a good basis for acceptance of the developed pages by a client, since the client knows how the pages will look. Otherwise a client would see the web pages for the first time when their development is finalized, and in the event that the client is completely dissatisfied with the result, you have to perform a lot of re-work. This risk can be mitigated when you discuss the storyboard with the client before coding is started.

13.1.3 Techniques

Configuration management

Configuration management is a technique to control different versions of deliverables. In principle it can be used for all kinds of project deliverables. However, it is mostly applied to control external technical project documentation. If several versions of a document exists, it is important to ensure that always the right version is used or handed over to the client.

Consider, for example, a deliverable like a business process documentation. A business process documentation is a recommendation to a client on how its business processes should be changed to fully deploy the benefits of the developed e-business solution. The process documentation is an important element for the success of the project and has to be approved by the client. Getting approval for such a description often involves some iterations with presentations, discussions, and re-work. In order to ensure that the latest version of the document is approved, making changes to the document and maintaining different versions of the document has to be controlled. Controlling changes and different version of documents in a systematic way is the objective of configuration management.

Configuration management controls the evolution of technical project documents and maintains their traceability and integrity. When project documents are placed under configuration management, it is possible to refer back to older versions of the documents to trace changes. Configuration management can also be used to restrict the access to documents to certain people. A restricted document access is useful when you want to allow only authorized individuals to make changes to specific documents.

Configuration management requires the definition of document handling procedures. These procedures have to cover aspects such as who is authorized to make changes in documents, which documents should be placed under configuration management, and a document identification scheme. Configuration management is normally performed with a software tool in order to support version control.

Document repository

Storing technical project documentation in a systematic and controlled way can be supported by using a *document repository*. A document repository is simply a central location where all project documents are filed. Technical project documentation is normally stored either electronically or in paper form. Sometimes both formats have to be considered. Often electronic documents are printed and the printouts have to be stored.

A document repository usually consists of two elements: (1) a defined document structure that is used to organize the documents in a systematic and consistent way and (2) a tool for storing the documents. For electronic documents a database or a file system can be used as the tool. Often a document repository is part of an overall *project management system* [38]. For paper documents, often a simple paper file or folder is used.

When documents have to be maintained in both electronic and paper forms, it is good practice to use the same document structure regardless of the tool used to store the documents. This eases searching and locating documents in the document repository. Having project documentation available in a central repository is also an excellent basis for archiving documents, because some documents – like lessons learned – might be useful long after project completion. It is therefore useful to archive relevant project documents for later usage.

13.1.4 Outputs

Technical project documentation

Not surprisingly, the primary output of the managing technical project documentation process are technical project documents. Those are either handed over to the client as official project deliverables or maintained in a document repository for internal purposes. After completion of a project, usually the technical project documents that might be of benefit to future projects are archived for later usage.

13.1.5 Key Success Factors

@ 92 Internal documentation is not a waste of time and money

Some people believe that internal project documentation in an e-business environment is a waste of time and money. They argument that e-business projects are too short to benefit from preparing internal documents. In their perspective internal documentation is simply a 'bureaucratic burden' that offers no value but only consumes resources and time. I do not share this view. Internal documentation presents value to a contractor company and the effort required to prepare it pays off.

What are the benefits of internal documentation for a project and for a contractor company? Internal project documentation is an excellent medium to share information among the project team members at a detailed level. Although information can be conveyed verbally, for many situations a written document is more expedient. e-business projects involve people from different disciplines where different terminology is used. When people from different disciplines talk to each other, often misunderstandings are provoked. Written documentation helps to avoid misunderstandings. Internal project documentation is also advantageous when new members enter the project team. New team members can utilize the internal project documentation to become acquainted to the project.

@ 93 Document and use lessons learned

A special form of internal project documentation are so-called *lessons learned.* Lessons learned are documented experiences gained from project execution. While many companies understand the value of reusing assets in terms of software components, concepts, and templates produced by a project, the value of reusing experiences is often ignored. Lessons learned are among the cheapest and easiest things that can benefit a future project. Experience is a valuable asset for performing similar projects in the future. Although each e-business project is unique, there are a lot of elements common to all – or almost all – projects. Documenting experiences gained in a project allows other project managers to benefit from those experiences. Even if an e-business project fails, documenting the things that went wrong can be of benefit in other projects. Knowing how previous problems were addressed can help you now. In your project the things that went wrong in other projects can be avoided – or at least you can try to avoid them.

For you, as project manager, lessons learned have two dimensions: (1) When your project is completed, you should gather and document the lessons learned in your project. Involving the project team members to recap and collect experiences will provide a wider view which things go well and which things could have been improved. Other project managers can benefit from the lessons learned in your project. (2) You can profit from lessons learned from other similar projects. Normally, a contractor company conducts numerous e-business projects. If all project managers document their lessons learned, you can read those documents to find out whether there are aspects that are applicable to your project. Decisions that have been made in other projects and the consequences that followed can provide valuable insights for you when you face similar choices.

The effort to document lessons learned is negligible compared to the possible benefits. If similar lessons learned are identified repeatedly in many projects of a company, this might indicate general problems and provides room for improvement at a higher company level. Adjustments to the overall company strategy or the way that a company is approaching its e-business projects might be the consequence triggered by elevating lessons learned.

@ 94 Establish proper configuration management

In many e-business projects no configuration management is implemented. Some of these projects suffer from uncontrolled dealing with different version of documents resulting in additional effort for the contractor and frustration for the project team. In other projects different versions of documents are not kept. There is only 'one' version of a document that contains the latest changes, so that previous changes are not traceable.

In discussions with clients on technical project documentation, it is often useful to have previous versions of documents available. Too often, the opinion of a client changes during the course of a project. When designing web pages, features that caused excitement to a client or were agreed on yesterday are no longer wanted today. In such a situation clients demand changes to coded web pages – free of charge. They often claim strongly that they "*never said anything else*" and that you "*did not listen carefully enough*" what they told you previously. Statements such as "*We did not know that we were going to get this!*" or "*This is not what we ordered at all*" are not so seldom. Although their requests might be completely contrary to what they wanted before, you often have to change deliverables in order to satisfy their expectations. This results in additional effort that has to be covered by the contractor – unless you can prove that the client's requirements have changed. I often achieved the commitment of a client to pay for such changes by producing previous versions of documents proving that their requirements were different some time ago.

Establishing and maintaining a proper configuration management involves some effort, but having previous versions available can be very useful politically, trust me.

@ 95 Make the amount of documentation proportional to client's expectation

In e-business projects the amount of documentation to be produced for a client is often a hotly discussed topic. How many pages should be produced for documents such as user manuals, installation instructions, or training materials? Some people argue that 'e-people' do not like to read documentation. They prefer to produce documents with only a few pages – or no documentation at all. Other people have a completely different view: they argue that e-business solutions are far more complex than, for example, a traditional IT solution, and the higher complexity requires a larger amount of corresponding documentation.

A general recommendation on the 'right' amount of documentation can not be given. The right amount may vary between different projects. While in one e-business project an administrator handbook of a few pages is appropriate, in another project hundreds of pages are adequate. So what amount of documentation is appropriate for your project? And what is a suitable approach to determine the 'right' amount of documentation? The answer is simple: ask your client!

The produced documentation has to satisfy the needs of your client. Your client will have specific expectations with respect to the amount of documentation that seems appropriate to fulfill its requirements. If a client expects detailed documentation you should produce a large amount of documentation. If a client expects only a few pages, you can limit your documentation efforts. Making the amount of documentation proportional to the client's expectations ensures that you chose the 'right' amount for your project.

@ 96 Keep track of documentation handed over to a client
When you hand over deliverables to a client, keep track of what you have handed over. This advice seems to be obvious, but I have seen many e-business projects suffer from exactly this pitfall. Keeping track of handed over documentation is especially imperative for preliminary or draft versions of documents that have to be discussed or reviewed with a client.

Keeping track of handed over documentation means logging the hand over date, the version of the document, and saving an exact copy of the handed over deliverable. What is the background to this advice? Often you or your team are improving or enhancing a document while the client is reviewing a specific version. There is nothing more frustrating than when a client wants to discuss with you specific details of a document in the version that was handed over, and you only have a version of the document available that was changed in the meantime. The attempt to match the two different versions is tedious and a meaningless effort. Having a clean copy of the handed over document version available – together with a proper configuration management – insulates you from such a frustrating experience.

13.2 Managing Legal Documentation

Managing legal documentation is the process of dealing with documents that are of a legal nature (see Fig. 37). What does *legal nature* mean in the context of project management? A legal document is a binding agreement that defines the legal relationship between two parties. In an e-business environment the two parties are either the contractor and the client or the contractor and a subcontractor. Legal documents defining the contractual relationship between two parties have to be handled with care, because a legal agreement is subject to remedy in the courts. The relevant project stakeholders should be aware of the legal implications a violation of a legal relationship can have.

Due to the binding legal nature of such documents, most companies have documented procedures, processes, and policies for dealing with these documents. This holds especially true for signing a legal document. Many companies have established a review and approval process that must be executed before a legal document can be signed. Signing a legal document is often restricted to specific persons who are authorized to sign agreements on behalf of a company.

To simplify the preparation, review, and negotiation of legal documents, some companies use templates with standard legal Ts & Cs that can be included in legal documents. The advantage of this approach is that standard Ts & Cs can be approved once by a legal authority and used several times without requiring fresh legal review and approval. However, a disadvantage of this approach surfaces when both parties have Ts & Cs that do not match. When each party insists on including its own Ts & Cs in a legal document, long and tedious negotiations are inevitable. Those negotiations are normally performed or supported by lawyers of the two parties.

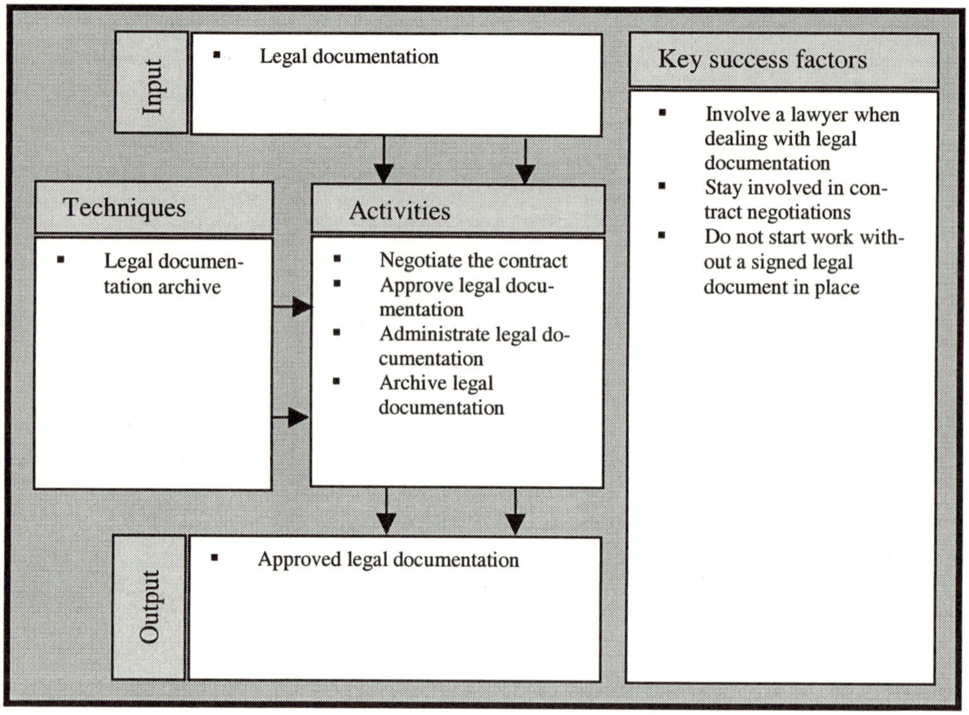

Fig. 37. Managing legal documentation

13.2.1 Inputs

Legal documentation

The input to the managing legal documentation process are all kinds of legal documents that are of relevance to an e-business project. Typical legal documents that you prospectively will have to deal with in your project are:

- **Contract.** The contract between a contractor and a client is probably the most important legal document. The contract defines the legal relationship and the responsibilities of both contractor and client. A typical contract for an e-business project usually contains four core elements:

1. A *Statement of Work* (SoW), describing in detail the work that a contractor has to perform. The SoW often includes a high-level project time plan specifying milestones at which project deliverables have to be handed over to a client.
2. *Ts & Cs*, the terms and conditions under which the work has to be performed. Here especially aspects like penalties for late delivery, intellectual capital and copyright rules, and rights to reuse the developed e-business solution in other projects, are specified.
3. *Client responsibilities*, specifying the contributions of a client that are required for successful project execution.
4. *Payment terms*, defining when and how much money has to be paid by a client to a contractor as compensation for the project work. The defined terms of payment lock up the contract type. For e-business projects mainly two types of contracts are commonly used: (1) *Firm-fixed-price* contracts under which the work defined in the SoW has to be delivered by a contractor to a client for a fixed price regardless the effort that is required to perform the work. With such a type of contract the financial risk is completely on contractor side. (2) *Time-and-material* contracts, under which the client reimburses the contractors costs plus a defined percentage of profit. With such a type of contract the financial risk is completely on the client side.

- **Subcontractor agreement.** A subcontractor agreement defines the legal relationship between a contractor and its subcontractor. Subcontractor agreements are discussed in detail in Sect. 11.1.4.
- **Letter of authorization.** A Letter of authorization (LoA), sometimes also called a *letter of agreement*, a *letter of intent (LoI),* or a *memorandum of understanding (MoU),* is a special kind of contract that is often used temporarily until a final, full-blown contract is signed and in place. When conflicting Ts & Cs of the contracting parties have to be negotiated, such negotiations can last for weeks or even months. In order to avoid delaying the project start until all legal issues are resolved, a LoA is signed by the parties. A LoA is a legal agreement between two parties expressing their intention to sign a contract. The important aspect is that a LoA allows a contractor or a subcontractor to start project work before the final contract is in place without a financial risk. In the case that an agreement on a contract can not be achieved, the LoA binds the client to reimburse the costs incurred by performing project work. In the event that an agreement on a contract is reached, the LoA is replaced by the contract.
- **Non-disclosure agreement.** A non-disclosure agreement, sometimes also called a *confidentiality agreement*, is a legal document that restricts the rights of a party to disclose information. Normally, a client demands that a contractor signs such an agreement. In order to perform the project work properly, a client often has to pro-

vide sensitive information to a contractor. Sensitive information might be specific technology, methodology, techniques, business processes, or plans that a client wants to keep secret. If this information became known to competitors or in the marketplace, the client would loose a competitive advantage. It can therefore be understood that a client wants to avoid certain information being communicated outside the client company. However, if this secret information is essential for a contractor to perform the project work, the client has to provide it to you in a written or verbal form. To reduce the risk that this information is disclosed, a client requests that a contractor signs a non-disclosure agreement. A non-disclosure agreement is a binding commitment of a contractor that sensitive information received from a client is not distributed to others, and is only deployed for project purposes. A breach of this agreement is usually punished by a penalty payment. While a non-disclosure agreement is usually requested by a client to be signed by a contractor, you can also request your subcontractors to sign such an agreement if you have to provide sensitive information to them.

13.2.2 Activities

Negotiate the contract

The activity to initially negotiate a contract between a client and a contractor usually takes place before a project is started or in the early project days when the work is already started under a LoA. Negotiating a contract can be facilitated by using contract templates, boilerplates, and standard Ts & Cs as a discussion basis.

When a contract is negotiated normally one party is responsible for creating and maintaining the physical document that is going to represent the contract. It is not important whether the client or the contractor is this responsible party. However, it is important that only *one* party maintains the document. Simultaneously modifying the document by both parties can prove extremely awkward and is a recipe for chaos. As a first step, usually one party will prepare details and make changes to the document. As a second step, the physical document is sent to the other party for review and comments. These two steps are iterated until all issues are resolved, everything is settled, and a document is achieved that both parties are willing to sign.

Contract negotiation can be long and tedious, but it might provide you with valuable insights into the priorities and attitudes of the other party. It requires both parties to discuss and agree on project details at a point when these may not be obvious. Contract negotiations between a contractor and a client can prove a harbinger of how the relationship between the two parties will most likely play out. Embittered disputes about contractual details and big differences in Ts & Cs of the parties are often an early indication that the 'culture' of the contract partners is somewhat different, which might cause problems during project execution.

If the negotiation effort is successful, it leads to a contract that is signed by the authorized representatives of contractor and client. Normally a signed contract covers the total project time frame. A contract is valid until all contractual obligations are fulfilled. However, special circumstances may suggest terminating a contract earlier than initially planned. As a contract is a mutually binding commitment, an early contract termination needs the agreement of both contract parties. Otherwise one party breaches the contract and can be prosecuted by the other in the courts. Also, in the case that a signed contract needs to be changed, this has to be mutually agreed upon by both parties. The process to change a contract should be covered by the overall project change management procedure (see Sect. 10.1).

Approve legal documentation

As outlined in Sect. 13.2.1, there are legal documents beyond the contract that have to be handled. The handling of subcontractor agreements is discussed in Sect. 11.2.2. LoAs and non-disclosure agreements are normally represented by standard templates or standard phrases that need not be negotiated in detail. However, it is important to sign these legal documents only after a careful and serious review. These documents are legal binding and commit you to certain responsibilities. It is your job to ensure that those documents are only signed after a serious evaluation of likely legal implications. Involving a company lawyer in approving legal documents is mostly advantageous.

Administrate legal documentation

The next step after legal documents such as contracts, subcontractor agreements, LoAs, or non-disclosure agreements are approved and signed, is to ensure that the defined contractual obligations are fulfilled. Administrating legal documentation usually includes applying at multiple levels many project management methods and techniques discussed in other project management domains.

When administrating legal documentation it is important that you and your team are fully aware of the legal implications that may be caused by actions taken during the course of a project.

When a project is completed or terminated, the corresponding legal documents have to be formally closed. Administrative closure, for example for a contract, is the activity of documenting formally that all contractual obligations of the two parties have been fulfilled and no open claims of one or both parties exist.

Archive legal documentation

In many countries rules for the preservation of legal business documents exist. Public legislation demands preserving legal business documents for a certain number of years after project completion to ensure traceability. Some companies have established their own rules and policies for document preservation. normally detailing or intensifying the public legislation rules.

You have to ensure that the public and the company specific rules for legal document preservation are fulfilled properly. At the latest at the end of an e-business project you have to select the documents that must be preserved. You should prepare a complete set of indexed legal documents that have to be preserved. Preservation of legal documents is usually performed via an archive. An archive is a repository that stores documents for a specified time frame (see Sect. 13.2.3). In principle, legal documents can be archived in any form, such as electronic, paper, or microfilm. However, public or company-specific rules might prescribe a specific form of preservation. It is your responsibility to ensure that all documents that have to be preserved are inserted into the archive.

13.2.3 Techniques

Legal documentation archive

A legal documentation archive is a repository for legal documents. Depending on the policies of your company, an archive for legal documentation might need to be set up for each single project, or your company might have established a central archive in which all legal documents of the company are stored.

In some countries public legislation demands that a legal documentation archive has to fulfill certain requirements. Such requirements might be, for example, protection of the archive against physical damages caused by fire, flood, and earthquakes, or the format in which the documents have to be preserved.

13.2.4 Outputs

Approved legal documentation

The final output of the managing legal documentation process are approved legal documents. After project completion the legal documents normally are preserved in a legal documentation archive.

13.2.5 Key Success Factors

@ 97 Involve a lawyer when dealing with legal documentation

Commitments given in signed legal documents are subject to remedy in the courts – and often they are in fact sued in the case of conflicts. Too often legal documents are signed by project managers who are unaware of the legal implications. Legal language is highly specific: phrases or terms might have a different meaning in legal terminology than what you think their meaning is. If you do not have, by fortune, a legal background, involve a lawyer when dealing with legal documents.

When preparing a contract for an e-business project there are different opinions on when and to what extent to involve a lawyer. Some project managers try to keep the lawyer's involvement to a minimum or refuse it completely. They suspect that the establishment of an e-business project stalls or even fails when lawyers are involved in contract negotiations. Together with sales people, they love to negotiate legal documents with their project manager counterparts and only ask a lawyer to formally approve the final document. Other project managers insist on having a lawyer participating from the initial discussions through to the end, until a written document is ready for signing.

The right point and the appropriate extent of a lawyer's involvement might differ in e-business projects. Influencing factors are the size of the project, the contract type, and whether or not the contractor and the client have done business before. The important point to remember is that you should not sign any legal document without a lawyer's review and approval.

@ 98 Stay involved in contract negotiations

In some companies negotiating a contract between a contractor and a client is delegated to company lawyers. Typically these lawyers are subject matter experts in legal issues with much experience in contract negotiations. Although you should appreciate the support of these experts, it is imperative that you stay involved. Do not leave the contract negotiation solely to the lawyers, because usually company lawyers are not familiar with the technical specifics of a project, especially with the technical project work that is specified in the SoW that is usually a decisive part of a contract.

Finally, it is you who has to deliver what is specified in a contract. It does not help you much when your company lawyers are proud of having achieved an agreement that seems favorable for your company from a legal point of view, if you are unable to fulfill the responsibilities specified in the SoW. Contract negotiation works best if it is performed as a joint effort between project manager, sales people, and company lawyers, so that the experiences and strengths of all parties are exploited to their best advantage.

The time you invest in negotiating a contract with a client often pays off. The contract is the basis for the formal contractor–client relationship. It should be as specific and detailed as possible. If an e-business project runs smoothly, you will seldom need to refer to the contract in your day-to-day business. Your project is most probably in a comfortable position when neither you nor the client have to refer to the contract. The best contract is one that the parties never have to refer to.

If you find yourself frequently arguing with the client over project disputes that have to be resolved by referring to the contract, the contractor–client relationship probably needs improvement. In such a situation you will appreciate your efforts spent on preparing a detailed and precise contract. You will be glad when project responsibilities are defined at a level of detail that clearly defines who has what obligations. Otherwise you or the other party have to refer to the 'spirit' of the contract, which is almost always an unreliable factor.

@ 99 Do not start work without a signed legal document in place

Time-to-market is key in an e-business environment. The earlier that an e-business solution can be launched the better. Too often, clients neither have a proper e-business strategy in place nor a firm idea of what they want to achieve with an e-business solution when they initiate it. This hurry results from the concern that they might put themselves out of business when they do not cope with competitors who are already present on the Web. When they start an e-business initiative, some clients do not have much more than a vague idea on the e-business project and the e-business solution to be implemented: project scope, project budget, technology, contractor, and many other project basics are unclear. Only one thing is definitely clear and absolutely fixed: the launch date of the e-business solution.

Driven by shareholders or competitors, the executive management of a client company often announce the availability and the 'go-live' date of an e-business solution long before a client is prepared to start a corresponding project. The amount of preparation and effort that is necessary on the client side to establish a project is frequently underestimated. Selecting an adequate contractor to perform the project work and agreeing on a contract can be very time-consuming.

While the client's and the contractor's lawyers are carefully discussing contractual issues to close the deal, the designated client project manager often feels like he or she is sitting on pins and needles. Having the announced deadline for solution launch in mind he or she becomes more and more nervous with each day that the technical project work is not started. The dilemma is obvious: the later the project work is started the higher the risk that the solution launch date "*that must be kept whatever happens*" is not met. You can count on that the enervated client project manager sometime will ask you the magic question: "*Could you please start the project work although the contract is not yet finalized?*" There is only one valid answer to this question: "*No*".

Starting project work for a client without a legal document in place is like sky-diving without a parachute or bungee-jumping without a rope. If a contractor starts project work for a client without a contract or a LoA, the effort and money spent performing the work is simply an investment. If the intended deal breaks and the project is not established – for whatever reason – this is a financial disaster for the contractor. Without a legal agreement, the total costs incurred by the performed project work remain on the contractor side. You do not have any chance of obtaining re-imbursement of the costs. Many companies have lost millions of dollars doing e-business work without a contract. Some smaller companies have even gone bankrupt.

Not surprisingly, the client project manager might give you an impression of absolute confidence that the project will take place, and that the work is in fact awarded to your company. However, unforeseen budget cuts, changes in e-business or overall client company strategy, changes in senior management, or company politics are only a few examples of innumerable events that can prevent a project from taking place. Do not allow the assertions of the client project manager to seduce you into starting project work before a legal document is in place.

Appendix A: List of Acronyms

This appendix contains a list of acronyms which are referenced throughout the book by their initials rather than their full term. This acronym list supplements the glossary of terms.

Acronym	Term
B2B	Business to business
B2C	Business to consumer
CEO	Chief executive officer
CMS	Content management system
COCOMO	Constructive cost model
CPU	Central processing unit
CR	Change request
CRM	Customer relationship management
C2C	Consumer to consumer
CV	Curriculum vitae
DB	Database
DoU	Document of understanding
e	Electronic
EMV	Expected monetary value
ETC	Estimate to complete
GUI	Graphical user interface
HR	Human resource
HTML	Hypertext mark-up language
ID	Identifier

IT	Information technology
ISO	International organization for standardization
LoA	Letter of agreement (or authorization)
LoI	Letter of intent
LoSC	Lines of source code
MoU	Memorandum of understanding
NLS	National language support
OO	Object oriented
OOD	Object oriented design
OOP	Object oriented programming
PC	Personal computer
PDA	Personal digital assistant
PMI	Project management institute
QA	Quality assurance
QAP	Quality assurance plan
RFI	Request for information
RfP	Request for proposal
RoI	Return on investment
SMS	Sort message service
SoW	Statement of work
SSL	Secure socket layer
SWOT	Strength, weaknesses, opportunities, threats
Ts & Cs	Terms and conditions
UI	User interface
XML	Extensible mark-up language
WBS	Work breakdown structure

Appendix B: Glossary

This appendix contains a glossary of terms which are used throughout the book. Only those terms are listed that have a unique meaning in a project management or an e-business environment. Terms whose use in this book does not differ from everyday use and whose meaning is clear without an explicit definition are not included in this glossary.

Where possible and useful, the definition given for a term is adapted from the PMI publication *"A Guide to the Project Management Body of Knowledge"* [32] or the international standard ISO 10006 *"Quality Management: Guidelines to Quality in Project Management"* [18]. However, the terms of the glossary are often defined with a narrower meaning than in general project management or e-business usage in order to reflect their specific usage in this book.

Acceptance	An acknowledgment expressed by a client to a contractor or by a contractor to its subcontractor to confirm that a project deliverable satisfies defined acceptance criteria.
Acceptance criteria	A set of quality criteria that define characteristics of a project deliverable which are used to evaluate whether or not a project deliverable is accepted by its receiver.
Additional costs	Project expenses that can neither be attributed to hardware, software, or services costs, nor are part of a planned expense reserve.
Assumption	A factor that, for planning purposes, is considered to be true, real, or certain. (PMI)
Audit	A special form of an independent review used to evaluate systematically whether a project is managed according to defined project management procedures.
Benefit–cost ratio	The ratio between project benefits – expressed in monetary units – and project costs, normally calculated by dividing the total discounted benefits by the total discounted costs.

Business need	A challenge, a problem, or an opportunity identified by a client that is the trigger for initiating an e-business project, and that can be partially or wholly addressed by the planned e-business solution.
Change request	An official request from one party – contractor or client – to change something in a project that can not be implemented without prior approval of the other party.
Client	The company that is the sponsor for an e-business project and which contracts another company – the contractor – to perform the project.
Client's responsibilities	Explicitly specified input and support required by a contractor from a client as its contribution to a successful project execution.
Configuration management	A tool-supported process of defining, monitoring, and controlling different versions of deliverables produced in a project.
Constraint	A restriction that limits the freedom of choice for a project manager or the performance of a project.
Contract	A legally binding mutual commitment between two parties that is normally based on a written agreement defining the obligations of the parties.
Contractor	The company which delivers an e-business project on behalf of and for another company – the client.
Corrective action	Changes planned to bring the expected future performance of a project in line with the plans and procedures. (PMI)
Cost–benefit analysis	A systematic, quantitative method of evaluating the costs and benefits of a project with a defined scope. It involves collecting and assessing tangible and intangible costs and benefits.
Cross-functional team	A project team consisting of people out of the creative, marketing, IT, and consulting disciplines.

Deliverable	A measurable, tangible, and verifiable outcome, result, or item that must be produced by a contractor or a subcontractor within a project. External deliverables normally have to be handed over to a client.
Dependency	A time or input–output–related relationship between two work packages (internal dependency), or between a work package and an event outside a project (external dependency).
e-business	The transaction of business over an electronic medium such as the World Wide Web.
e-business application	The software components of an e-business solution normally composed of a front-end and a back-end part.
e-business solution	The entirety of hardware and software components that have to be developed and integrated within an e-business project to satisfy a client's business need.
e-business strategy	An e-business strategy sketches the way that a client wants to implement its e-business vision.
e-business vision	The e-business vision of a client company determines the direction where it wants to go with e-business in general.
Effort	The number of labor units required to perform a specific piece of work. Effort is normally expressed in terms of person-hours, person-days, or person-months.
Finding	A result of a review or an audit indicating a discovered deviation between an actual situation or result and a planned or expected one.
Gantt chart	A method invented by Henry Gantt in 1917 to display a project time plan in the form of a graphical presentation of work packages, their sequence including start and end dates, and dependencies among work packages.
Gold-plating	The activity of a contractor to make an outcome bigger, with more features, or at a higher level of quality than planned, agreed on, and expected by a client.
Human resources	People with specified skills who are required to perform defined project work.

Human resource plan	A human resource plan defines the human resources requirements of a project. The human resource plan specifies for each job category the requirements of the number of required people, when the staff is required and for how long, special skills required, and the skills level.
Issue	Any event that can have a negative impact on a project if it is not resolved. The characteristic of an issue is that it surfaces unplanned and is mostly not foreseeable.
Kick-off meeting	A meeting that is normally conduced in the first days of a project to orient the project team in order to achieve team commitment to a project.
Lag	A modification of a dependency that results in a delay in performing a subsequent work package.
Lead	A modification of a dependency that allows an acceleration of a subsequent work package.
Lessons Learned	Experiences gained from executing a project that are worth documenting to ease the execution of other projects facing similar challenges.
Letter of intent	A special kind of contract that is used temporarily until a final, full-blown contract is in place. It defines the obligations of two parties – client and contractor – to allow project work to start while the negotiations on a final contract have not been completed.
Milestone	A significant event in a project, such as the completion and hand over of a major project deliverable to a client.
Non-disclosure agreement	A legal document that restricts the rights of a party to disclose information. A non-disclosure agreement is sometimes called a confidentiality agreement.
Project	A temporary endeavor undertaken to create a unique product, service, or result. (PMI)
Project budget	A spending limit for a project usually expressed in monetary units and set and approved by senior management. Normally there is a project budget on the contractor as well as on the client side.

Project management	The planning, organizing, monitoring, and controlling of all aspects of a project in a continuous process to achieve its objectives. (ISO)
Project management system	The methodology applied by a company to manage its projects defined and guided by a collection of plans, procedures, policies, tools, and experiences.
Project manager	The person responsible for managing an e-business project. Usually there is a contractor project manager with the authority to decide on all project-relevant aspects that arise on the contractor side in delivering a project to a client, and a client project manager with the authority to 'manage' the contractor and to deploy the project outcome on the client side.
Project office	A group of one or more individuals who perform administrative project management functions for one or more projects within a company. A project office releases a project manager from administrative project management work.
Project site	A web-based project management tool that can be used to enhance the communications with a client. A project site is maintained by a contractor and hosts the information a contractor wants to share with the client.
Project stakeholder	Individuals who are actively involved in a project or who are positively or negatively affected by the outcome of a project. Usually they have a certain level of influence on a project and its outcome.
Project status report	A document usually prepared by a contractor project manager to inform the stakeholders on project status and progress. A project status report is normally issued on a regular basis, for example, bi-weekly or monthly.
Project team	The people who are assigned to a project to perform defined project work. Besides the project team on the contractor side, there is often also a project team on the client side. The members of the project team are responsible for successful project delivery and deployment. A project team is usually headed by a project manager.

Project time plan	A project planning document usually listing the work packages that have to be performed in a project, a planned start and end date for each work package including dependencies among work packages, and an indication of which team members are assigned to perform particular work packages.
Prototype	A scale model of the intended e-business application normally used to verify, to experiment, or to visualize certain functions or features of the target solution.
Quality	The totality of characteristics of an entity that bear on its ability to satisfy stated or implied needs. (ISO)
Quality assurance plan	A project planning document defining quality criteria, quality targets, and the activities that are planned to be performed in a project to achieve the defined targets.
Quality criteria	A set of attributes by which the quality of a given deliverable can be described. These are used to evaluate whether explicitly specified or implicitly assumed quality requirements are satisfied.
Release	A specific version of an e-business application providing a specified set of functions to achieve defined objectives. Normally, consecutive releases provide an increasing level of functionality until the complete functionality of an e-business application is reached with its last release.
Request for proposal	A procurement document issued by a client to solicit proposals from potential contractors for delivering a project, or issued by a contractor to source and evaluate potential subcontractors for providing pieces of project work.
Reserve	A provision in the estimation of project costs to cover overlooked or incorrect cost estimates. Usually a reserve is determined by taking a certain percentage of the original cost estimate.
Review	A systematic examination and verification of a project deliverable – often performed in the form of a review meeting – to ensure that a deliverable possessed a set of desired or agreed attributes.

Risk	A potential event, condition, or future situation that, if it occurs, probably affects a project negatively.
Risk acceptance	A risk response strategy that consists of simply accepting the consequences if an identified risk occurs.
Risk avoidance	A risk response strategy with the objective of finding a way of avoiding the occurrence of an identified risk. This can be accomplished by taking appropriate countermeasures or by choosing an alternative approach.
Risk mitigation	A risk response strategy with the objective of finding a way to reduce the probability that a risk will occur, or to reduce the consequences to an acceptable level in the case that a risk occurs.
Risk transfer	A risk response strategy with the objective of finding someone outside the project to whom a risk can be transferred.
Skills	The totality of knowledge and experience of a human resource in a specific area that is required to perform a certain piece of work successfully.
Staff provider	A company that places human resources at the disposal of a contractor to perform project work. The individuals provided are usually integrated into the project staff of a contractor and managed directly by the contractor as members of the project team.
Storyboard	A design description of the front-end part of an e-business application. A storyboard describes at a detailed level the definite content and structure of each web page.
Subcontractor	A company that is contracted by a contractor to provide a defined piece of work on behalf of and under the supervision of a contractor. Normally a subcontractor is fully responsible for performing the subcontracted piece of work. A subcontractor is accountable to the contractor and not to the client of a project.

Subcontractor agreement	A document that defines the legal relationship between a contractor and a subcontractor.
SWOT analysis	A SWOT analysis is a systematic approach that can be used to explore how the outcome of different project options would influence the position of the client's company.
Template	A generic document, table, example, or guideline that can be used as the basis to develop a specific document, plan, or deliverable for a project. The objectives of using templates is to save effort by customizing generic outlines or structures instead of developing everything from scratch.
Testing	The process of executing an e-business application with the intention of finding errors. The level of quality of an e-business application can be improved by fixing the detected errors.
Vendor	A company that supplies standard software, hardware, or services that are used by a contractor to develop an e-business solution.
Workaround	A technique of overcoming a critical situation or a potential risk by taking an alternative approach or by implementing a temporary circumvention.
Work breakdown structure	A deliverable-oriented, hierarchical grouping of the work that has to be performed in a project.
Work environment	The technical and office environment comprising a collection of hardware, software, networks, and office facilities of any kind shared by the project team.
Work package	An identifiable entry in the WBS at its lowest level.

References

1. Archibald D (1992) Managing high-technology programs and projects. Wiley, New York
2. Auerbach Report (2000) Building an e-business strategy. Auerbach, New York
3. Barkley BT, Saylor JH (2001) Customer-driven project management. McGraw-Hill, New York
4. Boehm BW (1981) Software engineering economics. Prentice Hall, Upper Saddle River, New Jersey
5. Brooks F (1975) The mythical man-month: essays on software engineering. Addison-Wesley, Reading, Mass.
6. Department of Trade & Industry (2000) Information security breaches survey. DTI, London
7. Datta S, Mukherjee KS (2001) Developing a risk management matrix for effective project planning – an empirical study. Project Manage 32: 45–57
8. Ernst & Young (1998) Second annual global information security survey. Ernst & Young
9. Ferrara R, Lowery G (2000) Managing projects with Microsoft Project 2000. Wiley, New York
10. Fleming QW, Koppelman JM (2000) Earned value project management, 2nd edn. Project Management Institute, Pennsylvania
11. Fulmer RM, Vicere AA (1998) Leadership by design. Harvard Business School Publishing, Boston
12. Gartner Group (1999a) CEO and CIO alert: five mistakes that will derail an e-business. Gartner Group, Stamford
13. Gartner Group (1999b) e-business project planning: proceed at your own risk. Gartner Group, Stamford
14. Gartner Group (2000a) e-business services worldwide market forecast, 2000 – 2005. Gartner Group, Stamford

15. Gartner Group (2000b) The changing shape of e-business services: worldwide market trends. Gartner Group, Stamford

16. IBM (2001) Intense e-business: what a leader looks like. IBM Corporation, Armonk

17. International Function Point User Group (1994) Function point counting practice manual, release 4.0. IFPUG, Blendonview Office Park, Ohio

18. International Organization for Standardization (1997) Quality management: guidelines to quality in project management, International Standard ISO 10006. ISO Press, Geneva, Switzerland

19. International Organization for Standardization (2000) Quality management systems: fundamentals and vocabulary, International Standard ISO 9000. ISO Press, Geneva, Switzerland

20. Iyiguen GM (1993) A decision support system for R&D project selection and resource allocation under uncertainty. Project Management Journal, Issue December

21. Kaplan RS, Norton DP (1992) The balanced scorecard – measures that drive performance. Harvard Business Review 70: 71–79

22. Kaplan RS, Norton DP (1997) Why does business need a balanced scorecard? Journal of Cost Management 11: 5–10

23. KPMG (2000) Information security survey 2000. KPMG, London

24. Krammer M, Plummer D (2001) Ten imperatives for SMB e-business success. Gartner Group, Stamford

25. Lientz BP, Rea KP (2001) Breakthrough technology project management. Harcourt, Kent

26. Mazzarella J (2001) Usability is increasingly pivotal to e-business success. Gartner Group, Stamford

27. Meredith J, Mantel S (1995) Project management: a managerial approach. Wiley, New York

28. Myers GJ (1979) Software reliability: principles and practices. Wiley, New York

29. Nielsen J (1999) User interface directions for the Web. Comm ACM 42: 65–72

30. OConnell F (1999) How to run successful high-tech project-based organizations. Artech House, Norwood, Mass.

31. Oz E, Sosik J (2000) Why information system projects are abandoned: a leadership and communication theory and exploration study. Comput Inform 44: 66–78

32. Project Management Institute (2000) A guide to the project management body of knowledge. Project Management Institute, Pennsylvania

33. Pinto JK (1996) Power and politics in project management. Project Management Institute, Pennsylvania

34. Posner BZ (1987) What it takes to be a good project manager. Project Manage 3: 51–54

35. Putlock G (2000) The challenges of implementing an e-business initiative. Telelogic NewsByte, Kungsgaten, Sweden

36. Shields MG (2001) e-business and ERP: rapid implementation and project planning. Wiley, New York

37. The Standish Group (1996) CHAOS: a recipe for success. Standish Group, West Yarmouth

38. Suhanic G (2001) Computer-aided project management. Oxford University Press, Oxford

39. Tinnirello PC (2000) Project management. CRC, Boca Raton, Fla.

40. Whitaker K (1994) Managing software maniacs: finding, managing, and rewarding a winning development team. Wiley, New York

41. Wysocki RK (2000) Effective project management. Wiley, New York

Index of Key Success Factors

General

Managing the Scope

Managing the Schedule

Managing the Team

Managing the Cost

Managing the Client

Managing Risks

Managing Technology

Managing Quality

Managing Change

Managing the Subcontractor

Managing Communications

Managing Documentation

Index

A

B

C

D

E

F

G

H

I

J

K

L

M

N

O

P

Q

R

S

T

U

V

W

Druck: Strauss Offsetdruck, Mörlenbach
Verarbeitung: Schäffer, Grünstadt